Made-Up Minds

Made-Up Minds
A Constructivist Approach to Artificial Intelligence

Gary L. Drescher

The MIT Press
Cambridge, Massachusetts
London, England

This book was printed and bound in the United States of America.

Library of Congress Cataloging-in-Publication Data

Drescher, Gary L.
  Made-up minds : a constructivist approach to artificial intelligence / Gary L. Drescher.
    p. cm. — (Artificial intelligence)
  Outgrowth of the author's thesis (Ph. D.—Massachusetts Institute of Technology).
  Includes bibliographical references and index.
  ISBN 0-262-04120-0
  1. Artificial intelligence. 2. Schematism (Philosophy) 3. Human information processing. 4. Concept learning. 5. Piaget, Jean, 1896–   . I. Title. II. Series: Artificial intelligence (Cambridge, Mass.)
  Q335.D724 1991
  006.33—dc20   90-23653
                                                    CIP

To my new nephew, Josh—
  the real thing.

Contents

List of figures

Series foreword

Artificial intelligence is the study of intelligence using the ideas and methods of computation. Unfortunately, a definition of intelligence seems impossible at the moment because intelligence appears to be an amalgam of so many information-processing and information-representation abilities.

Of course psychology, philosophy, linguistics, and related disciplines offer various perspectives and methodologies for studying intelligence. For the most part, however, the theories proposed in these fields are too incomplete and too vaguely stated to be realized in computational terms. Something more is needed, even though valuable ideas, relationships, and constraints can be gleaned from traditional studies of what are, after all, impressive existence proofs that intelligence is in fact possible.

Artificial intelligence offers a new perspective and a new methodology. Its central goal is to make computers intelligent, both to make them more useful and to understand the principles that make intelligence possible. That intelligent computers will be extremely useful is obvious. The more profound point is that artificial intelligence aims to understand intelligence using the ideas and methods of computation, thus offering a radically new and different basis for theory formation. Most of the people doing work in artificial intelligence believe that these theories will apply to any intelligent information processor, whether biological or solid state.

There are side effects that deserve attention, too. Any program that will successfully model even a small part of intelligence will be inherently massive and complex. Consequently, artificial intelligence continually confronts the limits of computer-science technology. The problems encountered have been hard enough and interesting enough to seduce artificial intelligence people into working on them with enthusiasm. It is natural, then, that there has been a steady flow of ideas from artificial intelligence to computer science, and the flow shows no sign of abating.

The purpose of this series in artificial intelligence is to provide people in many areas, both professionals and students, with timely, detailed information about what is happening on the frontiers in research centers all over the world.

J. Michael Brady
Daniel Bobrow
Randall Davis

Acknowledgments

This book grew from my Ph.D. dissertation at the M.I.T. A.I. Laboratory; my research and writing on the subject then continued at Thinking Machines Corporation. I have had the pleasure and privilege to discuss this research with many friends, colleagues, and teachers. Danny Hillis, Marvin Minsky, and Seymour Papert (my thesis advisor) have offered volumes of valued advice, encouragement and criticism since the earliest days of this lengthy project, and Dave Waltz at Thinking Machines has been similarly supportive of the later portion of this work. My thesis readers—Hal Abelson, Ron Rivest, and Gerry Sussman—have likewise provided the most helpful guidance imaginable.

I am also grateful for discussions with Edith Ackermann, Phil Agre, Gunther Albers, Rick Alterman, Jon Amsterdam, John Batali, Anand Bodapati, Mario Bourgoin, Guy Cellerier, David Chapman, Jim Davis, Mark Gross, Ken Haase, Ed Hardebeck, Dan Huttenlocher, Bob Lawler, Henry Minsky, Margaret Minsky, Jerry Roylance, Alan Ruttenberg, Brian Silverman, Steve Smith, Cynthia Solomon, Mike Travers, Tom Trobaugh, Lucia Vaina, Sylvia Weir, Dan Weld, Stewart Wilson, Patrick Winston, and Ramin Zabih; their insights, and comments on drafts, have been valuable. I alone, of course, deserve credit for all errors, be they philosophical, typographical, or anywhere in between.

I thank my parents, Gladys and Irving Drescher, for their dedicated support, financial and otherwise, of my academic pursuits.

Were it not (still) inanimate, I would also thank the Connection Machine®, without which this book probably could not have been written.

Finally, as a now-adult child of the sixties, I gratefully acknowledge the continuing influence and inspiration of that era of wonder and change, concern and commitment, revision and renewal...what a long, strange trip indeed.

Preface

The schema mechanism is a general learning and concept-building mechanism intended to reproduce aspects of Piagetian cognitive development during infancy. A computer program that implements the schema mechanism has replicated several early milestones in the Piagetian infant's invention of the concept of persistent object.

The schema mechanism implementation connects to a simulated body in a microworld. The mechanism learns from its experiences by processes of empirical learning and concept invention, and uses what it learns to plan actions, often for the sake of explicit goals. Empirical learning is achieved by a novel induction technique, *marginal attribution*, that builds structures called *schemas*; each schema asserts that a given action, in a specified context, has particular results. Contexts and results are expressed in terms of binary state elements called *items*. Crucially, the schema mechanism not only discovers relations among existing representational elements (actions and items), but also constructs new such elements. Its learning is entirely autonomous and unsupervised.

For any achievable result, the mechanism can define a new, abstract action, the action of achieving that result. Most importantly, the mechanism invents radically novel concepts by constructing new state elements, *synthetic items*, to designate aspects of the world that the existing repertoire of representations fails to express. A synthetic item is defined with respect to a particular unreliable schema; the item designates whatever unknown condition must be satisfied for the schema to be reliable. Such a condition may differ fundamentally from any states previously represented by the mechanism.

The schema mechanism, like a Piagetian infant, initially represents the world only in terms of simple sensory and motor elements. At first, there is no concept of persistent, external objects—objects that exist even when not perceived. The schema mechanism recapitulates aspects of the Piagetian developmental sequence by inventing a series of approximations to the persistent-object concept. The mechanism discovers correspondences among touch, vision, and other modalities, and eventually represents an object independently of how, or if, the object is currently perceived. This designation is far removed from the original, sensorimotor elements of representation.

Part I Constructivist AI

1 Introduction and overview

The most wondrous quest of humankind remains its ancient and ongoing effort to understand the human mind. This book presents the *schema mechanism,* one of myriad attempted contributions to that effort. The schema mechanism proceeds from the work of the psychologist Jean Piaget, who sought the basic operational principles of the mind by studying the genesis of thought in infants and children.

Piaget's theoretical stance, known as *constructivism,* proposes that the newborn infant is virtually a solipsist, conceiving of reality exclusively in terms of sensory impressions and motor actions; the infant can learn that certain actions can create particular sensations, but lacks any idea that there are objects that exist independently of their perception. But although, by this account, the individual begins life with only sensorimotor terms of representation, she goes on to construct new representational elements as the prior repertoire proves inadequate to describe her experiences. Eventually, she is able to conceive of an object independently of how—or even *whether*—it is currently perceived.

The schema mechanism is a general learning and concept-building mechanism inspired by Piaget's account of human cognitive development. The mechanism is intended to replicate key aspects of cognitive development during infancy, with possible relevance to later development as well. This project serves two purposes: it takes Piaget's theory of human development as a source of inspiration for an artificial learning mechanism; and it extends and tests Piaget's theory by seeing whether a specific mechanism that works according to Piagetian themes actually exhibits Piagetian abilities. In fact, a computer program which implements the schema mechanism (along with a simple, simulated physical environment) has replicated several early milestones in the Piagetian infant's acquisition of the concept of physical object.

The schema mechanism practices a kind of learning that uses almost no *a priori* knowledge of the world. Starting without such knowledge is both a handicap and a source of power. A system that depends too strongly on built-in knowledge, and built-in terms of representation, will have difficulty ever making discoveries far beyond the scope of what is built in. But without already having a good idea of what relates to what, and how it relates, a learning system faces a formidable problem in interpreting its experiences well enough to learn from them in the first place; and without a built-in conceptual vocabulary suited to the problems it faces, the system needs a powerful facility for inventing concepts for itself. These are the two central challenges addressed by this research.

This chapter begins with an overview of the schema mechanism, and of the background of this research program—some basic concerns about the nature of learning that motivate and inform this work. A brief guide to the dissertation concludes the chapter. Subsequent chapters present a detailed description of the schema mechanism itself and of the results from experiments with its implementation. The final chapters discuss the schema mechanism in relation to cognitive science and to other research programs in the field of artificial intelligence.

1.1 The schema mechanism: an overview

This section summarizes the book. It spotlights the fundamental questions addressed by research with the schema mechanism, sketches the schema mechanism's implementation, and samples the results obtained.

1.1.1 Fundamental problems: empirical learning and concept invention

The schema mechanism controls, and receives sensory information from, a body. Based on its interaction with the world, the mechanism discovers regularities in the world, expressed in some existing representational vocabulary; and it constructs new concepts, thereby augmenting that vocabulary to make additional empirical discoveries expressible. The schema mechanism uses the knowledge it acquires to guide its actions, both for the sake of specific goals, and in order to gain further knowledge.

The mechanism expresses regularities as *schemas*, each of which predicts some effects of an action under specified circumstances; the mechanism expresses concepts as binary state elements called *items*, each of which can be *on* or *off* to assert or deny that some condition holds. Each item can have an associated *value*; an item's value can influence the selection of those actions which, according to extant schemas, may achieve the state designated by the item. The mechanism thus follows what we might call a *prediction-value* paradigm (see section 9.1), in contrast with a situation-action paradigm: the mechanism does not directly learn what action to take in a given situation, but rather learns what would happen next for each of several possible actions. It may then select what action to take based in part on the value of an achievable result.

The schema mechanism is principally concerned with empirical learning and with concept invention. For each of these intertwined processes, I identify a foundational problem, and propose and demonstrate a partial solution.

- The foundational problem in empirical learning is that the variability of the effects of the same action in different circumstances makes an action's results hard to notice as such in the first place. A solution to the empirical-learning problem, implemented by the schema mechanism's *marginal attribution* facility, is to use sensitive statistical measures to alternate between discovering a highly unreliable result, and then seeking conditions with respect to which the result follows more reliably.

- The foundational problem in concept invention is the need to define radically novel concepts—ones that designate entities fundamentally different from any that were previously represented (as, for example, a physical object is a much different sort of thing than a visual image or a tactile sensation). A solution is to define a new concept as the *potential to evoke a manifestation*, where the manifestation is described in terms of previously designated concepts; the schema mechanism's *synthetic items* define such concepts.

Empirical learning: marginal attribution

The first foundational problem concerns empirical learning. The schema mechanism's empirical learning facility faces a difficult chicken-and-egg problem. A given action may have a variety of different results in different circumstances; for example, moving one's hand incrementally backward can result in a tactile sensation on the chin, the shoulder, or elsewhere, depending on where the hand started. Even if a particular result follows a given action reliably under certain circumstances, that result may occur only rarely in general. Moreover, causes other than the given action may also give rise to the result; and even when that action does cause the result, the result may be buried among many unrelated events. Thus, even the most reliable results can be hard to notice as such, until the corresponding circumstances have been identified; but those, in turn, cannot be sought without first knowing what result they correspond to. That is the chicken-and-egg problem.

One solution would be to provide *a priori* constraint about what might be relevant to what. But in the interests of being able to transcend *a priori* domains (and in the interests of modeling Piaget's theory), the schema mechanism starts without such knowledge. This way, from the outset, the mechanism demonstrates the ability to learn in unprecedented domains—since, to the mechanism, all domains are unprecedented.

The schema mechanism's *marginal attribution* facility (section 4.1.2) tackles the chicken-and-egg problem by distinguishing the *relevance* of a result from its reliability. A result is relevant to an action if the result occurs more often when the action is taken than when not, however infrequent the result may be even when the action is taken. Requiring only that there be a significant difference in frequencies relieves the problem of a result's general rarity despite its following reliably under the right conditions. Requiring that the difference be significant quickly filters out merely coincidental co-occurrences. But detecting relevant results without *a priori* constraints requires looking everywhere—that is, maintaining relevance statistics for every pair of action and possible result. Section 5.1 argues that the burden of this exhaustive cross-correlation is acceptable.

Having identified a relevant result, the mechanism seeks conditions under which the result follows reliably. Here, too, distinguishing relevance from reliability turns out to be important, in order to build up to some necessary conjunction of context conditions by finding one conjunct at a time (as explained in section 4.1.2).

Concept invention: synthetic items

The second foundational problem is radically novel concept invention. Conventional learning systems define new concepts as boolean combinations, generalizations or specializations, or analogs or clusters of existing concepts. Any such variant of existing concepts resembles one or more prior concepts, differing only incrementally. Piagetian development, in contrast, requires the invention of concepts that differ fundamentally from all prior concepts.

For example, the schema mechanism—like an infant, according to Piaget—starts with only sensorimotor terms of representation—terms that designate sensory inputs and motor outputs. But the mechanism (again, like a Piagetian infant) develops important precursors of the concept of physical object, eventually being able to represent an object's continued existence even when the object is no longer perceived. A physical object that persists when not perceived is nothing like its various sensory manifestations: those are transient, variable, recurrent, and intangible, whereas an object is characterized by (among other things) its long-term persistence, its stability, its substance, its tangibility, its spatial locality, and its weight and volume.

The schema mechanism defines a new concept by building a state element called a *synthetic item* (section 4.2). The mechanism defines a synthetic item with respect to a schema that represents a *pattern of recoverability*. For example, returning the hand to where an object was last felt typically recovers the tactile manifestation of the object (because a nearby object typically stays put for a while, and thus will be felt again when the hand returns to where the object was recently encountered.) Upon discovering this pattern of recoverability, the mechanism defines a new synthetic item to designate *whatever unknown aspect of the world* assures this recoverability; in this example, the new synthetic item is thus defined to represent whatever aspect of the world assures that returning the hand to a particular location would in fact result in the tactile sensation in question.

In effect, this synthetic item thereby designates that there is, at present, a readily palpable object at a particular location. This English description—*object at a particular location*—is composed of designations of physical object, and of spatial location. But crucially, the mechanism itself does not define this synthetic item by composing prior concepts of object and location; the mechanism has no such prior concepts. On the contrary, this synthetic item may serve as a precursor of those very concepts.

Thus, the construction of a synthetic item starts from some previously conceived manifestation—in this example, a tactile sensation—which, however, had not been conceived of *as* a manifestation of anything. Working backward from the manifestation, the act of defining a synthetic item postulates a previously unconceived-of thing that is manifested (in this case, a physical object). Building synthetic items corresponds to Piagetian *conservation* phenomena, wherein an individual postulates some new kind of thing that remains invariant even when all manifestations of it change or cease. From early infancy to sophisticated science—from palpable objects to energy or quarks—such postulates can be revolutionary.

Having thus defined a new concept, the mechanism then tries to discover applicablity conditions for the concept—that is, conditions which distinguish instances of the concept from non-instances. In the present example, the applicability conditions are conditions under which the probing action of the hand would, in fact, result in the specified manifestation. These conditions are expressed as a function of other concepts represented by the mechanism (e.g., concepts corresponding to visual evidence for the object's presence). The applicability conditions serve to *operationalize* the new concept, to make it usable, by determining, albeit imperfectly, when the concept is and is not applicable. But the operationalizing function does not *define* the new concept, for the function is always subject to extension and revision when new experiences reveal a discrepancy between the function and the concept that it is supposed to operationalize.

1.1.2 The implementation: structures, machinery, and accomplishments

I intend *schema mechanism* to be a generic term (like *internal combustion engine*); it designates any learning mechanism that operates more or less as described here, no matter whether the mechanism is instantiated biologically, electronically, or is just an unimplemented abstraction. I advance the hypothesis that the schema mechanism may be implemented by the human brain, as a component of our intelligence. However, except where otherwise noted, I use the term *schema mechanism* in this book to refer to the mechanism as implemented by a particular computer program that is described here.

This section sketches the schema mechanism's data structures, its machinery for building and using its structures, and a synopsis of the learning actually achieved by the implementation. Chapters 3, 4 and 6 present this subject matter in greater breadth and depth.

Figure 1.1 illustrates the schema mechanism's robot body and *microworld* (i.e., a small, artificial world in which the body resides). These can be viewed on a computer screen, providing a way to watch the mechanism's actions. The body includes a crude visual system, and a single, mobile hand (detached from the body) with tactile sensors and the ability to grasp and move objects. Like a neonate's, this body lacks the ability to move itself from place to place.

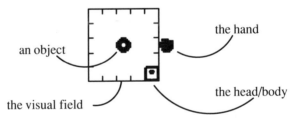

Figure 1.1 The microworld. The schema mechanism controls a simulated robot in a two-dimensional microworld. The visual field can move relative to the body. Here, the visual field encompasses the body and a round object, but not the hand.

Structures: schemas, actions, and items

The schema mechanism has three kinds of data structures: schemas, actions, and items.

- A *schema* is a tripartite structure comprising a context, action, and result. A schema asserts that if its action is taken when its context conditions are all satisfied, then the result conditions will obtain. (The assertion is subject to a reliability factor that the schema maintains). For example, the schema in figure 1.2 asserts that if the hand is just in front of the mouth (context), moving the hand incrementally backward (action) will precipitate a tactile sensation on the mouth (result).

- Each *action* designates an event that can affect the state of the world (as might be reflected in the state of some of the mechanism's items).

- An *item* is a state element. Each item corresponds to some proposition about the state of the world, and is *On* (or *Off*) to assert (or deny) that proposition. (An item can also be in an *Unknown* state.)

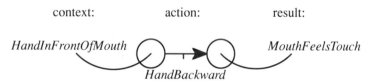

context: action: result:

HandInFrontOfMouth   *MouthFeelsTouch*

HandBackward

Figure 1.2 A schema. A schema asserts that taking its action when its context conditions are satisfied would achieve its result. This schema says how to move the hand backward to the mouth.

A schema is a unit of knowledge, both declarative and procedural. Declaratively, a schema makes a factual assertion, an assertion about what would happen under certain circumstances. Procedurally, a schema can say how to pursue a goal; the goal may be in the schema's own result, or the schema may facilitate the activation of some other schema whose result includes the goal. A schema is also a unit of experimentation, comparing what happens when an action is taken to what happens without it. As explained below, new schemas arise from such experiments.

Schemas' contexts and results are represented in terms of items. Each context designates zero or more items; some may be negated. In figure 1.2, the context consists of the (nonnegated) item *HandInFrontOfMouth*. A context is satisfied when and only when all of its nonnegated items are *On*, and all of its negated items are *Off*. A result similarly contains zero or more (possibly negated) items; in figure 1.2, the result consists of the item *MouthFeelsTouch* (also nonnegated). The result items are expected, subject to the schema's reliability factor, to turn On (or Off, if negated) when the schema completes its *activation*. To activate a schema is to initiate its action when the schema's context conditions are satisfied; the schema's activation finishes when its action terminates.

Primitive and acquired structures

The schema mechanism's primitively supplied items all correspond to perceptual information, such as *there's something touching the hand* or *there's some object at the upper left of the visual field*. Each primitively supplied action corresponds to some simple motor activity, like moving the hand incrementally forward or glancing incrementally to the left. Calling the initial actions and items *primitive* is just to say that they comprise the initial representational vocabulary, in contrast with later elements, which the mechanism itself constructs. What the primitive items designate, and how they are computed, need not be simple; the visual items, for example, may correspond to information that (in humans) is the result of a complicated analysis of a visual scene to extract information about three-dimensional structure.

However sophisticated the processing may be that supplies primitive information to the schema mechanism, the schema mechanism itself is, at first, wholly ignorant of what the primitive actions and items correspond to, or how they might relate to one another. It does not know, for example, which items are visual and which tactile, or even what it would mean to be visual or tactile. It does not know that two items designating similar kinds of information—for example, two tactile items corresponding to contact with adjacent regions of the hand—have any closer relationship to each other than to arbitrary other items. And the mechanism does not even *have*—let alone understand—any primitive items that designate persistent objects—objects that continue to exist even when not perceived. It is part of the schema mechanism's task to learn about the relations among its units of representation, both primitive and constructed.

A constructivist mechanism is like a programming language in that its character is defined not so much by its particular set of primitives as by its ways of combining structures to form larger ones, and by its means of abstraction—its means of forming new units of representation that allow the details of their implementation to be ignored.[1] The schema mechanism, like a good programming language, is *extensible*: instances of its basic units of representation—schemas, items, and actions—can all be constructed by the mechanism's means of combination and

---

1.   This analysis of programming languages is borrowed from Abelson and Sussman [1].

abstraction. More than this, the schema mechanism is *self*-extensible—it is the mechanism itself (rather than a programmer or other external agent) that manufactures these extensions.

The schema mechanism interacts with the world, and based on its experiences, constructs new schemas, actions, and items.

- The schema mechanism builds schemas that connect items and actions to express discoveries about regularities in the world. Such discoveries are made by the mechanism's marginal attribution facility, which, as mentioned above, addresses the chicken-and-egg problem of empirical learning: how to recognize an action's result without first knowing the necessary context conditions.

- The mechanism builds new state elements, synthetic items, to designate aspects of the world that are radically different from any that were previously represented.

- For any achievable result, the mechanism can build a *composite action*, defined as the action of achieving that result, regardless of just which schemas are used to achieve the result. Defining composite actions allows the mechanism to represent events at levels of abstraction higher than the lowest, sensorimotor level. Composite actions also allow for the designation of state transitions that are caused externally, rather than being under the mechanism's control (as explained in section 4.3.2).

Highlights of the implementation's accomplishments

Chapter 6 presents a detailed synopsis of the developmental progression achieved by the schema mechanism's computer implementation, emphasizing its recapitulation of some early milestones in the Piagetian development of the concept of physical objects. Here, as a preview, are some brief highlights.

The mechanism has ten primitive (i.e., built-in) actions: four to move the hand incrementally forward, back, right, or left, within a certain range of the body; four to shift the glance orientation incrementally in those directions, within a certain range; and actions of opening and closing the hand. There are three categories of primitive items: proprioceptive[2], tactile, and visual. For each possible body-relative hand position, there is a hand-position item which is On just in case the hand is in that position; similarly, there is an eye-position item for each possible body-rel-

2.   Proprioception gives an organism information about the orientation of its limbs and other body parts using direct cues such as muscle tension, as opposed to, say, visual evidence.

ative glance orientation. Various tactile items designate contact with parts of the hand or the body; some tactile items denote specific tactile details of objects being felt. The visual field comprises a number of regions; for each, there is a visual item which is On just in case an object appears at that region (every object's image occupies just one such region). Also, for each of several *foveal* regions, a number of other items designate visual details of an image appearing there; these details can help identify specific objects.

Among the mechanism's first achievements is a practical elaboration of the spatial relationship among the various visual-field items and proprioceptive items. That is, the mechanism builds schemas such as in figure 1.3, which describe the adjacency of certain hand-position, eye-position, or visual-region items with respect to incremental hand or glance actions. Such schemas chain together in networks that tell the mechanism how to move the hand from one body-relative position to another by a series of motions between adjacent positions, or how to direct the gaze to a given orientation, or change the gaze to shift an image to a given part of the visual field.

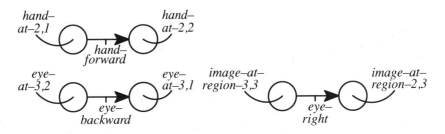

Figure 1.3 Adjacency schemas. These schemas help forge a practical understanding of locations' adjacency.

The mechanism learns about some visual effects of hand motions, as illustrated in figure 1.4. In addition, the mechanism learns to sometimes anticipate tactile contact when the hand is seen moved beside an object, also shown in figure 1.4. Such schemas begin to connect an object's visual and tactile properties—but without yet representing the object apart from its sensory manifestation.

It is not enough to discover such connections among existing representations. A constructivist system's greatest challenge is to transcend its initially supplied terms of representation, to extend its own ontological vocabulary, to designate kinds of things that are radically different from any that it had previously been able to represent. Beyond discovering intermodal coordination, the schema

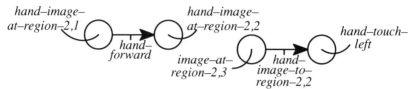

Figure 1.4 Intermodal schemas. These schemas anticipate some visual and tactile effects of hand motion. The notation *hand-image...* abbreviates visual-detail items that correspond to the hand; *hand-image-to-region-2,2* is a composite action.

mechanism builds synthetic items that begin to designate objects, as distinct from their current perceptions.

The first schema in figure 1.5 says that the action of moving the hand to body-relative position $(2,3)$[3] results in a tactile sensation. The schema's context is empty, so its assertion is unconditional, and very unreliable—the assertion is correct only when an object happens to be at the adjacent position $(1,3)$. The mechanism builds a synthetic item, which we might call PalpableObjectAt1,3 (the name, of course, has no meaning to the mechanism). The item is defined to represent whatever condition makes the schema reliable; we observers know (but the mechanism does not) that this condition is that there be an object at $(1,3)$.[4] As the mechanism discovers conditions under which the schema is reliable—for instance, if the schema happened to succeed just recently—it turns the item On when such conditions are met; whenever the item is On, the mechanism understands that moving the hand to $(2,3)$ will result in a tactile sensation.

Similarly, when the second synthetic item in figure 1.5 is On, the mechanism knows that looking directly at $(2,3)$ will produce an image just left of where the glance is directed; the item thus denotes a visible object at $(1,3)$. Each of these two synthetic items can remain On even when the eye and hand are both directed elsewhere, enabling the mechanism to represent that something persists in the absence of any sensory manifestation. Later developments coordinate these initially distinct items, so that they tend to turn On and Off together, reflecting, in effect,

3. This action is a composite action. The formation of composite actions is explained in section 4.3.1.

4. The reader may wonder why the synthetic item does not get incorporated into the context of the schema. The answer is that a given schema's context (or result) never changes, although a similar schema, but with something added to its context or result, may also be built. Thus, the synthetic item shown here may appear in the context (or result) of some other schema, but not in the very schema with respect to which the item is defined.

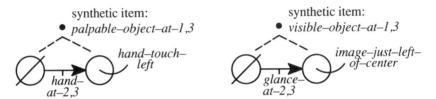

Figure 1.5 Persistent-object items. These synthetic items designate palpable or visible objects (respectively) at a certain body-relative position.

a discovery that the representations are coextensive—that a visible object at (1,3) is the same thing as a palpable object at (1,3).

1.2 Origins of constructivist AI: on the meaning of learning

A research program's aspirations are elucidated by its inspirations—by the prior investigations that pose basic questions and frame possible answers. This section presents some concerns about the nature of learning that motivate the schema mechanism, both in its broad outline and in many of its details.

The scope of human skill and knowledge is striking. For some domains of expertise, such as visual processing, it is clear that the human species is genetically endowed with hardware that embodies knowledge about the domain. For other domains, such as language, the question of built-in knowledge is controversial. But for many domains—physics, architecture, economics, chess, juggling, cinematography, computer programming, rock'n'roll—there can be no corresponding innate mental modules. The subject matter of these domains did not even exist (or become accessible) until so recently that evolution could not have learned how to preprogram the corresponding skills; and the complexity of those domains, along with the tight match of the corresponding competence, precludes the possibility that such preprogramming arose as an accidental side-effect of other evolutionary developments. Moreover, in those domains and myriad others, dramatic advances in knowledge occur within individual lifetimes—sometimes in mere years, days, even seconds. Uniquely, successive generations of human beings inherit a progressive accumulation of competence arising not by the rearrangement of genes but by the creativity of minds, and propagating not through biological reproduction but through the tutelage of culture.

We must, of course, be endowed with innate machinery that is responsible for our ability to construct and acquire such diverse knowledge. We may term such machinery a general learning mechanism—general in the sense that it spans a diverse, open-ended set of domains that were not specifically "anticipated" by evolution. It is natural to wonder what portion of human intelligence grows out of a general learning mechanism, and what part is due to innately specialized, domain-specific processing modules.

1.2.1 Learning in human beings: nativism and constructivism

Jean Piaget and Noam Chomsky stand at two extremes of the nativism vs. learning spectrum. Piaget's work is at the foundation of the modern empirical study of the genesis of intelligence in individual humans. Piaget proposes a radically *constructivist* account in which even the basic notion of an object—the notion that visual and tactile sensations are related to each other, as manifestations of some external thing; that this thing exists even when not perceived, etc.—is not innate, but is abstracted from the infant's interactions with its world. Similarly, notions of logic, classification, and number, conceptions of people and of self, and of the rest of the world, are all gradually constructed. Moreover, intelligence itself—seen as a gamut of strategies for pursuing goals or solving problems or exploring terrains, literal or figurative—is constructed, bit by bit, with ever-increasing sophistication.

At the other extreme, Noam Chomsky champions a radically nativist theory of cognitive development. Chomsky doubts the very intelligibility of the notion of learning [15, 54], particularly with regard to *cognitive universals*, that is, concepts normally acquired by all persons; virtually everyone, for example, comes to understand the rudimentary properties of physical objects, and gains fluency in speaking and understanding a language. It may be that such knowledge is not at first present, or is not present in a form that the infant can use (just as, for example, an infant's reproductive apparatus is not yet functional). But what is innately present, by any account, is a mechanism which, interacting with any normal environment, nearly inevitably develops a usable version of such knowledge.

Chomsky poses the rhetorical question: how does that nearly inevitable development differ from, say, the nearly inevitable development of limbs by a zygote? Limbs are not present at conception, nor any miniature model of limbs; nor is there even (necessarily) any local region of the genome specifically descriptive of limbs, i.e., specifically dedicated to the control of limb development but not of other body parts. Nonetheless, the growth of human limbs is an innately specified maturational process, merely by virtue of the fact that the human genome, placed in a normal environment, almost certainly will grow limbs. And, although natural selection undoubtedly shaped the evolution of limbs, many other physical structures (e.g., navels) were not specifically selected for, but developed instead as side-effects of other constraints; nonetheless, even navels are properly said to be innately specified, not learned by each individual. Why should the learnedness of cognitive universals be judged by different standards than morphological universals?

Escaping the snare of this clever, provocative question helps elucidate the meaning of learning, and prepares the way for more substantive investigations of the nature of learning. Here, I believe, is an easy, sensible way out.

Consider, for example, knowing the names and layout of the streets in one's neighborhood. This knowledge is untendentiously learned, in that *information is gained* when this knowledge is acquired (using Shannon's [62] technical sense of *information*). No examination of a zygote could yield a street map of its neighborhood; the information simply is not present. But examining the brain of a person who has acquired that knowledge could—in principle—reveal that information.

In contrast, the process of growing limbs yields no new information that limbs will exist. Looking at a zygote, one could already—in principle—deduce that the mature organism will develop limbs, if nurtured in a normal environment (presuming that one knows what such an environment is like). Thus, the information that limbs would develop is already present in the zygote; the mature organism bears no additional such information.

Let us say that a mechanism is a learning mechanism if its function is to gain and use information. Chomsky's point, recast in these terms, is that the acquisition of cognitive universals, like the development of limbs, entails no information gain; as much can be determined (in principle) about cognitive universals by examining a zygote (if the examiner has knowledge of the zygote's normal kind of environment) as by examining an adult. The same can be said for analytic—necessarily true—knowledge, such as 2+2=4. In the case of nonanalytic universals, either examination is fruitful; in the case of analytic knowledge, both examinations are superfluous (since we can know, for example, that 2+2=4, without empirical demonstration of that fact).

Nonetheless, in opposition to Chomsky's conclusion, universal or analytic knowledge might develop as the product of a learning mechanism. That is, a mechanism whose function is to gain and use information, to build and use knowledge structures that represent environmental contingencies (e.g., street names), might also, and by the same processes, build and use structures that represent features of the environment which turn out to be so ubiquitous, and so prominent, that any such mechanism, in a normal environment, will almost inevitably come to represent those features. Because they are inevitable, these structures do not add information (in the technical sense) to the system. Nonetheless, studying the knowledge structures built by a learning mechanism, one lacks any good reason to exclude those that turn out to be inevitable, hence universal (to mechanisms of that kind); all of a learning mechanism's similarly acquired and similarly used knowledge structures are sensibly called learned.

Thus, universal and analytic knowledge can be learned, if acquired by a learning mechanism—a mechanism for gaining information (even though the acquisition of universal and analytic knowledge is not itself an information gain). But even if cognitive universals are in fact learned, it remains sensible to say, as Chomsky does, that they are innately specified, in the same sense that limbs or navels are (even if, like navels, the cognitive universals were not specifically "anticipated," i.e., selected for, by evolution). The two apparently conflicting claims are reconcilable if the innately specified developmental process is a learning process, in the sense just given.

The substantive question, then, is which such knowledge, if any, is in fact learned by human beings, and which, if any, is either present at birth, or develops later by a nonlearning maturational process.

1.2.2 Learning in artificial systems

A parallel question arises when designing an artificial intelligence (AI). To what extent is it reasonable to seek powerful general mechanisms of learning; to what extent should research focus on more domain-specific mechanisms? The question about humans is distinct from the question about AI. Even if general learning mechanisms are feasible, human beings might not be designed that way; conversely, even if much of human intelligence does flow from a general learning mechanism, engineering a replica of that mechanism may be an intractable problem.

Indeed, early AI work, pursuing *self-organizing systems*, tried and failed to find just such a mechanism. As this approach became discredited, there followed a generation of *knowledge-based* AI, characterized by the principle that intelligence, especially learning, derives its power from knowledge: about specific domains, about reasoning, about space and time and so on. There must be a wealth of structure to support the acquisition of new structure. From this point of view, bootstrapping from meager initial knowledge seems unlikely.

On the other hand, the failure to develop *tabula rasa* systems may have been due to problems not intrinsic to the very attempt. In particular, the study of self-organizing systems (like some philosophical and psychological inquiries about the innateness vs.acquisition of human knowledge) has been handicapped by lack of attention to empirical evidence. The relevance of empirical data to the question about humans is clear: by observing the intellectual development of humans from infancy, one can hope to obtain evidence as to the early presence or absence of certain abilities or knowledge.[5] With regard to the AI approach, it is good to be reminded of a maxim of Seymour Papert: in order to think seriously about thinking, one must think about thinking about *something*. But what is a self-organizing system to "think" about? Not the things that human adults think about: adult tasks are predicated upon much acquired knowledge, not available to a *tabula rasa* machine. On the other hand, whatever it is that human *infants* think about is a plausible candidate for the subject matter of a learning-based AI mechanism. The infant's learning achievements offer target abilities for the mechanism, providing a basis for the mechanism's design. Without data about infants (and without a plausible constructivist theory to characterize that data) there is no good source of inspiration as to what, specifically, a constructivist mechanism ought to *do*.

The methodological flaw—not having a clearly specified target domain—is compounded by a second problem in research about self-organizing systems: it is traditional to set up a chaotic gaggle of interacting elements and then wait for order to emerge from the chaos. But extracting order from chaos is hard work. A mechanism to do this work must be designed not just to amass atomic facts, but to organize data into functional units, to abstract essential attributes and discard useless ones, to verify suspected regularities and pursue variations on them, to develop new kinds of representation as old ones prove inadequate—the sort of activity that must be involved in any serious effort to make sense of the world.[6]

---

5.   The interpretation of such evidence is not straightforward, though (see section 2.9.3). An infant might not yet manifest certain knowledge that is nonetheless present—or that will arise from an innately-programmed maturational sequence. Conversely, adultocentric interpretations may impart to an infant a more sophisticated understanding than is necessary to explain its actions.

6.   The resurrection of self-organizing systems in the guise of connectionism avoids the primary pitfalls of earlier such research. Present-day connectionism tends to focus more modestly on providing alternative computational goals for solving particular problems. Section 9.2 compares connectionist work with the approach advocated here.

1.2.3 Humanlike learning in artificial systems

Piaget's work offers an antidote to both the lack of a clear target domain and the naive-order-from-chaos problem. Piaget gives an elaborate description of the course of cognitive development from infancy through childhood and adolescence, taking account of the evolution of primitive problem-solving and domain-specific knowledge. Piaget characterizes ways in which, at a given point, a person uses existing knowledge and skills to achieve specific goals, and to create new knowledge and skills. Piaget's intricate road map of the course of development—especially during infancy—specifies a target domain for artificial systems, a sequence of cognitive acquisitions for a mechanism to achieve.

Piaget documents some striking uniformities throughout cognitive development, and refers to these as the *functional invariants* of intelligence. These invariants amount to a loose characterization of an underlying developmental mechanism. Departing from the older empiricist tradition, Piaget's characterization of developmental invariants emphasizes the importance of well-designed activities of organizing, structuring, and abstracting from experience, and of the purposive application of knowledge and exploration in the pursuit of goals, in contrast with merely accumulating data from and being conditioned by the environment. Piaget's loose description of functional invariants falls far short of a formal specification of a developmental mechanism; still, it furnishes an important alternative to naive order from chaos as a starting point for a precise specification.

My research program, then, is to design and implement a mechanism that corresponds to Piaget's sketch of the functional invariants of cognitive development. This endeavor has two broad goals: to help understand the human mind, and to help design an artificial mind. As mentioned above, questions about the nature of intelligence might have different answers for cognitive science than for AI. Nonetheless, the program advocated here (not as the sole promising approach, but as one of them) is to try to build an intelligent mechanism by taking human intelligence as the inspiration—that is, by trying to reverse engineer the mechanism of the human mind.

I presume, as a working hypothesis, the approximate correctness of Piaget's theory (subject to certain revisions in light of modern evidence, as discussed in section 2.9.3). That is, I assume that a general learning mechanism resembling Piaget's is indeed present in the human mind, and is of central importance to the development of intelligence during infancy (and quite possibly through adulthood). I present results to show that a mechanism designed along the lines of Piaget's theory can indeed account for some early aspects of the Piagetian developmental progression. The motivation for stressing early (rather than later) development is threefold: early development is simplest; the most detailed comprehensive observations of human development concern early development; and the developmental mechanism is most clearly discerned in its earliest operation, before its own constructs obscure it by complicating its observable activity.

The schema mechanism is a proposed approximation to the mechanism of Piagetian development. I make no a priori assumption about how uniform or complicated this mechanism must be; my method is to postulate as much built-in complexity as appears to meet the mechanism's design goals. Two fundamental influences contribute to the design of the schema mechanism: the Piagetian road map, and engineering requirements. The mechanism is intended both to help explain the themes of Piagetian development, and to be well-motivated from an engineering standpoint, given the computational demands of the learning tasks involved. I avoid machinery that accords with only one of these two principles—machinery that is rigged to replicate this or that developmental event, but without any good reason for a learning system to incorporate such machinery; or apparatus that builds in sophisticated abilities which, however, are not initially present in Piagetian development. These exclusions stem from the goal of reverse engineering the Piagetian mechanism. Replication of developmental events is of interest here only to the extent that those events reflect the operation of a reasonably designed learning mechanism; and reasonably designed mechanisms that do not correspond to the human apparatus are worthy of investigation, but belong to a different program of research. (See section 10.1 for elaboration on these methodological issues.)

Piaget's theory is symbiotic with the schema mechanism:

- As just noted, Piaget outlines the main themes of cognitive development, and details much of the content of its early learning. This gives a first approximation to the mechanism, and a set of target achievements.

- The schema mechanism adds precision to Piaget's characterization of constructivism. A more concrete statement of Piagetian theory makes possible more specific tests and evaluations of the theory.

- Implementing a mechanism for Piagetian development is itself a partial test of his theory. Successful replication of Piagetian milestones by a plausibly engineered learning mechanism is circumstantial evidence that such a mechanism is involved in human development. Unsuccessful attempts at such replication may point to places where the theory is wrong, or needs to be supplemented.

In sum, the project of *constructivist AI* is to explore Piaget's theory by the methodology of artificial intelligence: testing a theory of the mind by building a mechanism that works according to that theory, and seeing to what extent the mechanism displays the abilities that the theory was supposed to explain.

1.3 Guide to the rest of the book

Nine chapters follow the present one.

- Chapter Two gives a synopsis of the initial, *sensorimotor* period of Piagetian development (and touches briefly on subsequent periods); this developmental sequence is the target scenario for the schema mechanism. This chapter also addresses the the suitability of basing the schema mechanism on Piaget's theory, given strong contemporary challenges to that theory. (The reader who is concerned only with the schema mechanism per se may wish to skip this chapter.)

Part II: The schema mechanism

- Chapter Three describes the schema mechanism, its data structures, and its control.

- Chapter Four describes the mechanism's facilities for building new instances of its data structures.

- Chapter Five sketches the architecture (neural and computer implementation) of the schema mechanism.

Part III: Performance and speculations

- Chapter Six presents a synopsis of the schema mechanism's computer implementation's achievement of some of the developmental milestones described in the second chapter, and proposes a hypothetical scenario of further achievements.

- Chapter Seven raises the speculative possibility that the basic learning mechanism, acting in concert with its own constructs, can implement more sophisticated virtual structures and mechanisms.

- Chapter Eight addresses the problem of naive induction and its bearing on proposed learning systems, such as the schema mechanism.

Part IV: Appraisal

- Chapter Nine analyzes the schema mechanism in relation to other AI research programs.

- Chapter Ten offers a methodological critique of constructivist AI suggestions for future research, and an evaluation and summary.

2 Synopsis of Piagetian development

This chapter discusses Piaget's theory of the development of sensorimotor intelligence, as described in his volumes on infancy [50, 52]. I present a summary of the original theory, and suggest bases for reconciling Piagetian theory with modern evidence evidence which reveals infant knowledge that is apparently precocious by Piagetian theory.

2.1 Piagetian fundamentals

The point of departure of Piaget's theory is the schema: a unit of behavior and knowledge which, by Piaget's biological metaphor, interacts and evolves with its physical environment, and with other schemas. The initial schemas are merely those of reflex responses. For quite some time, the infant's schemas are closely associated with her own actions. Later sophistications, involving the combination of schemas, abstraction above specific acts and perspectives, and the *interiorization* of schemas' activity, will allow the schema to transcend a literal dependence on physical action, while retaining its procedural flavor. Schemas of looking, grasping what's seen, swinging, dropping, hiding one object under another, pushing one object with another, are examples of post-reflex schemas.

Piaget identifies *assimilation* and *accommodation* as the basic processes of intelligence:

- Assimilation is a schema's use of things in the world (including other schemas) as part of its own functioning; and

- Accomodation is the modification of schemas in adjustment to novelties in the world.

Piaget does not try to present complete, explicit rules governing the activity and modification of schemas. But his theory does try to characterize such rules and to give an intricate chronicle of the low-level results of their functioning.

The sensorimotor period (from birth until about age two) is the first of four broad periods of development in Piagetian theory. Sensorimotor intelligence is expressed solely in *actions* that affect the world. In the later phases—the *preoperational* phase, then the phases of *concrete operations* and *formal operations*—the *truth* of assertions about the world becomes the focus of intelligence, first for assertions about the *real* world, and later in the realms of the hypothetical and the abstract [53].

Piaget distinguishes six stages within the sensorimotor period. Each successive stage is characterized by schemas that embody a new elaboration of problem-solving activity (the infant's earliest behavior is only a zeroth-order example of problem-solving; later stages do greater justice to the term) or goal-pursuing activity (which never implies the eradication of less sophisticated schemas, or even that such schemas stop being created). The elaborations characteristic of a given stage do not appear simultaneously; the stage is just the period during which such appearances first peak. A stage's uniformity is thus a descriptive invention, and doesn't imply rigid chronological partitioning.

The infant's representation of reality—space, objects, causation, time—exhibits corresponding stages of development. In fact, Piaget argues that progressively more sophisticated techniques of intelligence, and progressively more sophisticated representations of reality, are two indissociable aspects of the same development. At the outset, problem-solving is just the dynamic expression of the infant's representation of reality—a natural enough idea, since the infant's schemas are procedural: a thing is understood in terms of what can be done to it or with it. So, more advanced problem solving results from the application of the same mechanism to more sophisticated representations of reality, and vice versa. Eventually, of course, the child acquires explicit knowledge *about* thinking that can be used to improve methods of thought; but there is substantial maturing of intelligence long before such meta-knowledge is evident in the child.

One critical feature of the infant's intelligence, not well captured by this summary, is the *incremental* quality of its development. At least at the outset, each new capability observed in the infant is only slightly different than what was previously exhibited; the infant shows only minor adjustments of activity, in apparent response to experience in prior activity. It should be kept in mind that the actual steps are of much finer grain than are presented here. As intelligence progresses and there come to be more powerful schemas for interpreting the world, the steps grow bolder, and, in ways that I'll discuss, less dependent upon specific experience. So, the change from trivial to powerful steps is a smooth one; the increments by which intelligence improves are, in effect, of size proportional to the power of existing schemas, so the development has an exponential character.

2.2 First stage: reflex activity, solipsist images[7]

The infant's initial schemas are those of reflex activity: for example, closing the hand in response to a touch on the palm, or sucking something that touches the lips. These schemas are exercised either in response to the appropriate stimuli, or else spontaneously, as though for play or practice.

From the outset, schemas admit of modifications in response to experienced results of their activity. For example, after many instances of disorderly reflexive groping for a nipple touching the mouth, an infant's sucking schema appears to notice that when the nipple touches (say) the left cheek, turning to the left will be propitious. Groping in adjustment to the nipple thus assumes a gradually more coherent appearance, as clues such as cheek-contact are exploited.

The early development of schemas also shows generalization and differentiation. For example, the sucking schema adjusts itself not only to the nipple, but also to other objects frequently presented to it: e.g., a finger or a toy. Often, the infant will suck such an object as contentedly as if it were a nipple. But when hungry, the infant responds with enthusiasm to the nipple while crying instead if given a finger to suck. The appearance of this discrimination suggests that, despite the production-like character of schemas' early, stimulus-triggered activity, the desired *result* of a schema's activity also affects its course.

The first few months of life also see the first so-called *primary circular reactions*. These are patterns of action, derived by gradual differentiation of reflex schemas, that tend towards repetition. For example, the grasp-reflex schema gives rise to a alternately-hold-then-release-object schema, and to a scratch-object schema, and so on. As with pure reflex schemas, these sometimes repeat "emptily," that is, without any stimulus or object to interact with.

Visual schemas developing at this time include those of tracking a slowly moving object, of visually exploring a stationary object, and of alternate glances between one object and another.

A striking feature of these early schemas is that they haven't yet "intertwined." For example, tactile stimuli elicit no visual response; things seen inspire no effort at prehension. Moreover, when for example a watched object passes beyond the infant's field of view, the infant either loses all evident interest in it, as though it no longer existed; or else, with apparent expectation of seeing it again, either continues to look off in the same direction, or gazes back to where the object was first seen. Similarly, an object that is touched but not seen may be repeatedly grasped then released; but if, say, it falls to a new position, the infant will neither search for it visually, nor move her hand to search for the object in a different position than where just grasped.

These observations imply that the infant's model of the world—in the sense of what aspects of the world the infant can react to or exploit—is (metaphorically)

---

7.   I am using a slightly different border between first and second stage than Piaget defines. This is of no importance; I mention it only to avoid confusion.

solipsist in nature: the infant's universe contains not objects of substance and permanence viewable from different perspectives, but rather images, some visual, some tactile, etc., that change state in response to personal actions (themselves known only by the transformations they produce). The infant's early schemas organize the world into various solipsist spaces, each giving a group (in the mathematical sense) of operations: the operations are primitive motor actions (or, sometimes, passive expectation), and the things operated on are sensory states.

2.3 Second stage: the coordination of primary schemas

As reflex schemas elaborate into primary circular reactions, they also begin to intercoordinate and thus to bridge the gap between sensory modes. The primary circular reactions, and their intercoordinations, both appear to have the same character of development: a schema acquires differentiated responses to, and anticipations of, sensory signals with which it was previously unacquainted. If the new signals of one schema are already familiar to another, then a functional coordination results, as when schemas of hand movements combine with sucking to form an integrated thumb-sucking schema.

Initially, an infant will suck her finger (or other object) only if it comes in fortuitous contact with the infant's mouth (or, slightly later, cheeks etc.). (Even then, the infant doesn't know how to keep her hand in place, and the hand is quickly pulled away.) But random hand movements may accidently brush the hand against the vicinity of the mouth. Not only will this trigger attempts to suck, but also, future hand trajectories will converge to the mouth more and more directly. Eventually, the infant can smoothly and spontaneously move her hand to her mouth, and insert and suck on a finger. Later, a more profound development is seen: the infant is capable of carrying a grasped object to her mouth and sucking on it; thus, prehension is coordinated with sucking.

More striking still is the coordination that develops between vision and prehension. Piaget discerns a number of milestones in this development:

- The infant watches the movements of her hand, and gradually learns to bring her hand into her visual field, and keep it there while watching it.

- The infant watches while grasping and releasing objects.

- The infant subsequently will turn to look at an object when the object touches her hand, or will move the object into her visual field to look at it.

- At some point, the infant will reach for an object, but only if the object and the infant's hand are seen together.

- Eventually, the sight of the object alone will suffice to trigger a successful attempt to grasp it.

Of course, each of these bits and pieces of eye/hand coordination develops not as a sudden leap, but by gradually improved groping.

The acquisition of visual/tactile coordination has an important consequence: hereafter, the infant's learning and attention become oriented around objects, not just particular sensory impressions. The appearance of this more objective behavior marks the onset of the next sensorimotor stage.

2.4 Third stage: secondary circular reactions, subjective permanence

The third sensorimotor stage usually begins four or five months after birth, and continues until eight or nine months of age.

Secondary circular reactions are characteristic of third stage behavior; these consist of the repetition of actions in order to reproduce fortuitously-discovered effects on objects. For example:

- The infant's hand hits a hanging toy. The infant sees it bob about, then repeats the gesture several times, later applying it to other objects as well, developing a striking schema for striking.

- A strange sound is made by accidentally striking the crib wicker with a toy. The infant reproduces the motion involved, and after more occasional fortuitous contacts, will rub the toy deliberately against the wicker. However, spatial contact between the objects is not understood as such. If the infant's position is changed such that the customary gesture fails to achieve contact with the crib, she repeats the gesture anyway, doing nothing that adapts to the altered situation.

- The infant pulls a string hanging from the bassinet hood, and notices that a toy, also connected to the hood, shakes in response. The infant again grasps and pulls the string, already watching the toy rather than the string. Again, the spatial and causal nature of the connection between the objects is not understood; the infant will generalize the gesture to inappropriate situations.

In these reactions, the infant responds quickly to a novel result by using a familiar schema to reproduce the result, even though the schema had never previously been used for that purpose. However, the effect is discovered by accident, and only the particular schema involved in the accident is used to reproduce the effect.

Nonetheless, thanks to the intersensorial schemas of the previous stage, the current schemas transcend particular primitive motor actions and sensory images. This, together with the more complex chain of actions involved in, say, seeing, grasping, moving, or rubbing an object, give secondary circular reactions the appearance of being goal-directed (where the goal is to reproduce the surprise effect), in contrast with the stimulus-bound appearance of the primary circular reactions.

The sense in which the third stage initiates the representation of objects rather than images is perhaps best described as follows: if one were to write a program that did the sorts of things that a third stage infant does (apart from learning), the program would most naturally be written on a level of abstraction that designated objects; a program to mimic earlier stages would most naturally lack such a level, and would instead be oriented around sensory images.

To the extent that they deal with objects rather than images, the secondary circular reactions can begin to designate interactions, and hence practical relations, between objects—but with the limitation that the relationship is given only by a schema with a particular motor action, implying both unnecessary restrictions, and inappropriate generalizations, of the relation (as in the wicker-striking and hood-pulling examples above).

Similar progress, and limitations, appear in the third stage representation of objects' permanence and position:

- *Deferred circular reactions* appear. An infant, playing with a toy (via a secondary circular reaction schema) is momentarily distracted but soon turns back to where the toy was left and resumes playing with it. This is similar to, but more complicated than, the earlier feat of looking again at one image after shifting gaze to another; here, a coordination of body and hand movements, guided by vision, is required to recapture the object.

- When the infant is watching an object that falls, moving too quickly to track so that she loses sight of it, she will look downwards for it. At first this happens primarily when it was the infant who held and dropped the object, and is also catalyzed by the sound of the fallen object, or by tracking it momentarily when it starts to fall. Eventually, the reaction becomes reliable even in the absence of such clues.

- Similarly, if the infant holds (without looking at it) an object that falls, or is taken, from her hand, she learns at this stage to extend her hand and reclaim the object.

Thus, the third stage infant apparently conceives of objects as occupying particular positions at which they can be reclaimed if they vanish from view. Moreover, in contrast with the previous stage, the object can be sought in a *new* position, rather than the first or last place that it was recently perceived. However, closer observation shows that this reclamation is only understood with respect to a particular schema of action. The infant confronted with an object's sudden disappearance tries to recapture it either by extending the activity of a schema already invoked to keep sight of the thing—e.g., for the falling object—or by reusing a schema just used to secure the thing in the first place—e.g., reaching to regrasp an unseen object removed from the hand. In this latter case, if that particular gesture fails to rediscover the object, the infant will *not* (until the next, fourth, stage) employ perpendicular motions in a systematic search for the thing, but may instead revert to looking for it in its original position. This reversion to cruder techniques when more advanced ones fail tends to occur through all stages of sensorimotor intelligence, and later intelligence as well.

That the position of vanished objects is first conceived only in terms of particular action schemas is further attested to by the reaction of an infant to the intervention of an obstacle. If an infant of this stage is presented with a toy which, as she watches, is covered with a cloth, the infant will not attempt to raise the cloth to recapture the object—despite the fact that the infant is quite capable of picking up a cloth when that itself is of interest. When the toy disappears, the infant either loses interest, stares at where it was, or looks back at where it was first seen (if that was a different place), but does not reach for it—or, if already reaching for it when sight of it is blocked, will immediately give up. In fact, even if the infant's attempt to grasp a toy is thwarted by a barrier that doesn't block sight of the toy, the infant appears to be oblivious to the barrier, making no attempt to displace it or move around it. The infant does, however, learn during this stage to grasp and extricate the hidden toy if *part* of it is visible.

The need to *rotate* an object presents intellectual difficulties similar to those posed by the need to move an obstacle. Suppose a third stage infant is presented with a bottle, but the bottle is held with the nipple facing away from the child, so that the nipple cannot be seen. Thus the important part of the bottle is obscured, not by a foreign object but by the rest of the bottle itself. The infant exhibits problems similar to those produced by a separate obstacle, giving up on the nipple when it is no longer perceived. The difficulty is not a lack of the motor skill required to rotate an object, since while the nipple is visible, the infant will turn the bottle to make the nipple accessible; this is done quite unsystematically, but persistently until fortuitous success is achieved. So the difficulty is again a representational one, characteristic of this stage: the potential nipple (as opposed to the nipple when actually perceived) is understood only in connection with certain schemas known to actualize it. There is not yet a schema of rotation; the successes in orienting a visible nipple appear to be due to a series of separate movements, each guided crudely by the current perception of the nipple, and not organized into a coherent activity of reorientation. When, in the next stage, these attempts are arranged in a coordinated structure, there will indeed be a schema of rotation, with respect to which the potential nipple can be represented.

Finally, it should be noted that during the third stage, a potential-X-with-respect-to-prehension is not strongly coordinated with a potential-X-with-respect-to-vision. For example, an infant of this stage who has looked at, but not touched, an object that falls below her gaze may look downward for it, but will not make any tactile search for it.

2.5 Fourth stage: coordination of secondary schemas

The fourth stage brings a coordination of secondary schemas analogous to the second stage's intertwining of primary schemas. Just as the second stage allowed the infant's representation of the world to transcend specific primitive motor sequences and sensory impressions, and abstract these to *acts* upon *objects* (the subject of third stage learning), so the fourth stage coordinations will allow the infant's understanding to become independent of particular acts, preparing for fifth stage elaboration of the activity of objects themselves, and their interrelationships.

The fourth stage infant is capable of using a familiar schema for a new purpose in a new situation. This contrasts with the previous stage, whose secondary circular reactions did allow familiar schemas to be used for new effects, but only if these effects had previously been empirically (and fortuitously) produced.

A classic example of this is the removal of an object blocking the prehension of a desired toy. This may be catalyzed by the accidental displacement of the intervening object when the infant initially ignores it. But at some point, the infant's attention is focused specifically on moving the obstacle (at first clumsily, but successive efforts develop a well coordinated schema of *displacement* by picking up and moving, or by striking). The infant's behavior makes clear that she is not interested in the obstacle itself, since it is discarded and the desired toy is then grasped. The obstacle displacement was thus subordinated to that goal. (Interestingly, it isn't until shortly after this displacement coordination that Piaget observes the advent of the infant's ability to release one toy being held in order to pick up another.)

An important variation of the above displacement coordination is the removal of an object that blocks the view of a desired toy. In transition between the third and fourth stages, an infant might continue to reach for and grasp a toy whose view was blocked, provided that the infant had already started to reach when the object disappeared from sight. This, along with the extrication of partially hidden objects (from the previous stage), and the displacement of non-hiding obstacles, leads to the ability to react to the complete covering of an object by removing the cover and claiming the rediscovered object. This is quickly generalized into a game of repeatedly hiding and recovering an object.

Recall the third stage inability to, say, respond with prehension to a potential visual object. During the fourth stage, potential (in contrast with actually perceived) objects with respect to different schemas are united in a way reminiscent of the second stage's marriage of visual and tactile perceptions. The ability to uncover a hidden object extends this unity: not only is there a prehensile remedy to a visual disappearance, but the remedy is complicated, involving a pair of secondary schemas that deal with two distinct objects. Thus, both the permanence and spatial localization of vanished objects are now understood, not just with respect to a given secondary schema, but with respect to coordinated pairs of such schemas. This begins to put objects in spatial relationship to one another. Similarly, the infant of this stage becomes capable of:

- Systematic search. E.g., when the infant drops an object, her hand will not only be moved down to find it, but will also be moved perpendicularly in exploration of the immediate vicinity.

- Systematic rotation. The infant can recover the obscured reverse side of an object.

- Exploitation of perspective. The infant can shift her head to look around an obstacle.

- Imitation of familiar but invisible movements. During the third stage, only visible actions, producible by existing schemas, are imitated—e.g., grasping a toy. (Interestingly, there is no imitation of a sequence, such as opening and closing a hand, that is exercised as a part of various familiar schemas, but not yet differentiated in its own right.) In the fourth stage, the infant will imitate an action (such as sticking out the tongue) that she has taken many times, but without having seen its effects. Prior visual and tactile exploration of faces, in conjunction with sounds sometimes accompanying the gesture, provide clues that assist that identification.

- Systematic exploration of novelty. When presented with a new object, the infant applies in succession many familiar schemas to the object: shaking, striking, rotating, etc. During the third stage, a new object would tend to excite some schema or other, but the current emphasis is different: the schemas now seem focused on the object, while previously, understanding of the object seemed focused on a particular schema. (An unexpected effect of some exploratory action—say, the production of an unusual sound—may give rise to a secondary circular reaction repeating that effect. Piaget calls such a reaction *derived* to denote that it arose in the context of more structured activity, namely the exploration.)

Despite these advances, the fourth stage representations of reality still exhibit many limitations of subjectivity. The most striking of these is the fourth-stage *place error*, shown by the following experiment. The infant plays with a toy that is then taken away and hidden under a pillow at the left. The infant raises the pillow and reclaims the object. Once again, the toy is taken and hidden, this time under a blanket at the right. The infant promptly raises, not the blanket, but the pillow again, and appears surprised and puzzled not to find the toy.

This sort of confusion is observed repeatedly during the fourth stage. It is a remarkable analog to the earlier reaction to disappearance by searching in the first or last place that the thing was recently perceived, or in a new position by extending a reclaiming schema. Then, hidden position was represented only with respect to the comparatively simple schemas that existed. Now, hidden position is understood in terms of combinations of such schemas, which relate pairs of objects. Although more complex, the representation is still procedural, and the procedures involved have only developed to the point of saying something like: "when this toy disappears, displacement of the pillow will rediscover it."

So the relationships among objects are yet understood only in terms of pairwise transitions, as in the cycle of hiding and uncovering a toy. The intervention of a third object is not properly taken into account. Moreover, the infant still comprehends the displacement of an object relative to herself rather that to another object. For instance, an infant who can easily turn a block around does not yet learn to orient it relative to a box so as to fit inside. Similarly, there is no comprehension of the need to put a stick in contact with a semi-distant toy in order to move the toy. These feats will be possible in the following stage.

2.6 Fifth stage: experiments on objects

During the fifth sensorimotor stage (usually beginning about a year after birth) the so-called *tertiary circular reactions* appear. These are little "experiments" that the infant conducts to see what an object will do. For example, an infant may repeatedly drop a toy, paying evident attention not to the act of dropping, but to the behavior of the *object* as it falls. Similarly, the infant experiments with varying ways of placing an object on an inclined surface to watch it roll, or perching it at the edge of a table so that it tumbles to the ground, etc.

These experiments extend the focus on an object's behavior, rather than personal action, noted during the last stage. But where fourth stage explorations merely use the object in existing schemas, the present experiments vary the exploratory schemas—not just in *response* to surprise results (as with the derived secondary reactions noted in the previous section) but in *provocation* of unexpected behavior. (Indeed, the specific autonomous activity of an object is yet unexpected by the infant, as evidenced by systematic inability to account for it when necessary. For example, an infant trying to dispose of an obtrusive cushion repeatedly pushes it back against a wall, but in such a position that it must fall back in the way again.)

Tertiary (like secondary) circular reactions can be coordinated with other schemas in a means-end relationship. For instance, an infant reaches through the bars of a playpen to grasp a long toy. The infant doesn't anticipate the solidity of the bars, which block the toy from being drawn closer. (The fourth stage infant learned about the solidity of an obstacle to prehension, but that was only with respect to movement of the hand itself! Here, the infant must learn that one object also blocks the motion of another object.) Although the infant already knows how to rotate an object (say to find its reverse side), there is not yet a schema for rotating one object relative to another, as is called for here so the toy can be oriented to allow passage through the bars. But, lacking such a schema, the infant nonetheless appears to identify the collision as the source of difficulty, and for a long while gropes for different ways of placing the object against the bars. Eventually, a successful orientation is found. On subsequent attempts, the infant's gropings converge more and more quickly to the solution, and a reliable schema of object-relative rotation evolves.

The gropings of this example are tertiary circular reactions, as they involve deliberate *variations* of a repeated action, and with interest in the effect on the object (i.e., whether it is making progress through the bars), rather than in the action itself. Now there is an additional feature: the experiment is directed toward the *goal* of bringing the toy closer. Thus, many schemas influence the activity:

- the grasping schema, which specifies the goal.

- the schema of turning an object, relative to one's self, which gives a point of departure for the new means needed to fulfill the goal.

- importantly, the many schemas that by now exist to describe objects and space; these are needed to interpret meaningfully the results of the experimental variations, to direct refinements of the evolving rotation schema.

- the intermediate approximations to the eventual object-relative rotation schema.

From the observer's point of view, the coordination of these schemas results in an important amplification of the infant's intellectual capabilities: for the first time, the infant responds to an unexpected obstacle by inventing a way to overcome it, rather than just relying on an already-existing schema. Piaget concludes that this capability essentially falls out of:

- quantitatively, the myriad schemas that can be brought to bear on a situation; and

- qualitatively, the higher level of abstraction on which the schemas now represent things, focusing on objects as such; thus allowing the same principles of interaction of schemas to yield more sophisticated results.

Similar examples of the invention of new means are found when the infant learns to use a stick, an underlying support, or an attached string, to move a given object. You may recall that some secondary circular reactions involved influencing one object by pulling another connected to the first by a string. But that effect was discovered entirely by accident, and with no appreciation of the physical connection. During the present stage, the infant wishing to influence a remote object learns to search for an attached string, visually tracing the path of connection. As with the object-relative rotation schema, a great deal of intermediate groping is required to develop schemas for using a string, support, or stick. One interesting intermediate situation that Piaget observes regarding the use of a stick is that an infant who is trying to grasp an object just out of reach, and who has previously succeeded in using a stick to draw the object closer, will not think of doing that unless she is already holding the stick, or unless the stick is presented to her. This is somewhat like the state of a second stage infant who is learning to grasp what is seen, but only when the hand is *seen* next to the object.

These developments add to the infant's conceptions of objects and space. Through the tertiary circular reactions, objects are endowed with autonomous behavior; and the direction of such reactions towards goals involving a second object teaches the infant about the solidity of objects, and relationships among objects themselves. This progress is also reflected in the fourth-stage place error, described above. During that stage, some improvement is made in selecting the right place to look for a vanished object, but the accomplishment has an empirical character and the selection is often wrong, as though the infant had learned that looking under the *blanket* sometimes works instead, but without really getting the point. On the other hand, the fifth stage infant learns reliably to search the place at which the object was seen to disappear.

2.7 Sixth stage: simulation of events

The fifth stage infant shows no sign of mentally simulating the activity of objects and learning from the simulation instead of from actual experimentation. But the sixth stage furnishes evidence of this ability. An infant who reaches the sixth stage without happening to have learned about (say) using a stick may invent that behavior (in response to a problem that requires it) quite suddenly, with dramatically less groping than for similar inventions of the previous stage. Piaget argues that the *interiorization* (a kind of internal reenactment) of physical activity is responsible for this capability.

In addition, the infant now becomes capable of interpreting situations whose understanding requires representation of events not actually observed. For instance, consider yet another form of hidden object confusion, which the fifth stage infant exhibits: A toy is placed in a small box, without a lid, so that the infant still sees it. Before the infant has a chance to recover the toy from the box, the box is moved beneath a blanket where, hidden from the infant's view, toy is dumped out. The box is brought to view again, empty. The infant is surprised that the toy is no longer in the box, and does not attempt to search under the blanket. Analogously to fourth stage progress with the place error, the fifth stage infant does learn, empirically and unreliably, to search under the blanket. But when *two* screening objects are used in succession, a remarkably parallel confusion results: the infant does not understand the need to look specifically under that cover from which the box emerged. But now, during the sixth stage, the infant deals successfully with these situations, apparently able to represent the unobserved displacement of the toy under the screen.

The above developments are a small sample of the explosion of intellect and knowledge of the sixth stage. The ability to represent one's own body in objective spatial terms, to understand personal orientation (for example, being able to point back to a house that's no longer in sight), and the beginning of language all arise during this stage. The sixth stage thus forms a bridge between sensorimotor intelligence and the later periods.

2.8 Subsequent periods: preoperational, concrete and formal operations

Throughout the sensorimotor period, the infant's intelligence is concerned with the effects of actions on present reality. Even the first manifestations of language, towards the end of the sensorimotor period, are concerned with the expression of desires and commands, rather than the communication of ideas. But in the period to follow—the preoperational period—the child begins to manipulate the truth of propositions, via inference and classification, just as earlier she had manipulated the state of objects via physical actions. The child begins to think and speak of past or distant events, of causation and number and time, of other peoples' perspectives.

During the period of concrete operations, the child becomes able to reason more systematically about the subject matter of the previous period; as during the various sensorimotor stages, previously uncoordinated fragments of representation become properly connected. A preoperational child, for example, confuses the relative duration of two time intervals with the ordering of their beginnings or ends; a child at that period tends to believe that the older of two people was born later. A preoperational child has not grasped conservation of number (or at least, conservation of 1-1 correspondence); consider the following fascinating (and typical) protocol, taken from a conversation with a child of five years ([51], p. 26):

> What are these?—*Little green* [A2]*and red* [A1]*beads.*—Is there the same amount in the two glasses?—*Yes.*—If we made a necklace with the red ones and another with the green ones, would they be the same length?—*Yes.*—Why?—*Because there's the same height of green and red.*—If we put the beads in there [L], what would happen?—*They would be higher.*—Would there be the same amount?—*No.* —Where would there be more?—*There* —[L].—Why?—*Because it is narrow.*—[A1 was poured into L] Do you really think there are more beads there [L] than here [A2]?—*Yes.*—Why? —*Because it is narrow and they go higher.*—If I poured them all out [making as though to pour the red beads on one side and the green on the other] would they be the same or not?—*More red ones.*—Why?——*Because that one [L] is narrow.*—And if I make a necklace with the red beads and one with the green beads, will they be the same, or not?—*The red one will be longer.*—Why?—*Because there'll be more in there* [L].—[The red beads were put back into A1.] And now?—*They're the same height again.* —Why?—*Because you've poured them into that one*[A1].—Are there more red ones or green ones? —*The same.*

These and other illuminating confusions are corrected during the period of concrete operations.

The final period of intelligence—the period of formal operations—begins approximately at the onset of adolescence. Just as the ascension from sensorimotor intelligence brought with it the ability to represent abstract truth instead of just current state, the passage to formal operations brings the capacity to represent abstract validity instead of just actual truth. Previously the individual could use one proposition to imply others in a variety of ways; but now implicability itself—i.e., validity—becomes an "object" about which the individual can reason. Reasoning about validity as such makes formal reasoning possible—reasoning separated from the content of the propositions reasoned about. In a similar vein:

- True hypothetico-deductive reasoning appears: a person gains the ability to devise appropriate experiments to test hypotheses, systematically varying one factor, then another, while holding the others constant. Previously the individual maneuvered in a space of propositions linked by (more or less) logical entailment; now, an entire such space is a single point in a new space, where going from point to point corresponds to changing a hypothesis.

- The ability to generate systematic permutations appears. The concrete operations individual could reason about sets of things; to generate all possible permutations among a collection of objects, a person must reason about a set of sets, each of the sets being one permutation of the objects. In all these examples, *relations* among concrete-operations objects in turn become the objects of formal reasoning.

Piaget describes the progression to concrete and then formal operations as the development of more powerfully expressive logics. In reply, Fodor [25] argues that such a progression, if indeed it occurs, cannot occur by learning. The essence of Fodor's argument is that less powerful logics, by definition, simply cannot express, and therefore cannot build, systems that embody more powerful logics. This objection, and a way around it, can be understood by an analogy between logics and classes of computational entities.

A finite-state automaton is strictly less powerful than a Turing machine: a Turing machine can simulate a finite-state automaton, but not vice versa [45]. Hence, a finite-state automaton cannot possibly learn to be a Turing machine. Nonetheless, any physically realized digital computer, though conventionally regarded as Turing-equivalent, is really just a finite-state automaton. It is considered Turing-equivalent via the reasonable and customary idealization that its memory is infinite. There are no precise rules governing the suitability of this idealization; roughly, the idealization is appropriate when a finite-state automaton has a large array of state elements that it uses more or less uniformly—elements that thereby serve as general memory.

A finite-state automaton might well have an initial state that does not lend itself to an infinite-memory idealization, but might later enter a state for which that idealization becomes suitable; this could happen, for example, if the automaton simulates a series of devices, and if an eventual such simulation, but not the ones that precede it, is of a device that is reasonably idealized as a Turing machine. Then, a Fodor-like argument is still correct, but only as a technicality: formally, there has been no increase in computational power. Nonetheless, for reasonable practical purposes, by plausible customary idealizations, the system has indeed changed itself from a finite-state automaton to (virtually) a Turing machine. An analogous possibility with regard to the development of logics of varying power suffices to escape Fodor's impossibility argument concerning the learning of concrete and formal operations.

2.9 Themes of Piagetian development

Several recurrent themes of Piagetian development are illustrated in the foregoing sections (in some detail for the sensorimotor stages, and hastily for the subsequent periods). These also serve as central themes for the design of the schema mechanism.

- Intelligence develops by building state-spaces to represent the world:

    - by discovering how states and transformations are related; and

    - by constructing new elements of the space, and new transformations, whose relations must in turn be discovered. From motions of physical objects to inferences among propositions, this theme is repeated throughout Piagetian development.

- New schemas form as incremental differentiations or generalizations of existing ones.

- Schemas coordinate to form composite structures that abstract above the details of the component elements.

- Another important kind of abstraction involves *conservation*—the discovery of a new kind of thing in the world, found by noticing the possibility of returning to some manifestation of it.

2.9.1 Fragmented representation

Perhaps the most powerful theme, composed of the above strands, is that the bootstrapping of intelligence involves the assembly of concepts from special-case fragments. That is, many apparently atomic or fundamental concepts are in fact composites of a large body of constituent schemas, from which the "atomic" thing arises. For example:

- Knowing that the ball is on the table entails the expectation that it can be detected there by sight, or by touch (or by weighing the table and noticing the extra weight...); and entails that it won't be found elsewhere at the moment (such as on the floor); and that it must have gotten there somehow, that it used to be in a different position but moved.

- Knowing that four things are present entails that adding another will make five; that if none are added or removed, there will still be four; that if they are counted, in any order, with each counted exactly once, the result will be "four;" etc. For each of these concepts (and many others), Piaget demonstrates that certain "entailed consequences" of the concept can be seen coming into use for the first time (thus, by implication, first existing) at different stages of development. Gradually, they are organized into a coherent whole. Only in the eventual mature result are the constituent parts of the concept so well coordinated, their mutual entailment so automatic, as to give rise to a functional unity.

2.9.2 Stages of development

The role of *stages* in Piagetian theory is often over-emphasized. As mentioned above in section 2.1, the apparent simultaneity of the innovations of a given stage is an expository device; the actual uniformity is only approximate. Moreover, even for some particular strand of development, the invariance of the ordering along the sequence is both less absolute, and less important, than is often thought. There are several reasons that development A might be observed to precede B, or on the other hand to be contemporaneous with B, in a typical individual's development. For example:

- A and B might each derive quickly and independently from some common ancestor C, and thus tend to appear at the same time.

- A and B might develop (mostly) independently, with A just being "simpler" than B, so that A would appear first.

- A and B might be comparable points along two similar but independent sequences of constructions, whose analogous developments are roughly contemporaneous.

- Some of A's structures might be included as components of B's; A's structures are then a prerequisite for B, so A must appear first. In the first three cases, it is plausible that the typical order of A and B might be altered by circumstances that cause the individual to focus an unusual amount of attention on one or the other. Thus, it is not surprising that White and Held [72], for example, have shown that by varying the prominence of a hanging, brightly-colored object in infants' early environments, experimenters can induce variations in the order of acquisition of hand-regard and swiping behavior. Even in the fourth case above, where the ordering constraint is the strongest, it is possible that alternative paths of development can bypass certain prerequisites, especially when unusual conditions (say, physical handicaps) block the typical paths.

Indeed, there is no *a priori* reason to expect a constructivist mechanism to exhibit stagelike regularities at all; the space of plausible developmental paths might be large enough for each individual to pursue her own idiosyncratic construction, in some or all domains. Alternatively, there may be domains where a particular next step is always so "obvious" that there is little room for variation. But in fact, some domains do show strong developmental regularities among different individuals, and it is natural for the study of constructivist mechanisms to begin there. For by observing similar developments among different individuals, the experimenter can partially compensate for being unable to repeat, with controlled variations, the same development for a given individual. Hence, a reason for the preponderance of stagelike developments in the discussion of constructivism.

2.9.3 Constructivism vs. nativism

A constructivist account of the development of intelligence holds that the difference between the mind of an adult, and that of an infant, lies in mental structures built by the individual. Even when a given concept is attained universally (e.g., the idea of a physical object), it is because the concept is prominent in reality, in a way that is accessible to the mechanism of learning (recall section 1.2.1). A nativist account, on the other hand, holds that universal knowledge is innate, and is either already operative in the neonate, or unfolds according to a predetermined, nonlearning process.

The debate between constructivist and nativist accounts of human intelligence extends back to antiquity. In a famous dialog, Socrates leads a student to a difficult conclusion by a series of leading questions; Socrates concludes that the student must have known the conclusion all along, since the teacher stated no facts, but merely asked questions (e.g., [58], p. 92).

Modern arguments on this subject often involve actual evidence. But the interpretation of such evidence can be difficult; it is easy to under- or over-attribute knowledge to an infant. The fact that a certain piece of knowledge does not show itself in an infant's behavior until a certain age does not guarantee that it was recently learned. Perhaps the infant had the knowledge sooner, but lacked some further capability needed to act on that knowledge. Or, perhaps the knowledge was recently acquired, but by a nonlearning maturational process. Piaget's strategy of observing infants' activity can give the false impression that learning occurs, by failing to detect the early presence of knowledge in some latent form.

On the other hand, it is also easy to overestimate an infant's knowledge, by presuming more awareness than is actually required to explain an infant's behavior. Consider an infant who sees an object, then reaches out and grasps it. This could be due to the infant's understanding that there are objects, that an object has a spatial location, that it has visual and tactile manifestations, that a certain visual pattern means object A is at position X, and that moving the hand to position X will therefore result in touching the object, which the infant desires. Alternatively, the infant might have no suspicion of the existence of objects, but might have noticed that a certain (visual) sensation, followed by a certain action (grasping), results in another (tactile) sensation (which the infant desires). A third possibility is that the infant is just exhibiting a reflex consisting of a motor response to a visual stimulus, without specifically desiring the result of that response, without even anticipating what the result will be, indeed without even knowing that there *is* any result.

In the present example, the Piagetian view is that all three interpretations are correct, each at a different stage of development. Mindless reflex activity yields to learned predictions that can be harnessed to pursue goals. These predictions are at first in drastically subjective form, expressed exclusively in terms of primitive perceptual inputs and motor actions. The predictions are then reformulated in gradually more objective terms of representation, terms that become progressively independent of personal action and perception.

What sort of evidence can be marshaled for or against such an interpretation? In principle, an examination of the infant's neural apparatus could reveal what sort of cognitive event was taking place; but that would require both a technology for monitoring the apparatus, and a theory for understanding what was being monitored, neither of which is forthcoming in the forseeable future. Thus, for now, we must settle for less direct forms of evidence.

- *Pro-Piagetian evidence.* Piaget chronicles a gradual elaboration of abilities, each step incrementally more advanced than the last. The themes of this process correspond to plausible learning methods, which the schema mechanism makes precise. That the incremental elaborations are consistent with the steps taken by a learning mechanism is circumstantial evidence that learning is in fact taking place.

• *Anti-Piagetian evidence*. Many recent experiments reveal infant knowledge that is expressed more subtly than by overt, purposeful action. Often, such expressions occur considerably prior to the first Piagetian manifestations of the corresponding knowledge, casting doubt on the Piagetian interpretation.

Some such evidence suffers from the problem of over-attributing knowledge to an infant. A clear example, I believe, occurs in T.G.R. Bower's description of a neonate's aversion to a looming object [9]. An infant sits in front of a screen that shows a projected outline of a rapidly approaching object. The infant exhibits an avoidance response: the infant closes its eyes, turns its head away, raises its arms in front of its face, and so on. Bower takes this as evidence that the infant interprets the visual information as an indication of an approaching object, anticipates that an unpleasant collision could occur, and takes action intended to ward off the collision.

Alternatively, the infant may have no such understanding of the movement and effects of objects, or even of their very existence. Instead, the infant may simply have a reflex that releases a particular motor response to a one simple class of visual stimuli. This more conservative attribution of knowledge indeed seems the more plausible, given the obvious benefit of having such a reflex, and the anomalous complexity of the infant's behavior by comparison with any other interactions with objects until several months later.

In other cases, however, Piaget under-attributes the infant's or child's abilities. For example, Piaget demonstrates that a preoperational child, when asked how a given scene (e.g., a model of some terrain) looks to an observer stationed somewhere in the terrain, instead describes how the scene looks from her own vantage point. Piaget infers a general inability to appreciate the difference of another's perspective; but experiments by Masangkay et al. [42] show that in simpler tasks—e.g., asking which of two sides of a card an observer sees when the card is placed between the child and the observer—children as young as two answer correctly. Still, in view of the Piagetian theme of assembling concepts from simpler fragments, it remains plausible that these special-case earlier abilities, overlooked by Piaget, are precursor components of a more general ability exhibited in the tasks Piaget describes. Taking note of the earlier abilities fine-tunes the Piagetian story, extending it rather than refuting it.

Some recent experiments, however, demonstrate early knowledge that is more difficult to reconcile with a Piagetian explanation. Here, the recent work of Baillargeon is exemplary. In one experiment [5], a five-month-old infant (third Piagetian stage) sits opposite a plywood board; the board attaches to a tabletop by hinges on which the board can rotate toward or away from the infant. Initially, the board is rotated flat against the table, tilting toward the infant. Just behind the board is a small toy. As the infant watches, the board rotates up, away from the infant, until it blocks the infant's view of the toy. The experimenter then surreptitiously removes the now-hidden toy (via a hidden trap-door in the table), and the board continues its rotation until it is again flat on the table, but now tilting away from the infant; the board could not have rotated that far if the toy were still in its way.

This seemingly impossible event surprises the infant, as determined by the infant's extended scrutiny of the apparatus, compared to (among other relevant controls) the time spent looking at similar rotation in the absence of an obstructing toy. Moreover, the infant takes into consideration such properties as the hidden toy's size and compressibility, showing surprise only if the board rotates further than those properties should allow.

Baillargeon's evidence thus reveals knowledge of hidden objects in infants who cannot yet retrieve such an object by displacing the barrier (despite being able to grasp and move the barrier object when that object itself is of interest). It remains an open question whether such knowledge is innate or learned. Clearly, however, Piaget's explanation for the third-stage obliviousness to hidden objects—that the infant simply does not represent that the object still exists—is contradicted by Baillargeon's evidence.

Baillargeon construes the evidence to demonstrate a failure of coordination between an infant's knowledge of hidden objects, and purposeful activity that rests on that knowledge. But that construal, I maintain, admits of three broad further interpretations, two of which are compatible with the constructivist view.

- One interpretation is not compatible: the infant's knowledge of hidden objects might be unlearned (or learned by a non-Piagetian process). The infant acquires the ability to recover a hidden object when some impediment to exploiting that already-present knowledge is overcome, perhaps by learning, or perhaps by a nonlearning maturational process.

- Alternatively, the persistence of hidden objects might be learned according to Piagetian developmental themes, albeit prior to the ability to exploit the knowledge by recovering a hidden object. That ability may be acquired by further learning along Piagetian lines. Section 10.3.1 illustrates this possibility in terms of the schema mechanism (although the illustration concerns intermodal coordination, rather than hidden-object persistence).

• It may be that the Piagetian story is true, not of the infant's cognition as a whole, but of the infant's central cognitive system. The central system, by this hypothesis, incorporates a general learning mechanism, and uses what it learns to guide its actions to achieve goals. True, the infant's peripheral, perceptual modules enjoy extensive, possibly innate knowledge about physical objects and their persistence (as reflected, for example, by the surprise exhibited by the infant in Baillargeon's experiment). But the central system, by this interpretation, lacks access to the knowledge embodied in the peripheral modules. Those modules use their knowledge to assemble the perceptual input to the central system, which, by this account, has no initial understanding of that input. The central system must recapitulate for itself much of the peripheral modules' knowledge (such as awareness of hidden objects), and does so in accordance with the Piagetian sequence. Observations of infants' purposeful behavior, in contrast with experiments that elicit subtle indications of surprise, reflect the Piagetian learning accomplished by the central system.

The first of these interpretations, if correct, would cast serious doubt on the constructivist theory, by refuting that account with respect to one of its paradigmatic examples. The second interpretation, like the perspective experiment cited above, extends the theory rather than refuting it. The third interpretation acknowledges a large exception to Piagetian theory, but salvages the essence of the theory.

It may seem implausibly wasteful for the central system to have to recapitulate knowledge already present in other modules, as stipulated by the third interpretation. But suppose that, in the course of biological evolution, a special-purpose learning system arose that became powerful enough to go far beyond its original special purpose—in particular, powerful and general enough to recapitulate *and transcend* much built-in knowledge from other cognitive modules. The knowledge in other modules would not be suitable for extension by this learning mechanism, because the independently developed representational formats used by the other modules would not be compatible with the module that happened to evolve into the general learning mechanism. (In particular, the peripheral knowledge would likely be implicit in procedures for, e.g., visual tracking, rather than explicit, as arguably required for nontrivial learning; see section 9.1) The built-in knowledge in the older modules would then be redundant—perhaps, in some cases, even becoming vestigial—as the learned recapitulation gained importance.[8] Built-in, biologically evolved knowledge of the existence of physical objects is then (partly) superseded by similar concepts re-invented by each individual; to put it succinctly, *ontology* recapitulates phylogeny.[9]

Postulating the learned recapitulation of apparently built-in competence may seem an unduly contorted effort to salvage Piaget's theory by explaining away the contrary evidence. In the absence of clear positive evidence for constructivism, this defense of Piaget would indeed be weak. One kind of positive evidence, though, is a demonstration that a plausibly designed learning mechanism would indeed have reason to exhibit the milestones of Piagetian development, as reflections of Piagetian learning processes. This book presents preliminary indications to that effect.

The research program presented here takes Piaget's theory as an approximate working hypothesis. This theory, even if diluted by the recapitulation interpretation of modern evidence, suffices to support the dual motivation for this research: using human cognition as inspiration for design of an artificial mechanism, and experimenting with an artificial mechanism in order to elaborate and demonstrate the possible workings of human cognition. If, on the other hand, the nativist alternative is correct after all, then these motivations collapse. In that case, aspects of the schema mechanism may still hold interest as artificial learning techniques, but the likelihood of their being prominent in human or humanlike development will be far smaller.

Even if the Piagetian account is essentially correct, there remain many possible versions of the account, with different balances of nativism and constructivism. Consider these illustrative points along a spectrum of possibilities:

- There is an invariant constructivist mechanism, and it is responsible for Piagetian development within the central system.

- The constructivist mechanism is invariant, except for some parameters or resource levels that improve maturationally. This maturational system

8.   Even if such recapitulation is thus required, might we not expect evolution itself to perform the recapitulation, building the duplicated knowledge directly into the central system, rather than requiring each individual's central system to re-learn it? Perhaps, eventually. But would that built-in recapitulation evolve before the central system became powerful enough to ask this very question? If not, the evolved recapitulation has not happened yet.

9.   This pun is due to Ed Hardebeck.

serves merely to *delay* cognitive development, compared to a system in which the full complement of resources was available from the outset. [10]

- Various auxiliary features are added maturationally, embellishing the the constructivist mechanism but leaving it qualitatively unchanged. As in the case just above, Piagetian development still results from the structures built *by* this mechanism, rather than from the predetermined changes *to* the mechanism.

- There is a preprogrammed succession of fundamentally different developmental mechanisms; for example, one for sensorimotor development, one for the concrete operations phase, one for formal operations.

- Much development is via structures built by a constructivist mechanism, but some major developments (say, instantiating a universal grammar) occur maturationally, due to other, more specialized mechanisms.

- No cognitive development is driven by learning. Acquired knowledge is tightly constrained, for a given domain at a given stage, to be of the sort that that domain's module is preprogrammed to accommodate at that stage.

Only the first of these possibilities is purely constructivist. But only the last three have *significant* maturational, nonlearning aspects; and only the last is entirely nonconstructivist. Any but the last of these possibilities preserves in full the motivations for building the schema mechanism. The schema mechanism itself, as currently implemented, is at the constructivist extreme of the above spectrum, but that can be regarded as merely a simplifying assumption. At this distance, the difference is not yet perceptible.

---

10. Conceivably, though, certain delays of complexity actively help subsequent development by providing useful simplifications to build upon.

Part II The schema mechanism

3 Representational elements: structure and use

The schema mechanism is engineered to pursue two fundamental, symbiotic objectives: to gain knowledge by constructing or revising symbolic assertions about the world, and to use those symbolic constructs to pursue specific goals and to gain further knowledge. The acquisition of symbolic constructs in turn has two principal themes: making discoveries expressed in terms of existing representational elements, and constructing new elements with which to express further discoveries. Figure 3.1 diagrams the major components of the schema mechanism, as explained in the next several chapters.

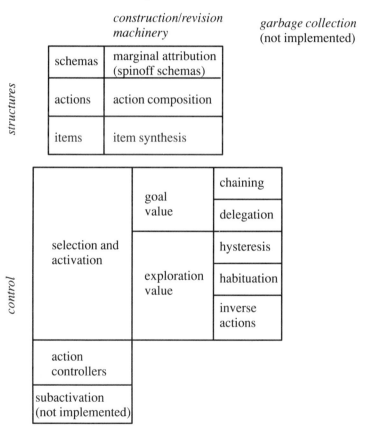

Figure 3.1 Organization of the schema mechanism.

This chapter and the next two describe the schema mechanism, and aspects of its present computer implementation. This chapter specifies the structure and function of the three kinds of representational elements used by the schema mechanism: schemas, actions, and items. Schemas express the effects of actions; items are state elements; and actions are conditions that are (sometimes) under the schema mechanism's control. This chapter describes the representational elements themselves, and the control of their use; the next chapter describes their construction and maintenance. There follows a chapter describing the schema mechanism's architecture—both the hypothesized architecture for a neural implementation, and the actual architecture of the computer implementation.

3.1 Schemas

A schema has three main parts: a *context*, an *action*, and a *result*. Contexts and results contain items, each of which designates a particular state or condition; an item's occurrence in a context or result may be negated, to designate the opposite or absence of a given state or condition. Figure 3.2 shows a schema with context *p~qr*, action *a*, and result *xy*. By notational convention, a schema's name is written in the form *context/action/result*; a negated item is preceded with a ~, and items conjoined in a context or result are separated with an & (ampersand) (or, if the items have single-letter names, they are simply concatenated). Thus, the schema in figure 3.2 is *p~qr/a/xy*.

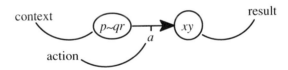

Figure 3.2 A schema. This schema has three context elements and two result elements.

A schema asserts that if its action is taken when its context conditions are all satisfied, then its result conditions will obtain. The assertion is subject to some auxiliary information that the schema maintains, including a reliability factor and a set of known overriding conditions, as discussed below. Four clarifications may circumvent some easily gained misconceptions about schemas:

- A schema makes no assertion about what happens if its action is taken when its context conditions are not all satisfied.

- A schema is not a rule that says to take its action when its context is satisfied; the schema just says what would happen if that were done.

- Satisfying a schema's context is not a prerequisite for being able to take the designated action; the context just designates a set of circumstances (possibly one such set among many) under which a particular result would ensue from the action.

- The schema does not assert that the effects noted in the schema's result are exhaustive; other events may occur as well, whether or not they are caused by the action.

As noted in the introduction (section 1.1.2), a schema serves as a declarative, procedural, and experimental unit of representation. Declaratively, a schema asserts a prediction about what would happen if a given action were taken. Procedurally, a schema directs activity, often in order to pursue a designated goal. Experimentally, a schema compares what occurs with vs. without a given action, or with vs. without a given condition's satisfaction (section 4.1.2). For an entity that must learn to take purposive action in its world, schemas' declarative, procedural, and experimental roles dovetail to make the schema both easy and useful to acquire.

A schema's context is a set of zero or more *items* (discussed in the next section), each included in either positive or negative form; a schema's result is another such set. An item can be in the state of being On or Off. (A synthetic item can also be in an Unknown state; see section 4.2.2.) A schema's context is *satisfied* when all the positively included items are On and all the negatively included items Off.

A schema is said to be *applicable* when its context is satisfied and no known overriding conditions obtain. An applicable schema is said to be *valid* at times when its assertion is in fact true—that is, at times when the result would indeed obtain if the action were taken.

To *activate* a schema is to initiate its action when the schema is applicable. A schema asserts that its activation culminates in turning On those items that are positively included in the result, and turning Off those items that are negatively included. An activated schema is said to *succeed* if its predicted results all in fact obtain, and to *fail* otherwise.

Schemas compete for activation on two bases: a schema may be activated for the sake of its own exercise, giving the mechanism a chance to test its validity and to extend or revise it; or it may be activated to help achieve a goal. When a reliable schema's context conditions are satisfied, and the schema's result items include some that are designated as goals (more on goals in section 3.4.1), the value of those goals contribute to the mechanism's incentive to activate the schema. More

generally, as shown schematically in figure 3.3, there may exist a *chain* of schemas from a current state to a goal. Such a chain has an initial schema whose context is satisfied. Its result conditions are a superset of the context conditions of the
next schema in the chain, and so on to the final schema, whose results include a
goal. If the chained schemas are reliable, activating each in succession should
achieve the context conditions of the next one, which can then be activated in turn,
until the goal is achieved.

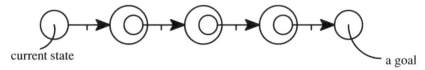

current state   a goal

Figure 3.3 Chaining. These schemas chain from a current state to a goal
state.

There are two kinds of activation: explicit and implicit. To explicitly activate
an applicable schema is to select it for activation and initiate its action. As a
side-effect of an explicit activation, other schemas whose contexts are satisfied,
but which are not themselves selected for activation, may have their actions initiated (if they happen to share the same action as the schema that was explicitly activated). Such schemas are said to be implicitly activated. As documented in section 4.1.2, schemas maintain some statistics that depend on activation, but that do
not distinguish between implicit and explicit activation; thus, implicit activations
contribute to these statistics. Keeping track of implicit activation also provides a
way to assess the *cost* of a given schema's activation on some occasion; its cost is
the minimum (i.e., the greatest magnitude) of any negative-valued results of schemas that are implicitly activated as a side-effect of the given schema's activation
on that occasion.

A schema maintains various auxiliary data, documented for reference in table
3.1, and discussed in this and subsequent sections. The data include a *reliability*
measure and a *correlation* measure.

- A schema's reliability is the probability with which the schema succeeds
  when activated. Each schema keeps track of its success rate when activated
  (biased toward more recent activations), which is taken to measure its reliability.

• A schema's correlation is the ratio of the probability with which a transition
  to the schema's result state obtains when the schema is activated to the frequency with which that transition obtains when the schema is applicable, but
  not activated (here again, a tabulation of actual frequency serves as a pre-
  sumptive probability). Thus, a schema's correlation indicates the extent to
  which the result depends on the action. Activating a schema for the sake of
  its result makes most sense when the schema's reliability and correlation are
  both high, so that the action is likely to be both sufficient and necessary.

Correlation	Ratio of frequency of result transition with vs. without activation.
Reliability	Rate of successful activation.
Duration	Average time from activation to completion of action.
Cost	Average cost (i.e., negative-valued side-effects) of activation.

Table 3.1 Schema data.

In addition to its three main parts, each schema has two large ancillary structures, an extended context and an extended result (figure 3.4). Each has a slot for
every item in the schema mechanism—not just the items appearing in that schema. (Each extended result also has a slot for certain context-like sets of items, as
explained below in section 4.1.4). Each such slot maintains some data about correlations between the schema and that item, and also, based on that data, specifies
whether that item's being On (or being Off) overrides the schema; if so, the schema is inapplicable whenever the overriding item is On (or Off, as specified), even
if the schema's context is satisfied.

A schema's auxiliary data (including the content of the extended-context and
extended-result slots) are subject to revision, but a schema's context, action, and
result uniquely identify that schema, and do not change.

Although schemas maintain some statistical information, such as the reliability
factor and correlations just mentioned, schemas are designed to provide symbolic, qualitative representations of the world. The schema mechanism endeavors to
build schemas that are of high reliability; there is no attempt to make accurate or
sophisticated models of the probabilities of less certain events. In particular, each

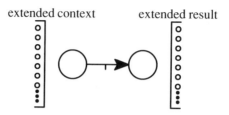

Figure 3.4 Extended context and result. Each schema has an extended context and an extended result.

schema's quantitative reliability measure serves mainly to exclude the schema if it falls far short of the ideal. Extended-context and -result correlations have a different primary purpose: to guide the construction of reliable schemas, as explained in section 4.1.2. The extended context also has several secondary uses: to discover or specify overriding conditions (section 4.1.5), sustained context conditions (section 4.1.6), and conditions for turing Off a synthetic item (section 4.2.2). A secondary use of extended results is to support the discovery of chains of schemas (section 5.1.2).

3.2 Items

An *item* is a state element. Each item represents some condition in the world, and has a state of On or Off to assert respectively that the condition does or does not currently obtain; an item can also assume a third state, Unknown, to indicate uncertainty. An item also maintains some auxiliary data, documented for reference in table 3.2, and described in the sections to follow.

Generality	Rate of being On rather than Off.
Accessibility	Rate of being at the end of some chain of schemas.
Primitive value	Built-in positive or negative desirability measure.
Delegated value	Acquired positive or negative desirability measure.

Table 3.2 Item data.

There are two kinds of items, primitive and synthetic. Primitive items are built into the schema mechanism—they are part of its initial endowment. Each primitive item corresponds to some sensory input; for the current implementation, the inputs are as shown in table 6.2. The state of a primitive item—that is, whether the item is On or Off—is maintained by the sensory apparatus.

It is plainly inadequate to represent states of the world directly in terms of primitive sensory elements. Even if, say, statements about physics, ballet, or politics could in principle be reduced to statements about the sensory manifestations of those domains, the reduction would be impossibly cumbersome. If a learning system's initial conceptual repertoire is indeed limited to sensorimotor terms, then a necessary condition for the system's eventual attainment of humanlike intelligence is the ability to synthesize much higher-level concepts.

Synthetic items are constructed by the mechanism itself. Each such item designates the validity conditions of a particular unreliable schema, called the item's *host schema* (figure 3.5); the synthetic item is called its host schema's *reifier*, because constructing the item treats the attainment of those conditions as a thing or state in its own right, thus reifying the validity conditions of the host schema. By notational convention, the default name for a synthetic item is its host schema's name, surrounded by square brackets; thus, the item in figure 3.5 is *[p/a/x]*. That item designates whatever (possibly yet-unknown, possibly yet-unrepresented) conditions must hold if the result *x* is to follow reliably when action *a* is taken under condition *p*.

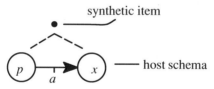

Figure 3.5 A synthetic item. A synthetic item reifies the validity conditions of its host schema.

The schema mechanism invents concepts by building synthetic items; as with primitive items, each synthetic item designates an aspect of the state of the world. Thus, there is no synthetic item whose meaning is *physical object*, which is a thing rather than a state; instead, there are various items with meanings such as *object A is at position X*. The systematic coordination of many such items amounts to the concept of physical object. Section 6.5.4 speculates as to the construction of abstract concepts, such as number, by means of synthetic items.

Primitive items are hardwired to sensory inputs that maintain their state. For each synthetic item, however, the schema mechanism itself must discover for itself the conditions under which the item should be On or Off, expressed as a function of the (past and present) state of other items. Section 4.2 describes the machinery for this discovery process.

3.3 Actions

There are two kinds of actions, primitive and composite. Primitive actions, like primitive items, are part of the schema mechanism's built-in endowment. Just as each primitive item is wired to a sensory input device, each primitive action is wired to a device that carries out a particular motor action. Table 6.1 documents the primitive actions used in the current implementation. Initiating a primitive action (by activating a schema which has that action) initiates the corresponding motor device.

Even for sensorimotor-stage schemas, primitive actions alone are insufficient, for two reasons: the schema mechanism needs to express actions at higher levels of abstraction; and it needs to discover the results of external events as well as of its own actions. Composite actions facilitate the abstraction and externalization of actions.

Consider, for example, the action of turning on a light switch. On a given occasion, that action might be accomplished by a particular low-level motor action, occurring in just the right context at the end of some chain of schemas that prepares for the final flick of the switch.[11] Rather than (or in addition to) such a representation, it is valuable for the schema mechanism to designate turning on the light switch as an action in itself. Such a designation offers three advantages:

- By abstracting above the action's implementation, the mechanism can learn about the results of turning on the light switch per se (e.g., that a light goes on), rather than just learning about the results of the particular motor action used on some occasion to turn the switch on; that lesson would not generalize to the next instance of turning on the light switch, if accomplished then by different low-level actions.

- Also, by abstracting above the action's implementation, the mechanism is able to organize activity hierarchically. A chain of schemas may incorporate the action of turning on the light switch—or much higher-level actions than that—as a single step, the details of which needn't be accounted for as part of

11. This hypothetical example is considerably beyond the implementation's actual achievements. Lower-level examples of the same principle appear in the synopsis of the schema mechanism's performance, in chapter 6.

that chain; the details may depend in part on circumstances that are yet unknown when that action is initiated

- Finally, representing light switch-on as an action enables the schema mechanism to learn about the effects of that action (e.g., a light going on) even
  when the action occurs as an external event, not under the mechanism's own
  control (as explained below in section 4.3.2). Thus, the schema mechanism's composite-action facility brings about a transition from representing
  the result of some action, to representing the external result as an action in
  itself—and in turn finding its own results. This facilitates the Piagetian progression from schemas of physical activity to schemas that are independent
  of personal action, via intermediate schemas that involve the effects of per-
  sonally-caused external events.

A composite action is defined with respect to some *goal state*; it is the action of
bringing about that state. Like a schema's context or result, a composite action's
goal state is a set of (positively or negatively included) items. A composite action
is essentially a subroutine: it is defined to be the action of achieving the designated
goal state, by whatever means available. The means are given by chains of schemas that lead to the goal state from various other states (figure 3.6); such schemas
are said to be *components* of the composite action. (A given schema may serve as
a component of arbitrarily many composite actions, or of none at all.)

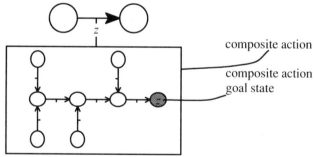

Figure 3.6 A composite action. The topmost schema has a composite
action whose goal state is z.

Each composite action has an associated *controller*. Just as a schema's extended context and extended result have a slot for every extant item, a composite
action's controller has a slot for every schema. Each slot contains data about
whether the schema lies along some chain to the goal state, and, if so, the *proximity*
to the goal that will be achieved if the schema is activated. Proximity is inversely

proportionate to the expected time to reach the goal state, derived from the expected activation time of the schemas in the relevant chain; proximity is also proportionate to those schemas' reliability, and inversely proportionate to their cost of activation.

Initiating a composite action (due to activating a schema which has that action) causes the controller to identify a component schema (among those currently applicable) with greatest proximity to that action's goal state; that schema is then activated. This process repeats until either the goal state obtains, or the composite action fails. The composite action is considered to have failed if either it has greatly exceeded its expected execution duration (a statistic that each action maintains, based on prior performance) without making much progress (that is, without much increase in proximity to the goal), or if a brief interval passes during which no component schema is applicable, so that no progress can be made.

The repeated selection of the most proximal component permits a kind of *opportunism* (e.g., [2]) in composite action execution: control may pass from one chain of schemas to another, if a more proximal schema along a different chain unexpectedly becomes applicable. The controller does not notice this shift as such; the shift is just a consequence of always selecting next the most proximal applicable component.[12]

3.4 Control

Schemas compete for activation. At top level, the schema mechanism selects a schema for activation. Selection occurs at each next time unit in the current, discrete-time implementation; a continuous-time version might perform this selection at regular, frequent intervals—perhaps a few times per second. In the present implementation, only one schema is activated at a time. However, the activation of a schema that has a composite action entails the immediate activation of some component schema; thus, the current implementation supports nested activations, but not parallel activations.

The top-level selection process chooses among applicable schemas according to the activation importance they assert. The importance of activating a given schema is based on two criteria: explicit goal-pursuit, and exploration. The exploration criterion boosts the importance of a schema to promote its activation for the sake of what might be learned by that activation. The goal-pursuit criterion con-

---

12. Work on *universal plans* [60] describes a planning scheme similar in this regard to composite-action control.

tributes to a schema's importance to the extent that the schema's activation helps chain to an explicit top-level goal.

Each explicit top-level goal is a state represented by some item, or conjunction of items. The schema mechanism explicitly designates an item as corresponding to a top-level goal by assigning the item a positive *value*; an item can also take on a negative value, indicating a state to be avoided. I use the qualifier *top-level* to refer to goals designated by a value level, as opposed to the goal states of composite actions. A composite action single-mindedly pursues its goal state when that action has been initiated. But the decision to initiate it, or any action, by the activation of a schema, is due to schemas' competition for activation, based on an exploration criterion and a top-level goal criterion. In what follows, the word *goal*, appearing alone, refers to explicit top-level goals.

Of course, the exploration criterion also serves a kind of goal, the goal of acquiring knowledge; but explicit goal-pursuit refers to achieving a state that is explicitly represented by some item—trying to achieve it *because* of its explicitly represented value. Exploration value *could* be made explicit; there could be a positively valued primitive item that asserts that interesting learning is taking place. Such an item would, in effect, create an explicit appetite for learning, similar to an appetite for food. Such a goal-based curiosity drive may well be present in higher organisms, and arguably should be present in the schema mechanism implementation (but is not currently).

To strike a balance between goal-pursuit and exploration criteria, the mechanism alternates between emphasizing goal-pursuit criterion for a time, then emphasizing exploration criterion; currently, the exploration criterion is emphasized most often (about 90% of the time). Also, rather than merely selecting the schema asserting the highest activation value, the mechanism chooses at random among those schemas whose value is close to the maximum value then asserted. This process prevents a small advantage from forever excluding schemas nearly as good as the best available; but limiting the selection to schemas close to the maximum value prevents highly valuable schemas from being passed over.

A new activation selection occurs at each time unit. Even if a chain of schemas leading to some goal is still in progress, each next link in the chain must compete for activation. Thus, as with the execution of a composite action, control may shift to an unexpected, new, better path to the same goal. Top-level selection carries this opportunism one step further: here, control may even shift to a chain that leads instead to a different, more important goal.

The mechanism also permits an executing composite action to be interrupted. A schema with a composite action, of course, may take arbitrarily long to complete, depending on the length of the chain of schemas used to reach the action's goal state, and on the duration of the activation of each schema in the chain. Even if a schema with a composite action is in progress, the cycle of schema selection continues at each next time unit. If the pending schema is re-selected, its composite action proceeds to select and activate the next component schema (which may recursively invoke yet another composite action, etc). If, on the other hand, a schema other than the pending schema is selected, the pending schema is *aborted*, its composite action terminated prematurely. The mechanism grants a pending schema enhanced importance for selection, so that the schema will likely be re-selected until its completion, unless some far more important opportunity arises. Hence, there is a kind of focus of attention that deters wild thrashing from one never-completed action to another, while still allowing interruption for a good enough reason.

3.4.1 Explicit goal pursuit

Kinds of explicit value: primitive, instrumental, and delegated

Three kinds of value may be associated with an item: primitive, instrumental, or delegated value. Each is a positive or negative quantity associated with an item or set of items.

- Primitive value is associated with certain primitive items. In biological systems, for example, representations of events beneficial to the organism or species (e.g., taste of food, sexual stimulation) ought to have built-in positive value, and designations of deleterious events (hunger, pain, etc.) should be negative. Correspondingly, the present schema mechanism implementation assigns positive primitive value to certain tastes, and negative primitive value to certain tactile sensations ("sharpness"). Inputs which represent states whose achievement is likely to be informative also have positive primitive value (these include items designating an image appearing at the foveal region of the visual field, where more visual detail is available than at the periphery; an item designating contact with the fingers, which provide tactile detail; and an item designating the sensation of grasping an object).

- A state is of instrumental value if its attainment is a specific prerequisite for achieving something else of value. When the schema mechanism activates a schema as a link in some chain to a positively valued state, then that schema's result (or rather, the part of it that includes the next link's context) is said to have instrumental value.

Instrumental value, unlike primitive (and delegated) value, is transient rather than persistent. As the state of the world changes, a given state may lie along a chain from the current state to a goal at one moment but not the next.

- Delegated value combines aspects of primitive and instrumental value. As with instrumental value, an item's delegated value derives from other things of value that that item helps achieve. But delegated value, like primitive value, is persistent. Delegated value is assigned as follows.

At each time unit, the schema mechanism computes the value explicitly *accessible* from the current state—that is, the maximum value of any items that can be reached by a reliable chain of schemas starting with an applicable schema. (Section 5.1.2 discusses the machinery for identifying such chains efficiently.) The mechanism also keeps track of the average accessible value over an extended period of time.

For each item, the mechanism keeps track of the average accessible value when the item is On, compared to when the item is Off. If the accessible value when On tends to exceed the value when Off, the item receives positive delegated value; if the accessible value when On is less than the value when Off, the item receives negative delegated value. The magnitude of the delegated value is proportional both to the size of the discrepancy of the On and Off values, and to the expected duration of the item's being On. For purposes of the value-delegation comparison, accessible items of zero value count as having slight positive value, thus delegating more value to states that tend to offer a greater variety of accessible options.

Rationale for delegated value

Delegated and instrumental value serve complementary functions: delegated value accrues to states that generally tend to facilitate other things of value; instrumental value is for states that currently facilitate other things of value, by a specifically forseen chain of events. Thus, delegated value may be said to be *strategic* whereas instrumental value is *tactical*.

An item does not (and should not) receive delegated value just by virtue of receiving frequent instrumental value. The state of, say, being in a standing position is often of instrumental value (as a prerequisite for walking somewhere, for instance); but it would be foolish (under most circumstances) to make a point of remaining standing just in case a contingency arose that required walking somewhere. The effort of standing all the time would be wasted, since it is enough to wait to stand up when the need to walk arises.

To generalize, if a frequently instrumental state (e.g., being on one's feet) is itself readily accessible, then the things it facilitates are thereby accessible even before the instrumental state itself has actually been achieved. Consequently, the value accessible when the state obtains does not exceed the value accessible when it does not; therefore, no value is delegated to that state.

Delegated value arises, and is useful, when a state is that is *not* readily accessible facilitates other things of value under circumstances that are likely to occur while the state still obtains (see figure 3.7). To an infant, for example, the presence of a parent may receive delegated value, even when there is no specific goal for which the infant needs the parent at the moment, because such a need arises often enough that it is good to have the parent nearby just in case. When a given state does not facilitate a specific goal at the moment, there is no chain of schemas to impart instrumental value to that state; consequently, delegated value is needed to promote the strategic pursuit of that state. The criteria mentioned above—delegating value to an item based on average value accessible when the item is On or Off, and the duration of its being On—are intended to promote delegation of value in a situation such as that of figure 3.7.

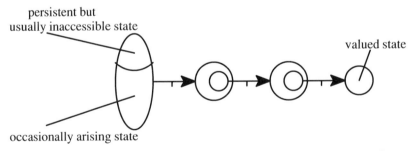

persistent but
usually inaccessible state

valued state

occasionally arising state

Figure 3.7 Delegated value. Here, a persistent but usually inaccessible state and some occasionally arising state together make a valued state accessible. The usually inaccessible state thereby receives delegated value from the valued state.

Delegating *negative* value to a state is appropriate if that state is, in effect, dangerous—if there is no *probable* negative value caused by its attainment, but there is a small possibility of large negative value arising. Here, too, there will be no chain of schemas that can reliably predict the unusual negative event; instead, delegating negative value to the state in question makes it something that is definitely somewhat bad, rather than something that is possibly very bad. The danger is thus avoided strategically, rather than tactically.

To designate goals only in terms of the mechanism's primitive lexicon would be as burdensome as having to represent all predictions and plans at that bottom-most level of abstraction. The delegation machinery allows higher-level, constructed concepts to acquire lasting value as well. At the same time, this machinery must ensure consistency between original and delegated value, so that pursuing the delegated value will continue to promote the top-level goals that the preassigned, primitive values are designed to coincide with. Arbitrary, unconstrained revision of the system's goals would be disastrous.

In particular, the mechanism must avert the danger of positive feedback in value delegation when two or more states are of mutual strategic value. Depending on how much value is delegated, each state's increase in delegated value could cause a similar increase in the other's, and so on without bound. To dampen such feedback, the value delegated to an item is only half of the difference between the unconditional average attainable value, and the value attainable when the item is on.

Of course, despite such safeguards, the delegation of value not only facilitates prior goals, but also changes the goal structure for the future. Thus, changes which locally do a better job of pursuing what is already sought may eventually culminate in additional goals which are far removed from what was originally pursued. This is not unlike biological evolution, in which the implicit goal of perpetuating an extant kind of organism is often most effectively achieved by making slight changes, thereby perpetuating inexact copies that are more robust than the original design; eventually, what is being perpetuated may bear little resemblance to its ancestors. (Indeed, biological cognitive systems' built-in values for certain primitive sensations may be regarded as having been delegated—not by the cognitive system, but by evolution—to various explicitly represented states—orgasm, tasting food, etc.—whose attainment strategically facilitates the implicit goal of perpetuating the genome.)

Rationale for numeric values

Numeric values are used to adjudicate the selection of a schema for activation. Yet this selection makes a qualitative decision: which of several eligible schemas to prefer. Basing this qualitative choice on a quantitative measure may seem inappropriate, particularly in light of the schema mechanism's presumption in favor of symbolic, nonnumeric representations. But I maintain that numeric values are appropriate to the selection task: given n explicit goals, n numeric values allow the derivation of n^2 preferences that might arise in pairwise choices between goals; they also permit the derivation of exponentially many (2^n) possible choices between sets of multiple goals.[13] Just as monetary exchange, as opposed to bartering, prevents having to trade one commodity directly for a preferred one, using quantitative values prevents having to make a direct qualitative comparison of each pair of results that the system can choose between. Still, delegated value derives from a particular qualitative relation, namely the facilitation of the accessibility of other things of value.

Although the current schema mechanism implementation includes primitive, instrumental, and delegated value, the mechanism's acquired skills to date are so unsophisticated that primitive and delegated value have little effect on the mechanism's activity; there simply are not any interesting things of value that the mechanism knows how to achieve. The mechanism's activity is influenced instead by instrumental value (in that the initiation of a composite action involves chaining to its goal state), and by exploration value, described below. Thus, in particular, the utility of delegated value remains to be demonstrated.

3.4.2 Exploration value

The schema mechanism maintains a cyclic balance between emphasizing goal-directed value and exploration value. The emphasis is achieved by changing the weights of the relative contributions of these components to the importance asserted by each schema. Goal-directed value is emphasized most of the time; but a significant part of the time, goal-directed value is diluted so that only very important goals take precedence over exploration criteria.

A schema's exploratory value is calculated to promote useful learning by the schema mechanism, rather than to pursue explicitly represented goals. Two chief components of exploration value are *hysteresis* and *habituation*: a recently activated schema is favored for activation (hysteresis), providing a kind of focus of attention that promotes repetition of a small number of schemas; but a schema that has recently been activated many times becomes partly suppressed (habituation), preventing a small number of schemas from persistently dominating the mechanism's activity.

---

13. The constraints of nonreflexivity, asymmetry, and transitivity imposed by numeric values ought to be respected by a rational preference system: it makes no sense to prefer A to itself (reflexivity), or to prefer A to B and B to A (symmetry), or to prefer A to B and B to C but not A to C (nontransitivity), given those pairwise choices all in the same situation.

A schema records its usage rate—its frequency of being selected for activation. Other factors being equal, a more frequently used schema is favored for selection over a less used schema. This factor mitigates possible redundancy among structures. Suppose there is some set of nearly-identical schemas—schemas which differ, say, by including different infrequently arising context conditions that only slightly affect reliability; or schemas that use different, effectively synonymous items to designate the same condition (see section 6.4.5). If one of these schemas, by chance, is used slightly more than the others, it accumulates greater usage—which, in turn, promotes its further usage (relative to those others), further increasing its value relative to those others. This deliberate instability carves out a situational niche in which only a few schemas, among all the similar ones, will dominate..[14] The instability is controlled by subordinating the usage factor to other components of a schema's value.

Another component of exploration value is designed to share activation among different actions. Without such a component, actions that appear in relatively many schemas tend to be initiated more often than others, which in turn promotes the construction of more schemas for those actions, leading to instability. To circumvent this problem, schemas with underrepresented actions receive enhanced exploration value. Similarly, a component of exploration value promotes underrepresented *levels* of actions, where a structure's level is defined as follows: primitive items and actions are of level zero; any structure defined in terms of other structures is of one greater level than the maximum of those structures' levels.

Inverse actions

The schema mechanism includes a facility to identify pairs of inverse actions, and to promote their successive activation; this promotion is part of the mechanism's exploration value. A pair of inverse actions is such that some schema with the first action reliably turns Off some item that some other schema, with the second action, reliably turns back On. For example, moving the hand backward, then forward again, reliably turns Off, then On, an item designating the original position of the hand; moving the hand forward is thus a inverse action of moving the hand backward.

The mechanism promotes the successive activation of inverse actions—especially if there is some other item which, in the same situation, the first action reliably turns Off and the second action *unreliably* turns back On. The hope is that this normally unreliable effect may be reliable when it immediately follows the

14. This trick also appears in [35].

first action. For instance, in the example just cited, an item designating tactile contact at the front of the hand is reliably turned Off by moving the hand backward, and unreliably turned On by the inverse action of moving the hand forward again—but moving the hand forward *reliably* turns the tactile item back On when the item had just been turned Off by moving the hand backward. Section 6.4.2 shows how the successive activation of inverse actions can catalyze conservation discoveries, such as object-persistence; and section 7.1.5 speculates about an unimplemented extension of the inverse-action facility which might promote conservation discoveries via thought experiments as well as by real activity.

4 Construction and revision

Above all, the design of the schema mechanism reflects the need for the mechanism to learn, to build its own structures for its own use, to come to represent the world in a way that is both practical and informative. The processes of constructing new schemas, actions, and items correspond roughly and respectively to empirical learning, abstraction, and conceptual invention. Schemas express discoveries about the relations among existing actions and items; composite actions designate the achievement of particular goals, abstracting above the details of how those goals are reached, permitting the goal itself to be seen as a cause of further results; and, especially, synthetic items represent aspects of the state of the world of which (some) previously represented states were mere manifestations.

4.1 Marginal attribution: spinning off new schemas

Piagetian development is rife with examples of generalizations and specializations of schemas. These examples involve the discovery of consequences of actions, and the discovery of the conditions that these consequences depend on. The schema mechanism tries to capture this sort of discovery with the process of marginal attribution, which constructs new schemas.

4.1.1 The problem: partially described regularities don't look regular

As noted in section 1.1.1, the task of constructing reliable schemas poses a chicken-and-egg problem. Even though the schema mechanism is designed to identify reliable results of actions—as opposed to making accurate probabilistic models of random events—a result that follows reliably under the right circumstances may follow only rarely in general. In addition, even when such a result does follow, it may be accompanied by dozens, perhaps thousands, of entirely coincidental state transitions at various levels of description. Therefore, identifying an action's result as such, before knowing the corresponding context conditions, is not a mere matter of noting that the result typically, or even occasionally, follows the action.

Thus, the chicken-and-egg problem: a result does not look like one except with respect to the appropriate context. Until the context is known, finding the result is difficult; but finding the context is impossible without knowing what result it is the context for.

Another, related chicken-and-egg problem arises even after a result has somehow been identified, if a conjunction of several conditions is required for the result to follow the action, so that the result does not follow if only some of the conditions are satisfied. Then, the relevance of any one of those conditions is difficult

to discern until the others have been identified—only when the last conjunct is
added does the schema become reliable. More generally, if the required context is
a disjunction of many conjunctions, the same problem arises for each of the conjunctions.

There is an obvious, but unworkable, brute-force approach to the conjunc-
tive-context problem: express all possible conjunctions of items, and for each
one, tabulate the probability of the result following the action when that conjunction is satisfied. In fact, this approach would solve the context-result problem too,
if all context-result pairs are similarly tabulated for each action. However, these
approaches are clearly intractable; the number of expressible context conjunctions, or of context-result pairs, is exponential in the number of items. If the conjunctions are limited in size to k conjuncts, only polynomially many (n^k, where n
is the number of items) need be monitored, as Littlestone [40] points out; still, if n
is on the order of a million or more, even a limit of, say, five conjuncts puts n^k
vastly beyond the number of synapses in the human brain.

The combinatorial problem would be eased if there were *a priori* constraints on
which items might be relevant to which schemas or actions. But it is impossible,
in a constructivist learning mechanism, to supply such constraints. To begin with,
there are no natural partitions among the primitive sensory items and motor actions. Hand motions, for example, can have tactile, visual, and auditory effects;
further, the effects might be contingent on conditions in any of those domains.
Similarly, vocal actions can have diverse effects—especially via people as inter-
mediary agents. (The discovery of such effects needn't entail awareness of that
agency; a neonate might discover that crying produces food long before understanding the existence of people.) As for constructed items and actions, as opposed to primitive ones, it is even harder to impose *a priori* constraints on relations among elements when the elements themselves are not present *a priori*, and
when those elements derive from primitive underpinnings which, as just argued,
are also without such constraints. (The need to be able learn without *a priori* relevance constraints does not, however, preclude the possibility of learned relevance
constraints assisting further learning.)

Fortunately, both chicken-and-egg problems—the context-result problem, and
conjunctive context problem—have a solution that does not presuppose *a priori*
constraints on relevance. The solution, as mentioned in section 1.1.2, is to identify relevant items by a subtle statistical comparison of their states' correlations
with schemas' activations (the specific comparisons and correlations are given
just below.) These comparisons are implemented by the schema mechanism's

marginal attribution machinery, which, to find the necessary correlations, requires the brute force of an exhaustive crossbar between schemas and items. For n schemas and items, only on the order of n^2 computational units are needed for an exhaustive crossbar, rather than an exponential number (or even just a larger-order polynomial number); as argued in section 5.1.4, a crossbar of that size is neurophysiologically plausible.

4.1.2 Marginal attribution: finding relevant partial descriptions

Marginal attribution initially identifies relevant but unreliable effects of a schema's activation, then searches for context conditions with respect to which those effects obtain more reliably. A series of intermediate, unreliable schemas serves as a scaffold for the construction of an eventual, reliable schema (when the process succeeds). Each schema keeps track of its own reliability, so the intermediate constructs are not mistaken for reliable assertions.

Initially, for each primitive action, the schema mechanism has a *bare* schema: a schema with empty context and result (e.g., at left in figure 4.1). Similarly, when a new composite action is defined, the mechanism constructs a bare schema that uses that action. A bare schema makes no assertion in its own right, but serves as a point of departure for the discovery of the effects of its action.

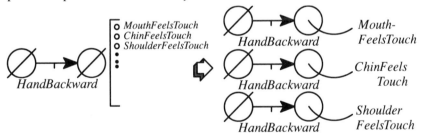

Figure 4.1 Result spinoffs. A bare schema discovers some results of its action and spins off other schemas.

Result spinoffs

A bare schema's extended result discovers effects of the schema's action. The discovery proceeds by way of two statistics maintained by each extended result slot.

- One statistic, the positive-transition correlation, is the ratio of the probability of the slot's item turning On when the schema's action has just been taken to the probability of its turning On when the schema's action is not being taken.

• The other statistic, the negative-transition correlation, is a similar ratio, but with respect to turning Off instead of On.

These statistics are tabulated over a number of trials in which the action is taken, and a number of trials in which it is not; the more trials there have been, and the more discrepancy there is between the two probabilities, the sooner the machinery will detect the difference (see section 5.2.2). The sampling is weighted toward the most recent trials.

Since the machinery seeks transitions to the result state, a trial for which the result was already satisfied before the action was taken does not count as a positive-transition trial; and one for which the result was already unsatisfied does not count as a negative-transition trial. Arguably, the mechanism should also look for a result that is kept constant by an action, when that item would otherwise have changed state. The present implementation does not do this—looking for transitions is more important, and memory and time are limited—but it could trivially be extended to maintain such statistics as well.

If some extended-result slot for a given schema shows that an item is significantly more likely to turn On (or Off) when the schema's action is taken, that item is deemed *relevant* to the action. A relevant item is a candidate for positive inclusion (if it turns On) or negative inclusion (if Off) in a schema that is said to *spin off* from the given schema. A spinoff schema copies the given schema's context, action, and result, but with the designated item included in the copy's result (or context, as discussed below). For example, in figure 4.1, the extended result of the schema */HandBackward/* discovers the relevance of items *MouthFeelsTouch*, *ChinFeelsTouch*, and *ShoulderFeelsTouch*. Correspondingly, the schemas */HandBackward/MouthFeelsTouch*, */HandBackward/ChinFeelsTouch*, and */HandBackward/ShoulderFeelsTouch* spin off from the bare schema */HandBackward/*. (These examples are not from the implementation, whose simulated body lacks a chin or shoulder; but these schemas are similar to ones built by the implementation, which are described at length in chapter 6.)

A relevant result need not follow an action reliably. In fact, its occurrence following the action may be arbitrarily unlikely, provided that its occurrence is even less likely in the action's absence. The relevance criterion uses the schema to specify a controlled experiment, comparing what happens with activation to what happens without (the control). Subtle but significant statistical differences then serve to identify a relevant but arbitrarily unreliable result, solving the context-result chicken-and-egg problem.

The machinery's sensitivity to relevant results is amplified by an embellishment of marginal attribution: when a given schema is idle (i.e., it has not just completed an activation), the updating of its extended result data is suppressed for any state transition which is *explained*—meaning that the transition is predicted as the result of a reliable schema whose activation has just completed. Consequently, a given schema whose activation is a less frequent cause of some result needn't compete with other, more frequent causes, once those causes have been identified; in order for the result to be deemed relevant to the given schema, that schema need only bring about the result more often than the result's other *unexplained* occurrences.

Context spinoffs

Once a relevant result has been so designated and a corresponding schema spun off, the induction machinery of the spinoff schema looks for context conditions with respect to which the result follows more reliably than it occurs in general; the spinoff schema's extended-context slots maintain statistics that identify such conditions. In particular, each extended-context slot records the ratio of the probability that the schema will succeed (i.e., that its result will obtain) if the schema is activated when the slot's item is On, to the probability of success if that item is Off when the schema is activated. As with extended-result statistics, these are weighted toward more recent trials; and the more trials there have been, and the greater the difference between the two probabilities, the sooner the machinery can detect the difference.

If the first (or second) of the extended-context probabilities is significantly higher than the other, the item is deemed a relevant condition for the schema's success, and is a candidate for positive inclusion (if the schema is more reliable with it On) or negative inclusion (more reliable when Off) in the context of a spinoff schema. In figure 4.2, the extended context of /HandBackward/MouthFeels-Touch discovers that HandInFrontOfMouth boosts the schema's reliability, spinning off HandInFrontOfMouth/HandBackward/MouthFeelsTouch; similarly, the discovery of the relevance of HandInFrontOfChin to /HandBackward/Chin-FeelsTouch spins off the schema HandInFrontOfChin/HandBackward/Chin-FeelsTouch.

A context spinoff schema, like a result spinoff, need not be reliable. For an item to be a relevant condition for a given schema, the schema need only be significantly more reliable for one state of the item than for the other, but even the greater of these reliability levels can be arbitrarily small. A context spinoff's own extended

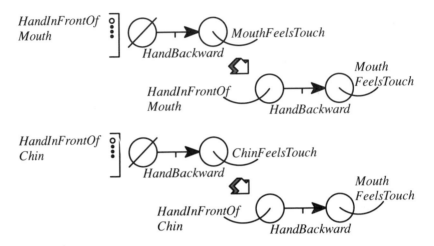

Figure 4.2 Context spinoffs. Each of two empty-context schemas discovers a relevant context item, spawning a spinoff schema.

context seeks conditions that further improve reliability; the discovery of such conditions spawns additional context spinoffs, as in figure 4.3. In this fashion, marginal attribution can build up to some conjunction of conditions that does make the schema reliable.

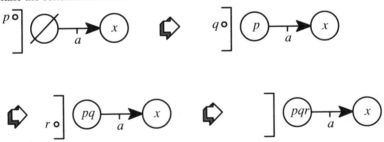

Figure 4.3 Context conjunctions. Successive spinoffs build up to a conjunction of context conditions.

Here again, distinguishing relevance from reliability solves a chicken-and-egg problem. If, say, items p, q, and r must all be On for result x to follow from action a, then the probability that the result follows if, say, p was On when the action initiated—call that $P(win/p)$, i.e., the probability of a win given p—is just the probability that q and r were On then too. If p, q, and r are statistically independent of one another, then $P(win/p)$ is the product of the individual probabilities of q and r being On; if p, q, and r are positively correlated, then $P(win/p)$ is even larger than that product. However small this probability may be, it is significantly larger than the likelihood that the result follows the action if p is Off—that likelihood is zero, given the above assumption that p, q, and r are all required. Hence, the relevance of p to the schema's context is detectable (and similarly for the other conjuncts; the one that makes the biggest difference will be detected first).

Critically, discovering the context-relevance of p does *not* depend on there being any nonzero chance that the schema succeeds when only p (but not q and r) is on. Even if p contributes nothing to the schema's reliability unless q and r are also on, p's relevance is noticeable without yet paying attention to q and r; it is noticeable because some of the trials for which p's statistics are collected do happen to have q and r satisfied as well.

As mentioned previously, for purposes of the statistics maintained by marginal attribution, a schema is considered to have been activated (*implicitly* activated) any time its action is taken when its context is satisfied, even if that schema was not selected for activation (to so select a schema *explicitly* actives it). Thus, many schemas' extended-context data may be updated at once. In fact, all activation-dependent schema data equates implicit and explicit activation; and the explainedness of a state transition, invoked just above, is also with respect to either kind of activation.

Most generally, there may be a disjunction of conjunctions of conditions under which the result x follows the action a. The schema mechanism does not represent disjunctive contexts as such; however, it may construct several reliable schemas that all have the same action and the same result, but with different contexts. This effectively expresses a disjunctive condition for the result to follow the action.

In that case, however, p's relevance is detected only if $P(win/p)$ exceeds the probability that some disjunct of the necessary condition is satisfied when p is not. If, on the other hand, some disjunct of the necessary condition—say, the conjunction of items d, e, f—is more likely to be satisfied when p is Off than is the conjunction of q and r when p is On, then the relevance of p will be obscured. (One way for the mechanism to circumvent this problem is to instead solve a differently formulated version of it; see section 6.3.3 for an example.)

4.1.3 Suppressing redundant attribution

There is an embellishment of the marginal attribution algorithm—deferring to a more specific applicable schema—that often enables the discovery of an item whose relevance has been obscured. Suppose, in the example just discussed, that the context-relevance of d to schema $/a/x$ is not obscured; the schema's extended context discovers this relevance, leading to the construction of the schema $d/a/x$. The extended-context slot for d in $/a/x$ records that a schema has been spun off from that schema for that (positively included) item. The following embellishment then occurs:

- All correlation data in all extended context slots of the schema $/a/x$ are reset to zero.

- Subsequently, whenever $/a/x$ is activated and d is On, the updating of all extended context data for that trial of $/a/x$ is suppressed. The effect of this embellishment is that the extended context of $/a/x$ now maintains correlation data only for trials for which d is not On (resetting the data erases correlations that had been tabulated without this condition). Thus, when d is on, attribution is deferred from $/a/x$ to the more specific applicable schema $d/a/x$. That schema, of course, can update its own extended context data for the trial, leading to the eventual construction of $def/a/x$.

Once the relevance of d has been thus recorded, the probability of $/a/x$ succeeding when a is On no longer has to compete with the probability of its success when d is On. The embellishment of deferring to a more specific applicable schema ensures that as some (conjuncts of) disjuncts of a disjunctive condition are identified, it becomes easier to detect the relevance of (conjuncts of) other disjuncts—the other disjuncts need only compete against the ''background'' probability of the schema's success due to yet-unidentified conditions. Not all conditions are thus discoverable, but many common and useful ones are.

Deferring to a more specific applicable schema also performs a second vital function. Consider again the sequence of constructions shown in figure 4.3, in which $/a/x$ spins off $p/a/x$, which spins off $pq/a/x$, which spins off $pqr/a/x$. If not for the provision for deferring to more specific applicable schemas, $/a/x$ would also spin off $q/a/x$ and $r/a/x$; schema $p/a/x$ would also spin off $pr/a/x$, and so on (figure 4.4).

With just three items in the eventual reliable context, such a proliferation of intermediate constructs is no crisis. In general, though, the number of such intermediate constructs is exponential in the size of the eventual context (the set of intermediate constructs corresponds to the powerset—the set of all subsets—of the eventual context). Fortunately, deferring to more specific applicable schemas prevents this exponential proliferation. If $/a/x$ has already spun off, say, $p/a/x$,

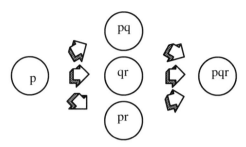

Figure 4.4 Powerset proliferation. Unembellished marginal attribution tries to build all subsets of an eventual context.

then /a/x's extended context slot for q will no longer be updated on trials when p is On; hence, /a/x will not redundantly discover the relevance of q.

A second embellishment also reduces redundancy: when a schema's extended context simultaneously detects the relevance of several items—that is, their statistics pass the significance threshold on the same trial—the most specific is chosen as the one for inclusion in a spinoff from that schema. Thus, if i is a special case of j (that is, i is On only when j is On), and the extended context of /b/z discovers the relevance of both simultaneously, i/b/z will spin off. (Both conditions' relevance will be discovered simultaneously if all encountered trials of /b/z when j is On also have i On.) If the more general condition j actually suffices, then /b/z will eventually spawn j/b/z as well, due to trials when j is On and i is Off. If, on the other hand, the more specific condition is necessary, j/b/z will not be built. (See section 6.2.4 for an example from the implementation's performance.)

Without this specific-priority embellishment, /b/z might first spawn j/b/z. Then, if the more specific condition i were actually necessary, /b/z would defer attribution to j/b/z, which would spawn ij/b/z. The unnecessary conjunction ij, appearing as the context of a reliable schema, would then be eligible for inclusion in the results of other schemas. The specific-first embellishment avoids this unnecessary proliferation.

An item is considered more specific if it is On less frequently. Although the specific-first embellishment is intended for situations in which the more specific item is a special case of the more general (as opposed to occurring disjointly), the embellishment is applied without checking whether the more specific item is in fact a special case. When it is not, the specific-first criterion amounts to an arbitrary choice among relevant items.

It may be of interest that, although the need for these redundancy-mitigating embellishments might have been anticipated a priori, it was not until I ran the unembellished implementation, and observed the proliferation, that I became aware of the problem.

4.1.4 Result conjunctions

In order for one schema to chain to another, its result items must include all the context items of the other (and with the same signs). Thus, for purposes of chaining, the schemas in figure 4.5a are not equivalent to those in figure 4.5b; the schema mechanism's chaining broadcast (described in section 5.1.2) identifies a chain to x in the second case, but not the first. Consequently, the marginal attribution machinery must be able to build schemas with conjunctive results, as well as conjunctive contexts.

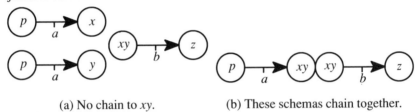

(a) No chain to xy.   (b) These schemas chain together.

Figure 4.5 Conjunctive chaining. Predicting two items separately does not chain to a context that requires their conjunction.

The mechanism might be designed to build conjunctive results incrementally, as with contexts. However, this approach would create a powerset proliferation problem, as above. And the above solution to that problem for conjunctive contexts—deferring to more-specific applicable schemas—does not suffice for conjunctive results; it fails to block a different exponential proliferation, as illustrated in figure 4.6. Suppose there exist reliable schemas $p/a/x$ and $q/a/y$. If $p/a/x$ sometimes activates when q is On, then if $p/a/x$ could have its own result spinoffs, it would discover the relevance of y as a further result, and would spin off the schema $p/a/xy$; similarly, $q/a/y$ could spawn $q/a/xy$. Either of these schemas, in turn, could spawn the reliable schema $pq/a/xy$, which combines the assertions of $p/a/x$ and $q/a/y$.

A combination of two such schemas is acceptable. But, here again, if n schemas thus combine, the number of such combinations is exponential in n. To prevent the explosive proliferation of such combinations, the schema mechanism does not build conjunctive results incrementally; only a schema with an empty re-

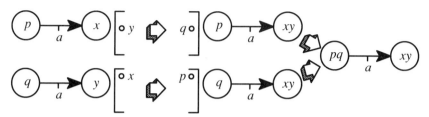

Figure 4.6 Combinational proliferation. Incrementally extending results would proliferate combinations of schemas.

sult can spin off a schema with a new result item. (Such a schema will be bare, since an empty result implies an empty context.) Chaining to contexts that have more than one items is made possible by permitting a schema to spawn a multiple-item result spinoff all at once, as follows.

A schema's extended result includes a slot for set of items whose appears as a context of a reliable schema (as well as a slot for every individual item). Marginal attribution treats each such conjunction just like an individual item with respect to maintaining extended-result statistics about the correlation between its transition and the schema's activation, and with respect to including a relevant conjunction in the result of a spinoff schema. Thus, when a conjunctive result is actually needed—to chain to a reliable schema's context—the marginal attribution machinery will permit that result.

Thus, a conjunctive result can form only if a conjunctive context has first been formed by some other schema; except in that case, a schema's result can include only one item.

4.1.5 Overriding conditions

Extended contexts, like extended results, identify relevant items for inclusion in spinoff schemas. Extended contexts serve a second function: identifying *overriding* conditions, that is, conditions under which an ordinarily reliable schema is invalid. A schema whose context is satisfied is nevertheless excluded from selection for activation when its extended context reports that a known overriding condition obtains.

The example in figure 4.7 illustrates the need to recognize overriding conditions. The schema *p/a/x* is very reliable, but fails when the (unusual) condition *w* obtains. The extended context of *p/a/x* duly discovers the relevance of *w* being Off—the schema has a much higher probability of succeeding if activated then than if *w* is On. Consequently, the schema *~wp/a/x* is spun off.

Figure 4.7 Override conditions. Here, condition *w* overrides schema *p/a/x*.

But merely creating the more specific schema *~wp/a/x* does nothing to suppress *p/a/x* when *w* is On; the mechanism needs to be able to learn not to trust the schema in that case. Permanently suppressing *p/a/x*, and relying instead on *~wp/a/x*, would solve that problem, but at an unacceptable cost: schemas chaining to *x* via *a* would now have to include *~w* in their results—and similarly for all other overriding conditions that may be discovered. But if these conditions arise rarely, the overhead of having to build new chains of schemas that explicitly include the negations of the overriding conditions is unacceptable; if the schema *p/a/x* shows itself to be highly reliable, the mechanism should be able to depend on it.

Instead of permanently suppressing the schema, the mechanism suppresses it whenever *w* is On. This temporary suppression is accomplished by the extended context's override machinery, which notes that item *w* is not in the state which makes the schema more reliable than otherwise by a significant factor; hence the mechanism deems the schema unreliable at the moment, and avoids selecting it for activation. At other times, however, the schema *p/a/x* may still be useful.

4.1.6 Sustained context conditions

Actions have variable execution times. In the present implementation, each primitive action takes one time unit to execute (though nothing depends on this). The time between a composite action's initiation and completion can vary considerably, even for different invocations of the same action, depending on the number of steps in the shortest chain to the action's goal state.

Some context conditions need only be satisfied when an action is initiated. Others need to be satisfied throughout the action's execution. The primary extended-context slot correlation, described above, compares two probabilities of a schema's success that are conditional on an item's state at the time that the schema's action is initiated. A second correlation, also maintained by each extended context slot, compares similar probabilities defined with respect to an item's state at the conclusion of the action. If both the initiation-time and completion-time correlations are significant, the mechanism presumes that the corresponding condition needs to be sustained throughout the action's execution.

If a context condition needs to be sustained until completion of a (composite) action, the mechanism obliges this requirement in two ways:

- When components of the composite action are selected for execution, actions whose results assert the negation of that condition are thereby suppressed. First, the activated schema informs its sustained context items of that status. Then, the mechanism identifies every schema whose result would negate a sustained item. Any such schema that is applicable, of nonnegligible reliability, and is not superseded by a more specific applicable schema informs its action of its status. The action then suppresses the activation of all schemas that have that action

- If such a condition becomes negated anyway (due to external events or to unanticipated side-effects of the mechanism's actions), the pending schema is aborted. (In that case, some chain of schemas that reestablishes the violated context condition and proceeds to the same goal may well be the basis for the next activation, effectively repairing the problem.)

Except for conditions that need only be satisfied initially, the mechanism does not seek context conditions that need to be satisfied for only part of the action-execution interval. This is in keeping with the use of schemas to chain to a goal—each prior link establishes the conditions needed for the next link to be applicable. A condition which is only necessary at, say, the completion of an action can be designated as a condition to be sustained throughout the action.

4.2 Synthetic items

Creating new state elements involves a more radical sense of novelty than building new schemas and actions. Schemas and composite actions are merely re-organizations of existing structures. But a synthetic item is a new element of the system's ontology—an element fundamentally different from the prior contents of the system's conceptual vocabulary. This section explains the schema mechanism's construction of synthetic items, and the subsequent elaboration of their meaning.

4.2.1 Constructing synthetic items

The mechanism's facility for building and maintaining synthetic items is designed to promote Piagetian conservation phenomena: conceiving of an underlying invariant when all apparent manifestations change or cease. Sometimes, as with conservation of object or of mass, what's required is the conception of some underlying physical reality. In contrast, conservation of number, for example, involves the conception of an underlying nonphysical abstraction. The synthetic-item machinery is designed to promote conservation discoveries of either kind (although the implementation has demonstrated only the first) by creating new items to represent newly-conceived aspects of reality.

The schema mechanism constructs a synthetic item to reify the validity conditions of an unreliable schema. That is, a new synthetic item is defined to represent whatever unknown aspect of the world governs the schema's validity. This is best explained by the example in section 1.1.2, whose illustration is repeated in figure 4.8.

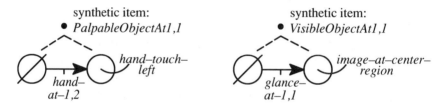

Figure 4.8 Synthetic items. These synthetic items designate palpable or visible objects (respectively) at a certain body-relative position.

The first schema in figure 4.8 asserts that moving the hand to the body-relative position (1,2) results in a tactile sensation at the hand. This schema is unreliable; it only succeeds when there happens to be an object at that position, waiting to be touched.

Significantly, however, the schema is *locally consistent*, meaning that if it happens to succeed when activated on some occasion, it is likely to succeed again if activated again within, say, the next several seconds. This consistency follows from the tendency of objects in our environment to stay put for a while. The schema mechanism, of course has no appreciation of this explanation; but it does keep track, empirically, of each schema's local consistency, the probability of its success when its last activation was successful; and, for a schema with high local consistency, the mechanism also tabulates the expected duration of the schema's consistency, the average interval during which the schema is observed to remain valid.

When a schema is found to be unreliable but locally consistent, the mechanism constructs a new synthetic item, called that schema's *reifier*; the schema is the new item's *host schema*. The host schema's reifier designates whatever condition makes the schema valid—in this case, roughly the condition that a palpable object is present at body-relative position (1,2).

In effect, the host schema associates its reifier with a *probing action*—the host schema's action—and a *manifestation*—the host schema's result. A synthetic item thus works backward from a thing's manifestation to define the very thing manifested. In the present example, an object at a given position is manifested by a tactile sensation when probed by putting the hand there. The reifying synthetic item represents the state of the world right now such that the probing action, if taken now, would yield the manifestation.

The concept of a palpable object being there says more than that the probe in fact yielded the manifestation—the concept further entails that, even when the probing action is not now carried out, it *would* yield the manifestation if it *were* now carried out (a so-called *counterfactual* assertion [39, 29], based on a hypothetical premise—that the probe is now carried out—which is contrary to fact). The synthetic item of this example, when it is On, asserts that, whether the hand is in fact moved there or not, the world right now is in such a state that moving the hand to the designated position now would result in a touch sensation; the item thus reifies that disposition of the world, regarding that disposition as a thing in itself—and that thing-in-itself turns out to be a palpable object's presence at the designated position.

What persists between probing actions and between manifestations is the fact that the probe *would* now yield the manifestation. This persistence is not merely the recency or recurrence of the manifestation; many states (e.g., television images or thunder) recur without there having to be an underlying entity which persists between recurrences and which the recurrent state repeatedly manifests. Thus, in the present example, asserting the persistence of a physical object goes beyond, say, having the memory that a particular sensation was felt a moment ago.

To repeat, the condition the condition that persists in this example—the condition that tends to be present after and between manifestations—is the presence of a palpable object at a particular position. From the mechanism's point of view, this concept is not composed from already distinguished concepts of *object* and *position* (as noted in section 1.1.2); rather, the synthetic item designating this condition is a rudimentary precursor of the concept of physical object (and of the concept of position). As section 6.4.5 illustrates, the development and intercoordination of many such fragments implements progressively better approximations to the concept of physical object.

Looking for persistence is built into the schema mechanism's synthetic item facility; thus, the significance of persistence it is innate to the mechanism, rather than being acquired. When the mechanism constructs a synthetic item, what is novel and learned is not persistence per se, but rather the very thing whose persistence is noticed—not the manifestation (which may recur, but does not persist between or after recurrences), but rather the state of the world such that the probing action would yield the manifestation.

4.2.2 Maintaining verification conditions

The state of a primitive item is set directly by some input module. In contrast, the state of a synthetic item must be maintained according to learned criteria for distinguishing whether the represented state currently obtains or not—that is, according to learned verification conditions.

The schema mechanism recognizes four kinds of verification conditions:

- *Host schema trial.* Each time the host schema completes its activation, it turns its reifier On or Off according to whether the schema succeeded or failed.

- *Local consistency.* When any of the conditions listed here turns a synthetic item On or Off, the item stays in that state for a period of time equal to the empirically determined expected duration of the host schema's local consistency (actually, two separate durations are used: one for staying On, the other for staying Off). If that period of time elapses without any further such condition, the item times out, reverting to the Unknown state. (An item also assumes the Unknown state if there is contradictory evidence as to its state—except that host-trial evidence simply overrides any conflicting evidence, since host-schema validity is the very definition of a synthetic item's referent.) Thus, local-consistency evidence is the memory of the most recent evidence for the state of an item—provided that there is some recent evidence.

- *Augmented context conditions.* A host schema's extended context may discover conditions that make that schema more reliable, leading to the construction of spinoff schemas (this is just the usual process of marginal attribution). For example, as illustrated in figure 4.9, the palpable-object schema shown above may be copied, with the addition of a context element that designates a visible object at the same position.

A reliable schema reports its applicability to its *parent* schema (the schema from which it spun off); in this example, when the visual-evidence schema is applicable, it reports that fact to the palpable-object schema. The applicability of this reliable schema implies that its action, if taken now, would yield its result; but that action and result are both shared by the parent schema. That schema—the palpable-object schema—thereby knows, without actually having to try, that its activation would succeed at the moment. Accordingly, the palpable-object synthetic item is turned On. If, however, some override condition currently obtains for the evidence schema (section 4.1.5), its report to its parent schema is suppressed. If an override condition obtains for the host schema itself, the host schema's reifier turns Off.

- *Predictions.* A synthetic item, like a primitive item, may come to be included in the results and contexts of many schemas. If a synthetic item appears in the result of a reliable schema, and that schema is activated, then in the absence of any evidence to the contrary, the mechanism presumes that that schema succeeded; thus the item is turned On (if positively included in the result, or Off if negatively included).

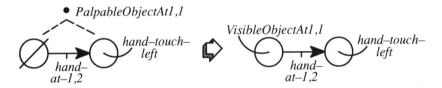

Figure 4.9 Context verification conditions. Context spinoffs specify evidence that helps maintain a synthetic item's state.

A synthetic item's verification conditions bootstrap from one another; the better an approximation they provide to the concept defined by the item, the better able the mechanism is to discover further correlates of that state, accordingly revising the verification conditions. The crucial step in this process is the initial one: defining the synthetic item in the first place. As noted in section 1.1.2, verification conditions operationalize a synthetic item—they make the item usable—by asserting when the state represented by the item does or does not obtain. But this assertion may be imperfect, and the state-maintaining function of verification conditions is always subject to revision upon the discovery of a discrepancy between what the function says, and the actual success or failure of the host schema. The latter is what actually defines the synthetic item; the state-maintaining function does not, for if a ''definition'' can change, but still correspond to the same concept, then it was not really definitive of that concept. In fact, it is typically impossible to fully define a synthetic item's meaning as a function of the mechanism's prior concepts, as the next section argues.

4.2.3 Irreducibility to any function of prior concepts

Verification conditions can be expressed in terms of nonprimitive items and actions, as well as primitive ones. Nonetheless, the state of every synthetic item, maintained on the basis of a function of the item's verification conditions, computes some boolean function of the past and present states of the schema mechanism's primitive items; functions of nonprimitive elements are ultimately expressible as functions of primitive ones, since the nonprimitive elements are themselves so expressible. Indeed, the state of any component of any deterministic machine must be some function of the cumulative (i.e., past and present) inputs to the machine; moreover, if the inputs are binary, the component's state must be given by a boolean function of those inputs.

Paradoxically, however, any given function of the system's cumulative inputs is inadequate to define many of the concepts that an intelligent mechanism that starts with only sensorimotor primitives needs to develop (as argued, for example, by Fodor [25]); Fodor pessimistically concludes that learning concepts is impossible, since he sees no alternative to defining a concept as some function of cumulative inputs). Even the most rudimentary conceptions of the physical object cannot be defined by the schema mechanism as any function of the sensory primitives. Consider, say, the concept that an object is present at body-relative position X. Two considerations make it impossible define this concept as any function of the cumulative inputs to the mechanism:

- *No manifestation.* Often, an object's presence at X has *never* had any sensory manifestation, directly or indirectly; on such occasions, the mechanism simply does not have the information needed to determine that the object is present. Moreover, even such manifestations as are available are often just probabilistic indicators of the object's presence; any function that relies on such indicators will sometimes be wrong

- *Unrecognized manifestation.* Even when manifestations are available, the mechanism cannot necessarily recognize them as such. The very question of what counts as a manifestation depends on physical regularities and states about which the mechanism may have incomplete information.

The no-manifestation problem has the consequence that no possible function of the cumulative inputs is coextensive with there being an object at X. Hence, there is no such function that *defines* what it means for an object to be there; a function that did define that could could never be incomplete or wrong—it would always, by definition, be correct. The unrecognized-manifestation problem implies that, even if there were some function of cumulative inputs that says precisely which manifestations are relevant, the mechanism may be in no position to find that exact function; the mechanism may forge an approximation, but that approximation is subject to change, and thus, once again, does not define the concept.

Furthermore, if we consider the need to represent more abstract concepts, an additional difficulty becomes apparent:

- *Logical inexpressibility.* Some concepts are uncomputable—e.g., the concept that the Turing machine in front of me will halt. This concept's uncomputability assures that the concept cannot be expressed as any function of my cumulative sensory inputs.

This problem is related to Fodor's argument that it is impossible to increase logical expressiveness via learning (section 2.8). If a new concept could be defined only as a function of the state of prior representational elements, such learning would indeed be impossible. Alternative means of definition, however, evade that objection.[15]

The schema mechanism, starting with only sensorimotor primitives, defines concepts that cannot be computed as any function of the cumulative state of those primitives. This apparent paradox is resolved by the observation that the mechanism does not in fact compute the meaning of these concepts. It does compute, for each item, a function of verification conditions, and this function maintains the item's state; but, as noted, that function does not actually define the concept—it only presents a changing approximation to the concept.

What, then, justifies construing a synthetic item as designating a concept other than what its state in fact computes? It is not merely that I, as the designer, intend synthetic items to designate the validity conditions of their respective host schemas. Rather, it is that the mechanism itself treats each item as having that mean-

15. For example, consider a schema whose context designates a Turing machine, whose action is running the machine forever or until it halts or repeats, and whose result is seeing it halt sometime. The synthetic item reifying the validity conditions for this schema defines the concept of the Turing machine halting predicate. Of course, the function computed by this item's verification conditions is computable (since it is, in fact, computed); but since that function does not define the concept, there is no contradiction of the concept's uncomputability.

ing, by systematically adjusting the item's state-maintaining function to better conform to that meaning, to better predict when the item's host schema is valid.

4.2.4 Intension, extension, and verification conditions

The analysis of a synthetic item's meaning is aided by the traditional distinction between two aspects of a concept's meaning: a concept's *intension* and *extension*. A concept's extension is the set of possible circumstances under which the concept holds. (This definition presumes that the concept is propositional, as is the case with concepts represented by primitive and synthetic items in the schema mechanism.) The intension of a concept is a particular designation or representation of that concept; in the schema mechanism, the intension of the concept represented by a given synthetic item is the item's host schema.

The state-maintaining function of an item's verification conditions changes; and, as noted above, it changes systematically in the direction of the extension given by the item's intension.[16] Thus, an item's state-maintaining function tends to converge to the item's extension. But the state-maintaining function needs not ever fully match the extension; they meet only at an imaginary limit.

The relation among an item's intension, extension, and verification conditions helps solve the puzzle of how a concept's extension can have psychological reality. It is well known that two concepts can have the same extension but different intensions (e.g., [26]). For example, section 6.4.5 discusses the formation of a synthetic item that designates a palpable-object-at-position-X, and another designating a visible-object-at-position-X. In a world without invisible or intangible objects, the two concepts are coextensive: there is a palpable object at X if, and only if, a visible object is there.[17] But they have different intensions: one is defined with respect to a host schema for reaching and touching something, the other for looking and seeing. At first, the schema mechanism does not represent the two concepts' mutual equivalence; indeed, it sometimes recognizes the applicability of one, but not the other. In what sense, then, is their coextension psychologically real at that time? That is, in what sense is their coextension, at that time, a property of the schema mechanism rather than just of the world external to the mechanism?

---

16.   More accurately, as Putnam's twin-earth parable demonstrates [55], extension is given both by intension, and by the physical circumstances of the agent entertaining the concept. But this subtlety is beside the present point.

17.   This example recasts philosophers' traditional morning-star example. The first star to rise in the evening may happen to be the same astronomical object as the last to set in the morning; yet one might separately define the last morning star and the first evening star, and fail to realize their synonymity.

Again, the answer concerns the state-maintaining functions of the two concepts, which soon become the same as one another. Even before the two functions come to coincide, it can be said that the mechanism is disposed to make them coincide, given suitable exposure of the mechanism to the world; and this dispositional property is reasonably regarded as a property of the mechanism, even though—like other dispositional properties, such as physical brittleness (a disposition to break easily)—it depends as well on external conditions.

4.2.5 The symbol grounding problem

The schema mechanism is one of many AI systems that build and use symbolic representations. When such systems organize their primitive structures into compound ones, it is relatively straightforward to express the meaning of the compound structures as a function of the meaning of the primitives, and of the compositional syntax. Often, however, there is no obvious basis—apart from the intentions of the system's programmer—for ascribing meaning to the primitives themselves. This is known as the *symbol grounding problem* (e.g., Harnad [32]): by virtue of what does a primitive (i.e., unstructured) symbol represent some concept?

For an embodied system whose primitives are wired to perceptions and actions, an obvious approach is to regard the primitives as representing those perceptions and actions. But then the problem becomes: how does the system acquire new concepts, other than boolean combinations of the primitives? As just argued in section 4.2.3, building new logical combinations of sensorimotor primitives is an inadequate basis for defining the sort of new concepts an intelligent entity must have.

A common proposal is to allow a symbol's meaning to be *adaptive*, in some sense or other; Harnad [32] and Edelman [24,56] (see section 9.9.4) exemplify this proposal. Harnad's adaptation is connectionist, Edelman's quasi-Darwinian. In both cases, a non-symbolic (e.g., connectionist) computational assembly receives inputs from the system's inputs and from other such assemblies; the assembly computes some function of its inputs, and that function can change over time, adapting to new contingencies. The assembly's *output* is a symbol, a primitive input to the symbolic part of the system; the symbol is grounded in part in the assembly's process of adaptation.

The adaptation of such an assembly is reminiscent of the updating of verification conditions for a synthetic item. But synthetic items, I believe, add a crucial further step. Whatever sort of adaptation an assembly performs must somehow be *trained* by an indicator of positive and negative instances of the concept being learned; the assembly adapts by changing itself to better conform to the indicator. Harnad's and Edelman's indicators, however, correspond only to sensorimotor inputs (Harnad's indicators include *iconic* representations, which are analog and/ or picture-like encodings of sensory data). Thus, their assemblies can only be trained to categorize such inputs, i.e., to build logical combinations of the inputs, and hence still fall prey to a Fodor-like anti-learning argument. The schema mechanism, in contrast, grounds its synthetic items in the reification of counter-factual assertions; the subsequent adaptation of its verification conditions is driven by that grounding.

4.3 Composite actions

As noted in section 3.3, a composite action is essentially a subroutine, defined by a goal state and implemented by component schemas coordinated by a controller. This section describes how the mechanism builds, maintains, and uses composite actions.

4.3.1 Constructing and maintaining composite actions

Whenever a bare schema spawns a spinoff schema, the mechanism determines whether the new schema's result is novel, as opposed to its already appearing as the result component of some other schema. If the result is novel, the schema mechanism defines a new composite action with that result as its goal state; it is the action of achieving that result. The schema mechanism also constructs a bare schema which has that action; that schema's extended result then can discover effects of achieving the action's goal state.

A composite action is *enabled* when one of its components is applicable. If a schema is applicable but its action is not enabled, its selection for activation is inhibited; having a non-enabled action is, in this respect, similar to having an override condition obtain. Usually, a newly formed composite action is seldom enabled, because few (if any) extant reliable schemas chain to it. But such an action may occur implicitly (see the next section) even before the mechanism can reliably bring it about; implicit activation suffices for the mechanism to learn about the effects of the action.

When a new composite action forms, the mechanism also allocates and initializes the new action's controller, which, as discussed in section 3.3, connects to all schemas, with a slot for each schema that records the schema's proximity to the action's goal state. To initialize the controller, the mechanism broadcasts a message backwards in parallel through chains of schemas that lead to the goal state (section 5.1.2). Occasionally thereafter, when the composite action is taken, the mechanism performs another such broadcast to update the controller information. Usually, though, the action executes on the basis of the already recorded controller data. Section 4.3.3 discusses some advantages of having a controller.

Recording proximity information in an action's controller is similar to *chunking* in SOAR [37]; both involve searching through a state-space, recording the points of departure, so that the path from those points to the goal is subsequently known without having to recapitulate the search. But the nature of the search that is thus abbreviated is different here; see sections 9.3 and 9.4 for elaboration.

4.3.2 Implicit activation and the representation of external actions

As noted in section 4.1.2, the marginal attribution facility considers a schema to have been implicitly activated if the schema's action is initiated when the schema is applicable, even if that schema was not selected for activation, and thus was not responsible for the action's initiation. Composite actions carry implicit activation one step further. A composite action is considered to have been implicitly taken whenever its goal state becomes satisfied—that is, makes a transition from Off to On—even if that composite action was never initiated by an activated schema—in fact, even if the goal state's achievement is due to external events entirely uninfluenced by the mechanism. Consequently, a schema whose action is composite is implicitly activated each time its action's goal state becomes satisfied when the schema is applicable. Marginal attribution can thereby detect results caused by the goal state, even if the goal state obtains due to external events.

Designating external events as actions combines with activation hysteresis (section 3.4.2) to promote *imitation* by the schema mechanism of external events that correspond to extant schemas. Hysteresis promotes the activation of a schema that has been activated recently. Hysteresis applies even to implicitly activated schemas, so if a schema is implicitly activated because an external event achieved its action's goal state, the schema's chances for selection for explicit activation are thereby boosted; its explicit activation would then repeat the achievement of that goal state.

4.3.3 Advantages of the composite-action controller

Using controller data has several advantages over performing a broadcast. The most straightforward advantage is that it is faster: a broadcast takes time proportionate to the maximum chain length searched for, whereas finding the closest applicable schema based via the controller only takes time logarithmic in the number of schemas.

Action controllers also facilitates the concurrent activity of several composite actions. (The current implementation only activates one top–level schema at a time, but many nested composite actions may run simultaneously; furthermore, the mechanism could be extended to permit several toplevel activations.) As noted in section 5.1.2, concurrent broadcasts would interfere with one another. Using prerecorded controller data circumvents such interference.

Using controller data also extends the length of chains that can be found by a broadcast, by means of an embellishment to the broadcast process. When a broadcast updates the information in a previously initialized composite action, the existing data serves as a point of departure. That is, rather than beginning the broadcast only from schemas whose results include the goal state, the broadcast also starts with schemas of already-known proximity to the goal. Schemas that had been at the fringe of prior broadcasts can now discover predecessor links in chains to the goal.

A second embellishment creates still other advantages. A composite action controller does not only record proximity information from broadcasts. It also averages in data from actual executions of the action. That is, each time a composite action is explicitly initiated, the controller keeps track of which component schemas are actually activated and when. (The present implementation only keeps track of the initial such component for each time an action is initiated; this lets the data be kept globally, instead of commanding space in each controller slot.) If the action successfully culminates in its goal state, the actual cost and duration of execution from each entry point are compared with the proximity information stored in the slot of each component actually activated; in case of discrepancy, the stored information is adjusted in the direction of the actual data. If the action fails to reach its goal state, the proximity measures for the utilized components are degraded.

Most straightforwardly, this empirical revision of controller data serves to correct false predictions based on proximity broadcasts. More subtly, the revision might foster the discovery of certain kinds of reliable paths that a proximity broadcast cannot identify as such (although such discovery is thus far undemonstrated by the implementation). In particular, it might be expected to foster the discovery of diverging and reconverging paths, of paths that require the repetition of a particular component, and of paths that involve on-the-fly repair of broken links in a chain.

- *Divergence and reconvergence.* Consider a set of three chains of schemas to a common goal, as shown in figure 4.10a. The three paths diverge, via three schemas with the same context and action as one another, but different results. Suppose it is reliably the case that one of these three results follows, but no particular one follows reliably; for example, each may have a 1/3 chance of occurring. Since each of the three results lies on a path that reliably reconverges to the goal, a chain that passes through the area of divergence and reconvergence is reliable.

(a)   (b)

Figure 4.10 Controller tricks. Composite-action controllers make possible the discovery of paths that diverge and reconverge, or that involve repetition.

However, the broadcast process misses this reliability. The cumulative proximity measure broadcast along each of the three chains is attenuated by the low reliability of each of the three diverging schemas. Thus, the broadcast proximity at and before those links in the chain underestimates the actual proximity of those links.

An underestimated component might nonetheless be selected by the controller, if no component schema with greater proximity is applicable. Each time such a selection culminates in reaching the goal state, the proximity measure for that component increases, until the estimate becomes accurate.

- *Repetition.* There may be a component schema that needs to be repeated several times until its result obtains successfully, enabling further progress along a chain (figure 4.10b). As in the previous example, the schema that is unreliable at each repetition (but which is, by assumption, reliable within several repetitions) attenuates the proximity measure that broadcasts backward through that link in the chain. But also as in the previous example, the empirical success of paths to the goal that pass through the underestimated link tends eventually to correct the underestimate.

- *On-the-fly repair.* Suppose a particular component schema is unreliable, and often fails when there is no other applicable component available, thus interrupting the composite action. It may so happen that certain schemas that tend to be applicable and to get activated at that point have the side-effect of making applicable some component of the interrupted action. It may even be the case that those schemas tend to create some new component schema, and create circumstances that make it applicable. The break in the original chain is thus repaired. If such repair follows reliably, the controller again comes to recognize empirically that the unreliable component, and its predecessor links, reliably lead to the goal state.

  By counting on this repair taking place, the machinery effectively invokes the system's overall intelligence as a subroutine to perform the repair. But this invocation is not explicit; it is just a consequence of the empirically derived high proximity value for an unreliable component which nonetheless leads to situations in which repair is typically possible.

4.3.4 Deterring redundant attribution of co-occurrences

An item may designate a state which is a special case of the state designated by some other item; for example, *SomethingSmoothTouchingHand* is a special case of *SomethingTouchingHand.* Both items may come to be goal states of composite actions. Then, a result of the special-case action will be redundantly attributed to the general-case action as well, and vice versa, since the two actions co-occur whenever the more specific occurs.

The schema mechanism tries to deter such redundant attribution by keeping track of actions that are special cases of others. Every schema with an empty context keeps track of the likelihood of its action occurring if its result obtains; if that likelihood is near unity, the schema's result is taken to be a special case of the action's goal state (unless the action has already been construed, via some other schema, as a special case of the result).

When one schema's action is a special case of another's, the special-case schema's extended result data do not update unless the general-case action has just completed. Recall that the extended result data compare samples taken both with, and without, the schema's action; by ignoring without-action samples unless the general action has occurred, the comparison finds the effect of the special action (if any) above and beyond the effect of the general action. If some result follows the special action only as often as it follows the general action, it will therefore not be seen as relevant to the special action.

There is a final, minor feature to mitigate redundant proliferation: by special dispensation, a bare schema with a composite action may not spin off a schema whose result includes an item in the composite action goal; for example /xyz/ cannot spin off /xyz/z.

5 Architecture

To be a viable partial theory of theory of human intelligence, or a viable model for artificial intelligence, the schema mechanism must not be intractably inefficient. A mechanism's efficiency depends in part on its presumed architecture; the schema mechanism's dual citizenship, in psychology and AI, requires two such substrates, which this section presents: a loosely envisioned neural architecture, and the actual architecture of the existing computer implementation of the schema mechanism.

5.1 Neural architecture

The schema mechanism is intended to explain aspects of human learning. The mechanism's design must therefore respect the constraints of neurophysiological plausibility; there ought to be a conceivable neural implementation of the schema mechanism, one that does not violate what is known about the human brain.

This section outlines a neurally plausible architecture for the schema mechanism. The outline is coarse—it is nothing more than a characterization of the sheer number of computational units involved, the required connectivity among them, and the time complexity of the required computations. I argue that these are plausibly within human-brainlike bounds. In contrast with connectionist [43] or neural-net models [4], the proposed architecture makes no attempt to indicate how specific functions performed by the schema mechanism might be implemented by vaguely neuron-like computational elements, such as linear-threshold units [47].

The presumed architecture supports one million computational units that are exhaustively cross-connected; that is, a separate physical pathway exists between each pair of units. (Some units, corresponding to sensorimotor primitives, also connect to peripheral modules.) The connections transmit data, both numeric and symbolic, the latter consisting only of a small number of discrete tokens (perhaps a few dozen); unlike, say, the letters of the alphabet, these tokens do not combine productively to form long composite structures (such as words or sentences). The connection points between units, and the units themselves, can each store some data, again consisting of numeric quantities and a small number of tokens (see figure 5.1). The connections between units, and the units themselves, operate in parallel.

Each unit and each connection point performs some simple, constant-time computations perhaps a few times per second; the results of the computation can affect the stored values, and can be output along the connection lines. The computation at each connection point is a function of the stored values there, and of data input from the two units that connect there. The computation at each unit is a symmetric function of the connection-line inputs to the unit, and of the stored values at the unit and at its connection points; the function might be the conjunction or disjunction of a binary value from each input, or to compute the sum, average, or maximum of a numeric value from each input, or from those inputs flagged by a particular token stored at or input to the corresponding connection point (such computations can be performed in time logarithmic to the number of inputs). A unit can output numbers and tokens along its connection lines, as well as receiving such data. There is also centrally coordinated global communication, such as broadcasting a message to every schema, every action, or every item.

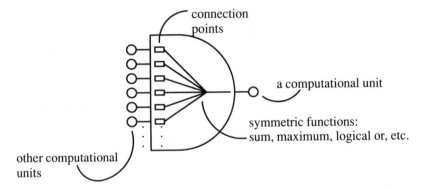

Figure 5.1 Cross-connection. Each computational unit connects to all others.

The above assumptions are similar to those of standard connectionist architectures, except for the presumption here of exhaustive cross-connectivity, and for the absence here of any attempt to reduce the computation performed by each unit to the behavior of linear-threshold elements.

Let us presume, for the sake of this analysis, that on the order of a few million schemas, items, and actions might suffice to implement adult-level intelligence. (At least on the order of a million cognitive units of some sort must be needed for human intelligence; that is the smallest round number that isn't clearly wrong. For comparison, the average vocabulary of an English-speaking adult is a few tens of thousands of words; and presumably there are many non-linguistic concepts for each one named by a word.) Assuming that each schema, action, and item is implemented by one of the computational units just discussed, I argue that something like the schema mechanism, with at least one million representational units, could fit in the neocortex of the human brain.

I have little to say about the computational units themselves, except that the 10,000 or so neurons available per unit are, intuitively, more than enough for the assigned computations. The more difficult matter is to account for the cross-connectivity that supports extended contexts and results, and action controllers; the identification of chains of schemas from current states to goals, noting the accessibility of goals from current states; and the definition new schemas in terms of actions and items.

The postulated crossbar connecting every unit to every other supports all four of these capabilities. (In fact, a slightly smaller crossbar, connecting all schemas to all items, and all actions to all schemas, would suffice; but the order of size of the required structures would not be much less.) The remainder of this section first describes how the crossbar supports these capabilities, and then argues for the neurophysiological plausibility of the crossbar itself.

5.1.1 Extended contexts, extended results, and action controllers

The exhaustive crossbar straightforwardly supports extended contexts, extended results, and action controllers. Each slot in an extended context or result, for example, is a connection point between a schema and an item; the slot computes and stores correlations between a schema's activation and the state of some item (as detailed in section 4.1.2). Each action controller slot connects a composite action and a schema. The connection point stores proximity information (described below), and receives data from the connecting schema as to whether that schema is currently applicable. The lines connecting to a given composite action collectively compute the maximum stored proximity among slots for schemas that are currently applicable.

5.1.2 Chaining

Identifying chains of schemas serves two functions: it propagates instrumental value to intermediate states between a current state and a goal; and it is part of the assessment of schemas' proximity to a composite action's goal state.

Finding a chain that leads to a particular item works by a parallel *broadcast*. The item sends a message to each schema asserting that that item is a goal; the item's value is also transmitted. A schema ignores this message unless the schema includes the item in its result; each connection point between a schema and item includes that information, stored when the schema is created (see below). If the schema does include the item that sent the message, and if the schema is reliable, then the schema broadcasts a message in turn to its context, making its context a goal; the value information is broadcast as well. Also broadcast is a proximity measure that takes account of the schema's reliability, expected duration of activation, and cost.

This process iterates, tracing backward along various chains in parallel, each schema along the way storing its proximity to the original goal, and the goal's value. The proximity measures computed by each link of the chain combine as the broadcast proceeds, diminishing the proximity at each step. When two or more items send converging messages to the same schema, the largest proximity measure is stored and propagated further; the others are ignored. The backwards iteration proceeds to some maximum depth of search; the time required is proportional to this depth.

A schema's context designates a conjunction of items, rather than just one item. Broadcasting a message to each item individually would not work, since arbitrarily many schemas might do so simultaneously. It is necessary to distinguish, say, between broadcasting to the items a and b from a schema whose context includes both, and broadcasting to those items from two distinct schemas, one with just a in its context, the other with just b. A chaining schema's result must include the entire context of the next schema in the chain; hence, in the first case, a schema whose result included only a or only b would not be a link in the chain, but it would be in the second case.

This problem is solved by broadcasting to the context set as a whole. As mentioned above in section 4.1.2, certain context conjunctions—specifically, those that are contexts of schemas of nonnegligible reliability—have extended result slots, just as individual items have. As with the slots for individual items, each such slot is set up, when a schema is created, to store a bit that says whether the schema's result items include all of that slot's conjunct items; a second bit indicates whether the result negates an included item.

When chaining is used to propagate instrumental value to help find the next schema to activate, the process proceeds not just from one goal item, but simultaneously from all items that have positive primitive or delegated value. When two or more goals' broadcasts converge to the same schema, the one with greatest value is stored and propagated; among converging broadcasts that have the same value, the one with greatest proximity is used, as above. A schema whose context is satisfied does not broadcast further, but rather competes for activation based in part on the instrumental value received from the broadcast. There is no need for the mechanism to keep track of which goal a particular broadcast is in aid of; keeping track of value and proximity provides the information needed by the selection for activation.

Chaining also serves a distinct but related purpose: determining each schema's proximity to a given composite action's goal, so that that information can be recorded in the slots of the action's controller (section 4.3.3). The broadcast process for this purpose proceeds as above, but for just one composite action's goal at a time, since in this case it is necessary to know what goal each schema is helping to chain to; broadcasts converging to a given schema from multiple actions' goal states would not all be able to propagate further back in the chain. (Of course, the mechanism could be extended to support simultaneous broadcasts for some fixed number of composite actions, but not for arbitrarily many, given the assumption that each computational unit can receive and store just a small number of distinct tokens.)

Finally, chaining is used to determine what states are accessible from the current state. (Accessibility is discussed above in connection with delegated value in section 3.4.1) To determine accessibility, the mechanism broadcasts messages forward along chains of reliable schemas (in contrast with propagating instrumental value and finding goal proximity, for which the broadcast goes backwards). To begin, each schema that is currently applicable broadcasts a message via its extended result to the items and conjunctions that are included in the schema's result. Any schema that has such an item or conjunction as its context broadcasts in turn via its own extended result, and so on, to some maximum depth of search. Any item or conjunction of items that receives a message by this process is currently accessible.

5.1.3 Composition

By the above architectural assumptions, the computational units that implement the schema mechanism do not support productive composition of symbolic tokens, as letters compose to form arbitrarily many words or sentences. Yet the schema mechanism presumes the ability to compose schemas from actions and items in just such a fashion. The exhaustive crossbar between schemas and items, and between schemas and actions, reconciles these two assumptions.

A schema designates its context and result simply by storing, at each connection point to an included item, the data that that item is included; whether it is included in the context, result, or both; and whether each such inclusion is positive or negative. Similarly, the schema designates its action at the connection point between the schema and the action.

Creating a schema with a specified context, action, and result has two steps: checking whether such a schema already exists (in which case it is not duplicated);

and allocating an unused computational unit, setting up the connection-point designations of the context, action, and result, and also the extended-result data designating items and some sets of items that are included in the result proper.

- To check if a specified schema already exists, the mechanism broadcasts to the action, and to each included item, its designation in the specified schema. The items and actions transmit this data along their connection lines to all schemas. If any schema finds a match, at all its item and action connection points, between the status of those items and actions for that schema, and their status according to the broadcast, then the specified schema already exists.

- Each reliable schema's context, if it is a set of more than one item, is allocated a computational unit that connects globally to every item in the mechanism; an item's membership in the set is flagged at the set's connection point to that item, along with a designation of positive or negative inclusion. Thus, wiring together a set of items does not require actually laying down a new wiring path; rather, bits on exhaustively connected, prewired units are set. The unit is also connected to globally by every schema, as part of each schema's extended result.

  - When a unit is allocated for a new such set, each schema's extended result must record, at the connection point to the new set, whether the new set is included in the schema's result. To this end, every schema is informed of the number of items in the new set. For each schema, each connection point between the schema and an item stores whether the item belongs to the schema's result (and, if so, its sign), and is told by the item whether the item is included in the new set (and, if so, its sign). On this basis, the schema counts how many of its result items also belong to the new set, with the appropriate sign. If that number is greater than or equal to the size of the new set, the schema's result includes the new set, and this fact is recorded at the connection point between the schema and the new set

  - When a new schema is built, its extended result must record, at each connection point, whether the item or set of items at that connection point is included in the schema's result. For individual items, that information provides the very specification of the schema's result, as noted above. For sets of items, each unit designating such a set deter-

mines (by a process similar to the one just described) whether it includes all the items in the new schema's result. If so, the unit thus informs the new schema via the extended-result connection line between
that set and the schema; that connection point then records the information.

5.1.4 Neural crossbars

An exhaustive crossbar between units of one type and units of another can be built
from a large number of fanout elements and fanin elements. Each unit of the first
type connects to the input side of a fanout element; the output side of the fanout
element has a separate connection for every unit of the second type. If there are
one million units being cross-connected, then the branching factor for a fanout
element far exceeds the 1,000-10,000 factor for neurons (see e.g., [17] for this and
other neurophysiological data cited just below). However, each element can be
constructed as a two-stage device comprised of elements that have a neurally
plausible branching factor, as shown in Figure 5.2; the first stage consists of a
single neuron, with 1,000-fold fanout, connecting to 1,000 second-stage neurons,
each with 1,000-fold fanout.

Input unit

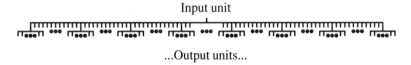

...Output units...

Figure 5.2 A fanout element. Each two-stage fanout element
connects one input unit to all output units.

A row of adjacent fanout elements, shown in figure 5.3, forms a sheet that extends from all elements of the first type to all elements of the second. The connection is accomplished by taking a similar sheet of fanin elements rotated ninety de-
grees from the fanout sheet and facing in the opposite direction, and placing the
two sheets together. A similar pair of sheets implements exhaustive cross-com-
munication in the other direction. Perhaps several such pairs of sheets would be
needed to implement various different crossbar computations.

The total number of neurons required for a million-by-million exhaustive
crossbar is about 2×10^9, which lies within the bounds set by the size of the human
neocortex. Furthermore, almost all the neurons comprising the crossbar are second-stage neurons, each of which needs to reach only a small fraction (1/1,000) of
the target volume. Consequently, although the crossbar crossbar implements ex-

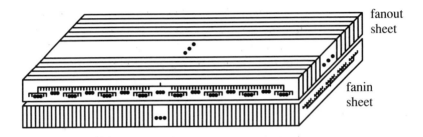

fanout sheet

fanin sheet

Figure 5.3 A neural crossbar. A sheet of fanout elements atop a sheet of fanins forms a full crossbar.

haustive cross-connectivity with regard to the million computational units, it exhibits almost exclusively local connectivity with respect to individual neurons. Only the first stage neurons—one crossbar neuron in a thousand—makes a distant connection. This locality accords with observations of the wiring of the human cortex.

I do not claim that there is positive evidence from neurophysiology that the human neocortex implements a million-by-million exhaustive crossbar. The foregoing merely argues that there is no neurophysiological basis to dismiss the hypothesis that such a crossbar exists. In the absence of such a basis, it is as reasonable to postulate the crossbar, if required by a plausible theory of intelligence, as there is to postulate any other structure or algorithm of intelligence, without positive neurophysiological evidence.

Still, the crossbar may seem counterintuitively exorbitant—one may envision ways to be more efficient (e.g., using a priori relevance constraints, although section 4.1.1 argues against that approach); and, even without a specific alternative in mind, the crossbar may just seem hopelessly large. But this intuition, I suspect, results only from thinking on the scale of present-day digital technology. A theory of human intelligence, I maintain, should not be constrained to be implementable on twentieth century computers, for there is no good reason to suspect that such an implementation is possible. Indeed, our only reason to believe that intelligence can be implemented on a device with the computational power of the brain is that we see that it already has been; and it is eminently plausible that the brain is as large as it is because it has to be—or, at least, because that is the simplest course, even if there are more sophisticated and more efficient alternatives.

One final consideration arises in defense of the crossbar. I originally postulated the crossbar to support marginal attribution, but subsequently found it important for other parts of the schema mechanism as well: composite action controllers, chaining and broadcasting, and implementing composite structures. The last of these is especially noteworthy, for it shows that an exhaustive crossbar effectively erases the distinction between connectionist and symbolic systems; that is, a crossbar permits a connectionist architecture to implement arbitrary, nested syntactic entities, which are the hallmark of symbolic systems. If a device so powerful can fit within the brain, we may well expect to find it there.

5.2 Computer implementation architecture

The computer program implementing the schema mechanism runs on a Thinking Machines CM2® computer [33], using a dedicated Symbolics® Lisp machine as front end. The CM2's salient architectural features are as follows:

- There are up to 65,536 physical processors that operate in parallel. The machine portion available for this research had 16,384 processors. Each processor has 262,144 bits of memory.

- The CM2 is a SIMD machine (Single Instruction, Multiple Data streams), which means that all processors execute the same instruction at once, each on its own data.

- Some instructions operate locally to each processor, affected by or affecting that processor's data alone. Other instructions act globally, computing, for example, the sum or maximum of some specified processors' values for a given numeric datum, or the logical conjunction or disjunction of some specified processors' values for some logical datum. Some global instructions act in the other direction, sending a value to all processors

- Finally, there is a class of *communications* instructions, which send messages from one or more source processors to one or more target processors per source processor. A source processor may designate its target by address, or by coordinates in an n-dimensional grid into which virtual processors can be organized. A message may be sent to an entire row (or even hyperplane) of such a grid at once. Most of the program is written in *LISP [67], a parallel extension of LISP [63]. Some inner-loop code is written in PARIS [68], an assembly-language-like instruction set for the CM2.

5.2.1 General program structure

The program allocates virtual processors for each schema, action, and item, and for the connection points in the schemas-items crossbar and the actions-schemas crossbar; the connection-point virtual processors are organized into two-dimensional grids for purposes of the communications instructions. (Due to memory limits, there are 64 connection points per virtual processor; the program iterates serially through updating each of those 64.) The basic computations performed at each time unit by each schema, action, item, and by each crossbar connection point, are cycled through in sequence, all instances of the same kind of structure performing their computation together. The crossbar connectivity is simulated by using CM2 communications instructions to transmit data from one kind of structure to another.

Each of the 16,384 CM2 processors can designate about half of a schema or composite action; these are large structures because of the extended contexts and results, and controllers. Ninety percent of the processors are reserved for schemas, the remainder for composite actions. Available memory for schemas is the limiting factor in the implementation's performance.

5.2.2 Compactly storing correlation data

Each schema has an extended-context and extended-result slot for every item (and, in the case of the extended context, for certain conjunctions of items). Almost all of the memory required by the schema mechanism's data structures is devoted to the correlation statistics in schemas' extended contexts and extended results; a naive representation of these statistics would be so bulky that the schema mechanism could not be implemented on present-day hardware. Hence, this section descends well below the level of abstraction at which the rest of the mechanism is described here, to explain a low-level scheme for compactly representing correlation statistics.

Every extended-context or extended-result slot maintains two correlation statistics, each of which is the ratio of two probabilities, a *with-probability* and a *without-probability*. For extended-result slots, these are respectively the probabilities of particular state transition with or without activation of the schema; for extended-context slots, these are the probabilities of successful activation with or without a particular item being on. *Positive* trials are the events whose probability is tabulated. For extended results, positive trials are ones for which the state transition does occur; for extended contexts, positive trials are ones for which the activation is successful.

Naively, each correlation statistic could be represented by a pair of probabilities (figure 5.4), each represented as a rational number, with fixed-length numerator (corresponding to the number of positive trials) and denominator (the total number of trials).[18] The size of the smallest detectable probability then depends on the number of bits used for each probability; for example, sensitivity to about one event in a million requires a numerator and denominator of twenty bits each, for each of the two probabilities per correlation statistic.

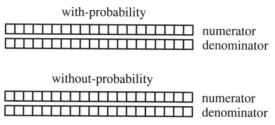

Figure 5.4 Full correlation representation. Representing a correlation as a pair of probabilities, each with a 20-bit numerator and denominator, has a resolution of 1/1,000,000.

The representation can be made more compact by alternating between one with-sample and one without-sample (figure 5.5); an alternation bit is added to the representation to indicate which of the two kinds of samples should be counted next. If the next trial is not of the indicated type, it is ignored. Alternating between the two types of samples assures that the two probabilities have the same denominator. Then, since only the ratio of the two is of interest, the denominators needn't be stored.

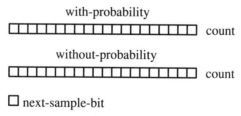

Figure 5.5 Correlations without denominators. Alternating between the two samples eliminates the need for the denominators.

18.   A floating-point representation might be used instead. However, incrementing the number of trials by one then becomes impossible when the exponent is larger than zero, so that the least significant bit of the mantissa is greater than one.

A provision for overflow offers further improvement. If either numerator reaches its maximum value, both numerators shift right by one bit (that is, divide by two); this operation preserves their (approximate) ratio. Moreover, the representation now has sensitivity to arbitrarily small probabilities—not merely, say, one in a million—since precision is no longer limited by the size of the numerators. The number of bits per numerator can thus be reduced sharply (figure 5.6). As information about earlier trials vanishes when the numerators shift, the sample is biased toward more recent trials. This bias is arguably desirable: circumstances change, and if the two probabilities significantly differ in the course of recent trials, it is likely that the item in question is indeed relevant now.

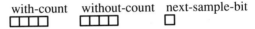

Figure 5.6 A truncated correlation. Right-shifting to prevent overflow requires fewer bits per count.

Unfortunately, this alternation scheme unacceptably slows learning when a large number of consecutive with-samples tend to alternate with many consecutive without-samples. Extending the next-sample-bit to be a two-bit count mitigates the problem. Unless the next-sample-count is zero, another with-sample can be tabulated, and the next-sample-count is decremented; unless the next-sample-count is three, another without-sample can be tabulated, and the next-sample-count is incremented. Thus, up to three samples of one type can be taken before having to wait for a sample of the other type.

A final improvement, due to R. Rivest (personal communication), compresses both counts into one signed count; the current implementation uses a four-bit count, plus sign bit, as in figure 5.7. The count increments for a positive with-sample, and decrements for a positive without-sample. To attenuate random drift (which otherwise would soon bring the count to one of its two extrema even if the two probabilities were equal), increments (and decrements) are of different sizes. In particular, if the count is positive, then a positive with-sample increments the count by a smaller amount (three, in the present implementation), but a positive without-trial decrements by a larger amount (presently two). Similarly, if the count is negative, positive with-trials increment the count by the larger amount, and positive without-trials decrement it by the smaller amount. This disparity exerts pressure toward zero, so that the with-probability must exceed the without-probability by the ratio of the two increments for it to be likely that the value steadily diverges from zero. If the value reaches the positive extreme, the corresponding item is deemed relevant (and, for extended-context slots, reaching the negative extreme indicates the relevance of the item's negation).

Figure 5.7 A single-count correlation. Two counts collapse into one signed count which increments and decrements, with a bias towards zero.

The actual ratio of the two probabilities cannot be recovered from the single-count representation; that representation indicates only whether the ratio's magnitude exceeds a threshold determined by the ratio of the two increments. For a given probability ratio, the ratio of the larger increment to the maximum count magnitude determines how many positive trials are required before relevance is detected. When two probabilities are actually equal, the likelihood of a false indication of relevance decreases exponentially with the number of trials required (double-exponentially with the number of bits in the count). Hence, although the small parameters used by the current implementation are no doubt adequate only because of the unrealistic simplicity of the microworld—which thereby requires fewer trials to distinguish real correlations from coincidence—scaling up would not strain computational storage or time resources.

Part III Performance and speculations

6 Synopsis of schema mechanism performance

The schema mechanism is designed to recapitulate significant milestones of the Piagetian developmental sequence in infancy, in a manner consistent with the Piagetian developmental themes, and thus to explain how that development might in fact come about. This chapter presents a synopsis of the actual developmental progression exhibited by the current computer implementation of the schema mechanism, followed by some speculations about further development.

A caveat concerning experiments with computer programs is in order. In sciences such as physics, experiments must be replicable; published descriptions must have enough detail to support such replication. Apart from safeguarding against outright error or fraud, this policy helps determine that observed results indeed follow from the factors described, rather than from extraneous, unnoticed conditions.

Computer experiments in AI, however, are seldom subject to systematic attempts at replication.[19] This may be due in part to the nature of computer programs; a deterministic program that once produces a given output for a given input will always do so again. In this sense, replication is trivially guaranteed.

On the other hand, the slightest change to a program revokes the trivial guarantee. One would like to know what characteristics a program must have—short of being identical—in order to behave similarly to a given prototype. The preceding chapter is an attempt to so characterize the schema mechanism implementation; as in the hard sciences, this attempt needs validation by independent replication.

The schema mechanism has been run from scratch on several dozen occasions, with minor variations of the mechanism or the microworld from one run to the next. The synopsis describes a particular *reference run*; in fact, all mention throughout this book of the implementation's accomplishments, except where otherwise noted, regard the reference run. Informally, the results of the reference run are typical of many other runs of similar versions of the mechanism. But there is no attempt here to quantify the consistency and variation of results from different runs. The synopsis may be regarded as a pilot study in preparation for a more rigorous analysis, which could be carried out in conjunction with independent replication efforts.

6.1 The microworld

The computer program that implements the schema mechanism operates in a discrete, two-dimensional microworld (figure 1.1). The program controls a simu-

---

19. See McDermott [44] for discussion; Haase's [31] reworking of Lenat's Eurisko [38] is a noteworthy exception.

lated robot that has a body, a single hand, and a visual system. The hand can touch and grasp objects, and move them about. The visual system maps a visual field onto a region of the world in the immediate vicinity of the robot body; the visual field provides a bird's-eye view of that region. The simulated robot can shift its gaze, changing the body-relative orientation of its visual field. (The visual system is designed to provide a bird's-eye view, rather than a projection onto a one-dimensional retina, because of the paucity of information in a one-dimensional projection.) Objects in the microworld (including the robot's body, and the hand) are of uniform size. They can move but cannot rotate, and their motion occurs in discrete units of the same size as the objects themselves. The microworld is *energetic*, meaning that objects can move spontaneously, not just in response to the simulated robot's actions.

The schema mechanism's data structures—primitive and constructed—are available to the experimenter for direct examination; in effect, there is a monitoring tool for reading the mechanism's mind. Since the internal representations may be observed directly, we need not try to infer them from the simulation's external behavior. Thus, it is much easier with the schema mechanism than with infants to determine what the system knows, and when it knows it.

The primitive actions supplied to this implementation of the schema mechanism are summarized in table 6.1. The hand can move about in a particular three-by-three unit region relative to the position of the body, as shown in figure 6.1a. Similarly, the visual field can have nine body-relative orientations, within a range of three units in each dimension (figure 6.1b); the coincidence of the range of eye and hand movements is not important. The potentially visible body-relative region is seven units on a side, since the five-by-five visual field can assume each of three by three orientations.

Two objects are present near the body, and are often seen, or within range of being touched. Each has four contiguous home positions among which it circulates spontaneously (figure 6.2); at random intervals averaging 200 time units, each object moves to its next home position. The object at left may also be moved by the hand when the hand grasps it; the object at right is out of the hand's range for grasping, but may be moved by being pushed by the other object when the other is grasped by the hand.

There are four primitive actions, called incremental hand actions, for moving the hand one unit forward, backward, right, or left (table 6.1). The actions are effective as long as the hand stays within the permitted body-relative range; an action that would move the hand beyond that range has no effect. Similarly, four

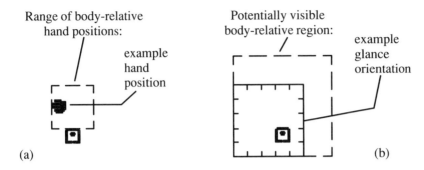

Figure 6.1 Hand and glance ranges. The hand and glance each have a three-by-three range of possible orientations.

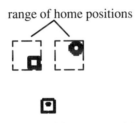

Figure 6.2 Objects' home positions. Two objects occasionally circulate among their home positions.

incremental eye actions shift the glance orientation one unit in each direction, within the permitted range. Two other actions close or open the hand; these actions can cause objects to be grasped or released. For each of these primitive actions, the mechanism has an initially supplied *bare* schema (empty context and result) with that action.

The mechanism's primitive items present visual, tactile, and proprioceptive information (table 6.2). Proprioception is the direct perception of the orientation of limbs or eyes via muscle tension and the like. For each of the nine body-relative hand positions, there is a proprioceptive item that is On just in case the hand is at that position; similarly, there is a proprioceptive item for each of the nine visual-field orientations.

There is one coarse tactile item for each of the four sides of the hand, designating contact with that side of the hand. (Contact occurs when an object occupies an adjoining position; objects never overlap at the same position.) In addition, the left side of the hand (the edge with its "fingers") has four tactile detail items that

- *handf, handb, handr, handl*: These actions move the hand incrementally forward, backward, right, or left.

- *eyef, eyeb, eyer, eyel*: These actions shift the glance orientation incrementally forward, backward, right, or left.

- *grasp*: This action closes the hand, grasping any object touching the hand's "fingers" (its left edge) unless the hand was already closed. Once closed or grasping, the hand remains in that state for a small number (two) of time units, unless explicitly opened in the interim. Moving the hand moves any grasped object; but any other object cannot be displaced by the hand, and will instead block the hand's motion if the hand moves into it.

- *ungrasp*: This action opens the hand, releasing any object that had been grasped.

Table 6.1 The primitive actions.

report on the texture of any object that makes contact there; each such item designates an arbitrary, unspecified textural property. There is also an item that is On whenever the hand is closed, and another that is On whenever the hand is grasping something.

Similarly, there are four tactile items designating contact with the four sides of the body; and the front of the body (where the "head" and "mouth" are) has four items that designate arbitrary, unspecified aspects of an object's taste.

There are 25 coarse visual items, one for each of the five by five visual field regions. Each coarse visual item is On just in case an object's image appears at the corresponding region. Coarse visual items thus report only the presence or absence of an object at each region; there is no information as to the specific appearance of the objects. For objects appearing in any of the five *foveal* regions of the visual field (figure 6.3), that information is provided by visual detail items.

There are 16 visual detail items for each foveal region. The items present information intended to be analogous to real-world visual details concerning shape, texture, color, and other aspects of appearance. Rather than being faithful to aspects of real-world appearance, however, the visual detail items, like the texture and taste items, denote arbitrary, unspecified properties. The designation is consistent, in that an object that turns On a given detail item at one foveal region turns

- *hp11,...,hp33*: Haptic-proprioceptive (hand-position) items, one for each possible hand position. Position (1,1) is the lower left corner of the range; in figure 6.1a, the hand appears at *hp12*.

- *vp11,...vp33*: Visual-proprioceptive items, one for each possible glance orientation. Coordinate designates center of visual field, using same conventions as for hand position; in figure 6.1b, the glance is oriented at *vp11*.

- *tactf,tactb,tactr,tactl*: coarse tactile items, one for each side of the hand (front, back, right, left).

- *text0,...text3*: Detailed tactile items, denoting arbitrary textural details of an object touching the ''fingers'' (left edge of hand).

- *bodyf,bodyb,bodyr,bodyl*: Coarse tactile items, one for each side of the body (front, back, right, left).

- *taste0,...taste3*: Taste items, designating arbitrary surface details of an object touching the ''mouth'' (front edge of body/head).

- *hcl*: Hand closed.

- *hgr*: Hand closed and grasping something.

- *vf00,...,vf44*: Coarse visual-field items, one for each of 25 regions. Region (0,0) is at the lower left; in 6.1b, the body appears at *vf31*.

- *fovf00,...fovf33,fovb00-33,fovl00-33,fovr00-33,fovx00-33*: Visual details corresponding to each of five foveal regions (figure 6.3): front, back, left, right, and center. Each has 16 arbitrary details: 00,...,33.

Table 6.2 The primitive items.

On the corresponding detail item at any other such region to which the image shifts. (In fact, the visual detail items are implemented as a low-resolution rendition of the pixel appearance of each object.)

   The coarse and detailed visual-region items are entirely unlike pixel-level information from the human retina. Rather than designating something analogous

Figure 6.3 The fovea. Five foveal regions—front (F), back (B), right (R), left (L), and center (X)—in the center of the visual field provide detailed visual information.

to the intensity of light at a particular spot on the human retina, the visual items convey information similar to the output of sophisticated processing in human vision, involving the detection of edges, the distinction of figure and ground regions, and the formation of 2.5-dimensional sketches of objects [41]. The end product of this processing encodes the existence, appearance, and location of objects in space (three-dimensional space in the real world, or two-dimensional space in the microworld).

Of course, the simulated robot's visual system does not perform comparably sophisticated computations to arrive at this encoding. Rather, the computation is trivial because of the simplicity of the microworld—in particular, the uniformity of objects' size, units of motion, and mapping onto visual-field regions. Furthermore, because the visual field enjoys a bird's-eye view, it need not recover information from a collapsed representation, as with the interpretation of depth from a real-world two-dimensional projection. Thus, the design of the simulated visual system deliberately bypasses the difficult problems of real-world vision; the artificial system merely provides information about nearby objects that is roughly similar to real-world visual information.

Notice what is and is not hardwired about the nature of physical objects. The visual system itself may be regarded as being rigged to know much about objects, by virtue of the close correspondence between the appearance of objects in the visual field and their actual spatial arrangement in the microworld; as just noted, this correspondence stands in for elaborate, visual domain-specific computations in real-world vision. Nonetheless, the schema mechanism, as opposed to its visual subsystem, does not know about objects. That is, the mechanism does not know that some of its sensory primitives designate visual information, or that there are categories of inputs that correspond to different modalities; the mechanism starts out knowing nothing about what each item or action represents, or how they might be related to one another. It is up to the mechanism itself to derive the meaning of the items and actions by learning about their interrelationships.

From the mechanism's initial point of view, each primitive item and action is a featureless entity, rather like a *gensym* in the computer language LISP [63] (a gensym is a symbol with a unique but arbitrary, automatically generated name). Whatever innate, domain-specific knowledge about objects and space the visual system uses to maintain the state of the visual inputs, this knowledge is *encapsulated* to the visual system, and is not available to the schema mechanism. (Similarly, of course, for the tactile and other domains.) This encapsulation corresponds to the working hypothesis put forth in section 2.9.3, that the Piagetian constructivist account is approximately correct with respect to the acquisition of knowledge by a central, general learning mechanism, although peripheral modules embody more innately specified competence than Piaget acknowledged.

6.2 Learning spatial substrates

6.2.1 Initial schemas

As noted in section 4.1.2, there is an initial, bare schema for each primitive action. Figure 6.4 shows the mechanism's initial schemas.

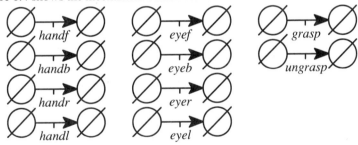

Figure 6.4 The initial schemas.

6.2.2 Grasping

The first schema built is /*grasp*/*hcl* (figure 6.5), which asserts that the grasp action results in the sensation of the hand being closed. This schema is unusual in that its result follows from its action unconditionally; hence, the schema is reliable despite an empty context. That the result follows unconditionally also makes the schema easy to discover quickly by marginal attribution, since every occurrence of the action produces a transition to the result state (unless the hand is already closed, in which case the action's occurrence does not count as a trial); and a transition to the result occurs only when that action is taken. Thus, the significant difference between the result's occurrence with and without the action becomes apparent more quickly than in the case of a relevant result that follows only infrequently, or that occurs under other circumstances as well.

Figure 6.5 A hand-closing schema. The grasp action closes the hand.

Similar schemas describe the ability to close the hand and grasp an object that touches the hand's "fingers" (figure 6.6). The mechanism builds the unreliable schema /*grasp*/*hgr*, which designates the relevance of the grasp action to the sensation of grasping. That schema's extended context discovers the relevance of the condition *tactl*, spinning off the schema *tactl*/*grasp*/*hgr*, which denotes the necessity of being in appropriate contact with an object in order to grasp.

Figure 6.6 A grasping schema. The grasp action grasps an object in contact with the fingers.

6.2.3 Elaborating the visual field

Often, it happens that an object is in the visual field when an incremental glance action occurs. Suppose, for example, that on several occasions, an object appears at *vf21* when the action *eyer* is taken (figure 6.7). As a result of the action, the image shifts to the adjoining visual region to the left, and *vf11* turns On.

before glance-right: after glance-right:

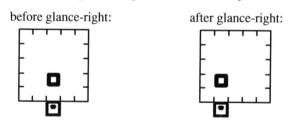

Figure 6.7 Glance shifting. A glance action shifts a visual image to an adjoining region.

The transition to *vf11* is an infrequent result of the action of glancing rightward; it results only if an object happens to be within view, and at just the correct region of the visual field, when the action occurs. Moreover, that transition also happens, on occasion, in the absence of the action in question—if, say, a forward glance brings an image from *vf12* to *vf11*, or if a moving object's image passes through that region while the glance is stationary.

Nonetheless, the transition to *vf11* happens more often when the action *eyer* is taken than when not:

- When *eyer* is taken, a transition to *vf11* follows if:

  - A stationary object appears at *vf21* before the action starts, and the glance is not already at its rightmost orientation; or

  - A moving object arrives at the projection of *vf11* as the action concludes (regardless of whether the glance orientation changed, or was already at its rightmost extreme).

- When *eyer* is not taken, a transition to *vf11* follows if:

  - Some other glance action moves the image of a stationary object to *vf11*; or

  - A moving object arrives at the projection of *vf11*, regardless of whether a glance action was just taken.

Transitions to *vf11* brought about by moving objects happen about as often when the *eyer* action is taken as when not; in either case, what is required is that the object's image move to wherever *vf11* ends up being mapped. Since objects are stationary most of the time, the comparison between the likelihood of transition with and without the action is dominated by the case in which the object does not move.

Transitions to *vf11* due to a stationary object require that some incremental glance action be taken, that the visual field is not already in its most extreme orientation in the direction of that action, and that the object's image is in the appropriate adjoining region just before the action. The glance-orientation and image-position requirements are as likely to be met in the case of the *eyer* action as in the case of any of the other three incremental glance actions; therefore, these factors attenuate the probability of the *vf11* transition equally whether or not the *eyer* action occurs. The only remaining factor is whether a glance action occurs, and this occurrence is significantly more likely (in fact, certain) if the action *eyer* is taken than if not. Thus, the transition to *vf11* is significantly more likely when *eyer* occurs.

As indicated in figure 6.8, the extended result of /*eyer*/ discovers the relevance of *vf11*, spinning off the schema /*eyer*/*vf11*. Of course, the relevance of other visual-field items is similarly discovered by the extended result, leading to spinoffs for those items as well.

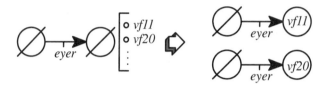

Figure 6.8 Glance results. A glance-action schema discovers visual-field results.

These schemas, with empty contexts, are all unreliable. But their extended contexts each identify the appropriate context condition, designating the visual-field region immediately to the right of the result item (glancing left shifts an image to the right). So, for example, /*eyer*/*vf11* spins off the reliable schema *vf21*/*eyer*/*vf11*, and similarly for the other schemas showing results of glancing left (figure 6.9), except for those glance-left schemas that result in a visual appearance at the leftmost edge of the retina.

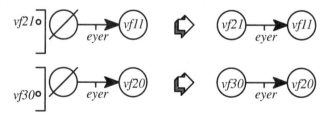

Figure 6.9 Glance contexts. Schemas expressing visual results identify corresponding context conditions.

Similar schemas form for each of the other three incremental glance actions. Eventually, these schemas link together to form a network that elaborates the spatial structure of the visual field (figure 6.10). The spatial elaboration is practical; the adjacency of visual-field regions is designated by their connection via an in-

cremental glance action. The network comprises chains of schemas that say how
to shift an image from one visual-field region to another by a series of incremental
glance actions.

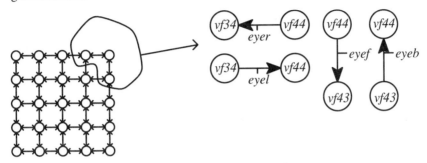

Figure 6.10 The visual-field network. These schemas with incremental glance actions link adjacent visual-field items.

The schema mechanism constructs most of the schemas shown in the network
of figure 6.10, but it does not realize the entire network by the time the reference
run ends. Rather, the mechanism builds 55 of those 80 schemas; in addition, there
are 24 schemas such as *vp32/eyeb/vf11*, which corresponds to the special case of
moving the body's visual image to *vf11* from *vf10,* which is where the image appears when the glance orientation is *vp32.*

6.2.4 Foveal relations

Each of the schemas in figure 6.10 fails when the visual field cannot shift further
in the direction of the action. The mechanism begins to learn about these overriding conditions, building, for example, the schema *vf21 &~vp32/eyer/vf11.*

The visual-detail items in the fovea also have adjacency relations; when an
image shifts from one foveal region to another, the details of its appearance shift
correspondingly. The extended result of the bare schema for each incremental
glance action (such as */eyer/* in figure 6.11) notes the relevance of each visual detail item, spinning off schemas such as */eyer/fovx12* and */eyer/fovf32.*

The extended context of each such schema seeks conditions that make the schema's result follow reliably. For some schemas, such as */eyer/fovx12,* a corresponding visual-detail item in an adjoining retinal region serves as such a condition; thus, for example, the schema *fovr11/eyer/fovx12* spins off (figure 6.12a),
and similarly for other actions, regions, and details. (It so happens that detail *11*
and and detail *12* tend to co-occur among the objects encountered, so *fovr11* and

Figure 6.11 Foveal glance results. A glance-action schema discovers visual-detail results.

fovr12 are equally correct context conditions for */eyer/fovx12*; */eyer/fovx12*'s extended context discovers the relevance of both items simultaneously, and arbitrarily chooses *fovr11* for the spinoff schema.)

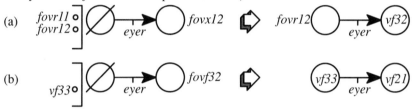

Figure 6.12 Foveal glance contexts. These glance-action schemas discover contexts for visual-detail results.

For other schemas, such as */eyer/fovf32*, there is no visual-detail item to confer reliability, since *vf33*, the region immediately to the right the forward foveal region, is not itself a foveal region, and thus conveys no visual detail. The extended context of */eyer/fovf32* does identify the coarse item *vf33* as a relevant condition, leading to the construction of *vf33/eyer/fovf32* (figure 6.12b). This schema, though still unreliable, is much more reliable than the unconditional */eyer/fovf32*.

The extended context of */eyer/fovx12* also identifies the result's adjoining coarse item (in this case *vf32*) as a relevant context condition. If *vf32* spawned a spinoff schema *vf32/eyer/fovx12* before *fovr11* spun off *fovr11/eyer/fovx12*, then the extended context of *vf32/eyer/fovx12* would itself discover the necessity of the condition *fovr11*, constructing the schema *vf32&fovr11/eyer/fovx12*. (Since *fovr11* is never On unless *vf32* is On, */eyer/fovx12* would never, once *vf32/eyer/fovx12* had formed, spawn *fovr11/eyer/fovx12*, due to the provision, discussed in section 4.1.3, for suppressing redundant attribution by deferring to a more-specific applicable schema.)

Two factors make it likely that */eyer/fovx12* will spawn *fovr11/eyer/fovx12* before spawning *vf32/eyer/fovx12*. First, the mechanism may encounter an object lacking the visual features *11* and *12* whose image passes from the right-foveal region to the central-foveal region when the action *eyer* is taken. In that case, *fovr11* contributes more to the observed reliability of */eyer/fovx12* than does *vf32*, so the extended context will detect the relevance of *fovr11* sooner. Second, if instead the relevance of the two items is detected concurrently, the mechanism prefers to create a spinoff for the more specific context condition (section 4.1.3 again), again favoring *fovr11*.

Once *fovr11/eyer/fovx12* exists, the context condition *vf32* does not give rise to further spinoffs for the action *eyer* and result *fovx12*: */eyer/fovx12* cannot spawn *vf32/eyer/fovx12*, because of redundant-attribution suppression; and *fovr11/eyer/ fovx12* does not spawn *vf32&fovr11/eyer/fovx12*, because there is no measured improvement in the reliability of *fovr11/eyer/fovx12* when *vf32* is On rather than Off (indeed, *fovr11/eyer/fovx12* cannot even be tested when *vf32* is Off, since *fovr11* must then be Off too, making the schema inapplicable). Thus, the mechanism avoids the inefficiency of building a conjunctive context here when a single item suffices.

For similar reasons, the mechanism avoids building *fovr12/eyer/fovx12*, as long as details *11* and *12* co-occur. But suppose the mechanism were to encounter an object that has feature *12* but not *11*. If, on some occasions, glancing left shifts that object's image from the rightmost foveal region to the central foveal region, */eyer/fovx12* can spawn *fovr12/eyer/fovx12*; since *fovr11* was Off on those trials, it does not suppress the attribution of relevance on those trials to *fovr12*.

6.2.5 Elaborating the proprioceptive fields

Incremental glance actions affect visual proprioceptive items as well as visual-field items. Schemas such as *vp21/eyef/vp22* express the adjacency of visual proprioceptive items by designating their connectivity with respect to incremental glance actions. (I omit the details of this schema's derivation, which is similar to the examples above.)

Such schemas link the visual proprioceptive items into a network (similar to the visual-field network in figure 6.10) that elaborates their spatial structure (figure 6.13). This network provides a chain of schemas from any given eye orientation to any other, conferring the ability to shift from any orientation to any other. In the reference run, the mechanism builds 17 of these 24 schemas. In addition, there are seven pairs of schemas such as *vf20/eyeb/vp21* and *vf20&vp22/eyeb/ vp21*, in which the body's image for a given glance orientation is initially designated as the context condition in lieu of the orientation itself; later, the actual orientation, specified proprioceptively, is added as a condition.

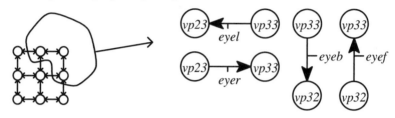

Figure 6.13 The visual proprioceptive network. These schemas with incremental glance actions link adjacent visual proprioceptive items.

Similarly, incremental hand actions affect haptic proprioceptive items; for example, *hp23/handl/hp13* shows the adjacency of *hp23* and *hp13*. Such schemas form yet another network (figure 6.14), which implements a practical description of the spatial arrangement of the haptic proprioceptive items. The mechanism constructs the entire haptic proprioceptive network, except that the schemas *taste2/handl/hp11* and *taste1/handr/hp31* appear in lieu of *hp22/handl/hp11* and *hp22/handr/hp31*; these two schemas substitute designations of the taste of the hand when it is at (2,1)—touching the mouth—for the proprioceptive designation of the hand's position. (These taste items are chained to from the haptic proprioceptive network; see figure 6.19.)

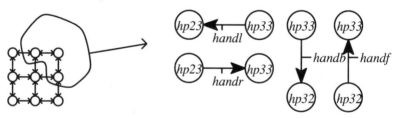

Figure 6.14 The haptic proprioceptive network. These schemas with incremental hand actions link adjacent haptic proprioceptive items.

6.2.6 Negative consequences

Shifting the position of the hand, the glance, or a visual image not only establishes a new position, but also eradicates the prior position. Schemas like those in figure 6.15 designate such consequences.

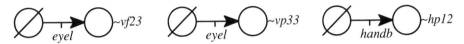

Figure 6.15 Moving away. Moving to a new position eradicates the old one.

6.2.7 Positional actions

Each of the proprioceptive items linked in the above networks is an achievable result; as such, it becomes the goal state for a composite action—the action of achieving that glance or hand orientation. As stated in section 4.3.1, for each newly defined composite action, the mechanism also builds a bare schema which has that action. Figure 6.16a, for example, shows the bare schema with a composite action whose goal state is *hp22*; the action's component schemas are those of the network in figure 6.14 above. The action *hp33*, shown in 6.16b, has the same component schemas—as do all the other composite actions with haptic proprioceptive goal states.

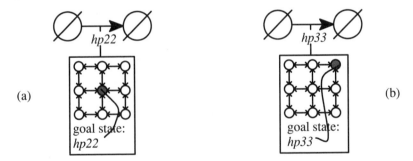

(a)

(b)

Figure 6.16 Positional hand actions. Composite actions form for various hand positions. Each defines the action of bringing the hand to that position. The schemas shown in the controllers are from figure 6.14.

These hand actions, with proprioceptive goals, are *positional*, in contrast with the primitive hand actions, which are incremental. Activating a given positional hand action moves the hand to a particular position, regardless of where the hand started.

Similarly, each of the visual proprioceptive items becomes a goal state of a composite action, as illustrated in figure 6.17. These composite actions are positional glance actions, again in contrast with the incremental primitives.

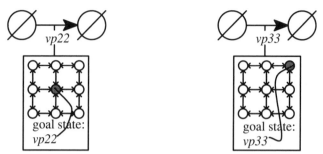

Figure 6.17 Positional glance actions. Composite actions also form for various glance orientations. Each defines the action of bringing the glance to that orientation. The schemas shown in the controllers are from figure 6.13.

Finally, the schemas that link adjacent visual-field items also provide a basis for the definition of composite actions with those items as goal states (figure 6.18). Each such composite action is the action of shifting an image to a particular region of the visual field. Of particular interest are the *foveation* composite actions: a foveal action (e.g., *vf12*) shifts an image to one of the foveal regions of the visual field. Foveal actions permit the visual details of an object to become apparent.

Many visual-detail items themselves become goal states of composite actions. Most objects exhibit a number of visual details, which therefore tend to co-occur when the object's image appears at some foveal region. This could lead to an n^2 proliferation of schemas, in which each visual-detail action claimed each co-occurring visual detail as a result. The mechanism's provision for suppressing redundant attribution to special-case actions (section 4.3.4) substantially mitigates this proliferation (since visual details are special cases of coarse-visual information; also, for any pair of visual details that almost always co-occur, one will arbitrarily count as a special case of the other). Still, more than a thousand such schemas do form, in part because some special-case actions acquire attributed results before being acknowledged as special-case actions.

6.3 Steps toward intermodal coordination

The schemas documented above set forth a substrate for the practical representation of visual and proprioceptive spatial knowledge. Other schemas begin to describe the relationships among these domains—including coordination of the

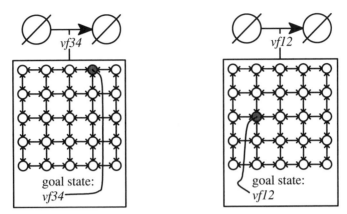

Figure 6.18 Visual-position actions. Composite actions form for various coarse visual items as well. Each defines the action of shifting an image to the corresponding region. The schemas shown in the controllers are from figure 6.10. Some schemas for moving the hand—with visual side-effects—are also in these controllers (but are not shown in this diagram).

haptic and buccal (mouth-oriented) domains; the visual manifestations of moving the hand; and coordination between sight and touch.

6.3.1 Moving the hand to the mouth

The schema *hp22/handb/taste1* (among other such examples) anticipates the taste of the hand when the hand moves to touch the mouth (figure 6.19). Schemas of the haptic proprioceptive network—e.g., *hp12/handr/hp22*—chain to this schema, allowing the mechanism to suck its thumb (as it were), wherever the hand may be initially. Schemas such as *hp22/handb/taste1* implement a rudimentary form of intermodal coordination; with the advent of these schemas, the haptic and buccal realms are no longer separate and unrelated. Rather, the mechanism now has a practical elaboration of their interconnection, by knowing, in effect, where in haptic space the taste-producing location is.

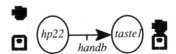

Figure 6.19 Hand-taste coordination. The schema mechanism learns to suck its thumb.

The mechanism also learns about the tactile effects of moving the hand to the mouth, building schemas such as *hp22/handb/tactb*.

6.3.2 Visual effects of incremental hand motions

Moving the hand while it is in view affects where the hand's image appears in the visual field. If the motion occurs within the foveal region, the visual change can be reliably predicted (if the hand is only peripherally visible, its identity as the hand is uncertain). As shown in figure 6.20, a bare incremental hand-motion schema such as */handl/* spawns schemas that show the hand, or its visual details, appearing at various visual-field regions—e.g., */handl/vf01*, */handl/fovx02* (visual detail *02* happens to be part of the hand's appearance); other schemas are similar, but with other hand actions, visual regions, and visual details.

Figure 6.20 Seeing the hand move. These schemas depict some visual effects of a hand motion.

Some of these schemas denote effects of the motion of the hand from a foveal visual region, others from a peripheral region. In the case of a peripheral origin, the best that the extended context can do is to discover that an image at the appropriate adjoining region is a relevant context condition; for example, */handl/vf01* spawns *vf11/handl/vf01* (figure 6.21). This schema is unreliable, since the object seen at *vf11* need not be the hand.

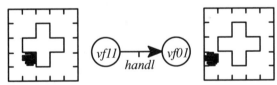

Figure 6.21 Peripheral hand motion. The motion of the hand's visual image is unreliably predicted from its peripheral appearance.

In contrast, the extended context of, say, */handl/fovx02* discovers the relevance of various visual features of the hand when it appears at the adjoining foveal region *vf32* (figure 6.22a). The relevance of the item *vf32* itself is also noticed, but only after some of the details that are unique to the hand are found relevant; *vf32*, and details less specific to the hand, also obtain when objects other than the hand are at *vf32*, and thus make a smaller difference to the with-without comparison made by the extended context data. Therefore, */handl/fovx02* spawns a context that best distinguishes the hand from other objects seen at *vf32* just before moving the hand to the left. This process culminates in the schema *SeeHand@3,2/handl/ SeeHand@2,2* (figure 6.22b), where *SeeHand@x,y* is shorthand for a conjunction of one or more visual features that jointly distinguish the hand's image at visual field region *(x,y)* from the images of other objects seen there.

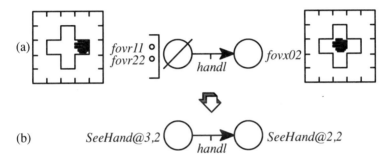

Figure 6.22 Foveal hand motion. When the hand appears in the fovea, the destination of its image is reliably anticipatable when the hand moves.

That schema, and others such as *SeeHand@2,3/handb/SeeHand@2,2* in figure 6.23, chain together to say how to move the hand so as to move the hand's image among the foveal regions. And each achievable result such as *SeeHand@2,2* defines a composite action—the action of bringing the hand's image to a given region of the visual field.

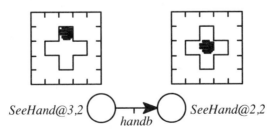

Figure 6.23 Seeing the hand move. Moving the hand moves its image across the fovea.

6.3.3 Touching what is seen, and vice versa

Touching what is seen

Sometimes, moving the hand not only shifts its visual image, but also results in tactile contact. The schema in figure 6.24a, for example, reflects the discovery of this result. That schema's extended context is able to discover a condition that confers reliability on the tactile result: that an object be seen next to where the hand will move. The schema in figure 6.24b incorporates that condition in its context (for a specific visual detail, *02*, exhibited by the object being touched).

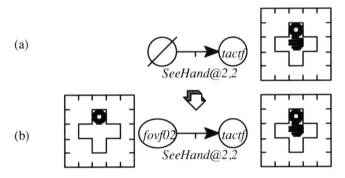

(a)

(b)

Figure 6.24 Seeing contact. Moving the hand, and its image, results in tactile contact if an object is present next to the hand's destination.

This schema tells the mechanism to anticipate the tactile resulting from moving the hand beside an object that is seen. However, as of the end of the reference run, the controller for *SeeHand@2,2* had not incorporated many schemas with hand-motion actions (although some other *SeeHand* action had)—most of *SeeHand@2,2*'s component schemas used eye-motion actions, moving the hand's image by shifting the glance rather than the hand. But shifting the glance does not bring the hand into contact with an object. The schema *fovf02/SeeHand@2,2/tactf* needs to sustain its context (recall section 4.1.6) until its action completes; sustaining the condition *fovf02* would tend to inhibit schemas with glance actions, since a side-effect of those actions would be to turn *vf31* Off. If the controller for *SeeHand@3,2* were to incorporate components for moving the hand's image to visual-field region (3,2) from immediately adjacent regions, the mechanism would be able to use the schema *fovf02/SeeHand@2,2/tactf* to touch an object, provided that the hand was already seen near (2,2). This ability would correspond to an intermediate development described by Piaget, in which an infant can only grasp an object if the hand is seen in the vicinity of the object.

As more components linked into the controller, grasping would become possible from more starting points. And the construction of schemas for bringing the hand into view when it is not seen at all—described in the following section— could create the ability to grasp an object even when the hand is not at first seen.

Seeing what is touched

Because the composite action *SeeHand@3,2* has eye-motion components as well as hand-motion components, it can serve to look at what is touched, as well as vice versa. The schema *tactf/SeeHand@3,2/vf33* in figure 6.25b is works inversely to the schema in figure 6.24b; *tactf/SeeHand@3,2/vf33* anticipates seeing an object that the hand feels, if the glance is directed at the hand. This schema's success depends on sustaining the context condition *tactf* by using only eye-motion components of *SeeHand@3,2*, inhibiting hand-motion components.

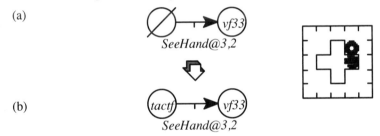

(a)

(b)

Figure 6.25 Touching then seeing. Looking at the hand when it touches something results in seeing the object that is touched.

Other descriptive levels

There is an alternative route by which the mechanism starts to develop a schema for touching what's seen near the hand, but which turns out to be a dead end. The schema */handb/*, for example, spawns the unreliable schema */handb/tactl*. That schema, however, is unable to make progress toward identifying visual conditions that confer reliability on the schema. The problem is that the object being touched could appear anywhere in the visual field (or could fail to appear at all); its appearance at a given visual region makes tactile contact no more likely than its appearance at any other region (and not measurably more likely than when it does not appear, given that an object is likely to be nearby even if not in view). Similarly, the hand's appearance at a given region makes tactile contact no more likely than for another hand position.

Any *conjunction* of an image's appearance at one region and the hand's appearance at the appropriate nearby region would confer reliability on the schema */handb/tactl*. But, in this case, the marginal attribution facility is unable to build incrementally to any of the required conjunctions, because the conjuncts, taken individually, do not enhance reliability. In effect, the schema mechanism breaks this impasse by reformulating the problem at a more suitable level of description—expressing the relevant action in terms of moving the hand's image, rather than as a primitive motor action. With respect to that description, the relevant context condition is straightforwardly discerned by marginal attribution—the mechanism can discover where in the visual field an object must appear to be touched when the hand appears at a given visual-field region.

In contrast with, say, the Minsky's Society of Mind theory [46], the schema mechanism lacks any specific reformulation machinery that detects and reacts to the need to look afresh at a recalcitrant problem. Rather, the facilities for defining new actions and items develop a variety of levels of representation; and the marginal attribution facility filters out levels of representation that are irrelevant to a given schema—not by recognizing levels of representation as such, but rather the same way it filters any irrelevant events: by requiring statistical evidence of relevance.

6.3.4 Bringing the hand into view. and looking at the hand

The schema mechanism learns how to bring its hand into view. Unreliable schemas such as */hp23/SeeHand@22* reflect the fact that seeing the hand at the center of the fovea sometimes results from that positional hand action. This schema is reliable for a particular glance orientation (which must be sustained through the positional hand action's execution); thus, the above schemas spawns *vp23/hp23/SeeHand@22* (figure 6.26a). By constructing a number of such schemas, the mechanism in effect builds a dispatch table that says, for each of several glance orientations, where the hand must be put (relative to the body) to appear in the visual field when the glance is in that orientation. These dispatching schemas chain to *SeeHand@22*, and so become components of that composite action.

Similarly, the mechanism builds a number of schemas that say how to shift the glance to look at the hand when it is out of view (figure 6.26b). These schemas dispatch from the current hand position, specifying the appropriate glance orientation for each.

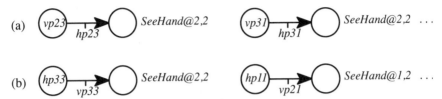

Figure 6.26 Viewing the hand. Schemas that dispatch from glance orientation move the hand into view (a). Schemas that dispatch from hand orientation direct the glance to the hand (b).

6.4 Beginnings of the persistent-object concept

At this point, schemas are structured so as to provide rudimentary representations of the spatial relationships of both external and proprioceptive sensory data, both within and between the various sensory modes. This knowledge was acquired through action, and its embodiment is practical: it is knowledge of how to act and what to expect to happen. But the content of these schemas is not only procedural: the coordination of hand motions and eye motions, of seeing and feeling, begins to describe the nature of objects and space; sight and touch begin to be known as coordinated properties of external objects.

All of this boasts respectable progress from the schema mechanism's initial endowment of knowledge, in which all actions and items were devoid of any meaning to the mechanism. Still, it remains to transcend the rendering of reality only in terms of sensory and motor primitives. If an object is not perceived, then as far as schema mechanism is concerned, it has ceased to be—there are no items whose state signifies the thing's continued existence. And similarly, an object's specific identity is immediately forgotten when its distinguishing features (e.g., visual details) cease to be perceived, even when some (partial) perception of the object persists. Next, the schema mechanism begins to synthesize items to represent these persistent states in their own right.

6.4.1 Palpable and visible persistent objects

Various positional hand actions, e.g., *hp23*, sometimes result in tactile contact, e.g., *tactl*. The schema /*hp23*/*tactl* reflects this occasional result (figure 6.27). As in the example of section 4.2.1, this schema is unreliable—it only succeeds when an object happens to be present at position *hp13*. But the schema is locally consistent—if it succeeds on some occasion, it probably will succeed again if activated again soon, since nearby objects tend to stay put for a while. Without understanding that reason, of course, the schema nonetheless discovers, over a number of trials, that it is indeed locally consistent; and the schema determines the expected duration of its local consistency, the average time that the schema remains valid (in this case, the average time that an object stays put there).

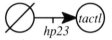

Figure 6.27 Positional contact. Moving the hand to a particular position sometimes results in tactile contact.

Such schemas develop for other hand positions as well. Each such schema serves as host to a synthetic item that designates a persistent palpable object at a particular body-relative position. For example, the host schema /*hp23*/*tactl* acquires a reifying synthetic item that we may call *PalpableObj@1,3* (figure 6.28); when the hand is at *hp23*, the hand's left edge touches the object at position (1,3). The host schema's positional hand action serves as a probe, and the schema's tactile result as manifestation, of the condition reified by the synthetic item—the condition of there being a palpable object beside that hand position.

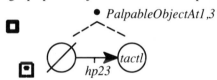

Figure 6.28 Persistent positional palpability. This synthetic item designates a persistent palpable object at a particular position.

Analogous synthetic items designate persistent visible objects. For example, the unreliable, locally consistent schema /*vp21*/*vf14* (figure 6.29) reveals a manifestation of a visible object—seeing it at visual-field region (1,4)—by the probing action of glancing at a particular body-relative position. The reifying synthetic item, which I'll call *VisibleObj@1,3*, designates a persistent visible object at that position.

A clarification about notation is warranted here. By convention, persistent-object synthetic items—both palpable and visible—are named with respect to the body-relative coordinates of the object designated; visible-object items are not named with respect to visual-field coordinates. For visual orientation *vpxy*, the central visual region, *vf22*, maps to body-relative position (x,y). Thus, for glance orientation *vp21*, an object whose image appears at *vf14* is at body-relative posi-

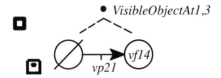

Figure 6.29 Persistent positional visibility. This synthetic item designates a persistent visible object at a particular position.

tion (1,3). This is the same body-relative position as that of *PalpableObjectAt1,3*; thus, the notation uses the same coordinate frame for naming both palpable and visible persistent-object items.

6.4.2 inverse actions and persistent objects

The successive activation of schemas with inverse actions (section 3.4.2) promotes the formation of synthetic items by demonstrating the local consistency of their host schemas. Consider, for example, the inverse actions of the schemas *hp23/handb/hp22* and *hp22/handf/hp23* when there happens to be an object at (1,3). Those schemas' successive activation, starting and finishing with the hand at *hp23,* implicitly activates the schema */hp23/tactl.* The implicit activation is successful—the schema's result does obtain—and several repetitions of the pair of successive activations thus amount to successive successful activations of */hp23/tactl,* exhibiting that schema's local consistency, and spurring the construction of a synthetic item for that schema (if none exists already). Similarly, of course, for other hand positions (and for visible-object items; for those, inverse eye actions, rather than hand actions, give aid.)

The ability to repeatedly touch and then withdraw from an object appears early in Piagetian development (section 2.2). This pair of actions implements a special case of recognizing object persistence—the actions repeatedly recovers the tactile manifestation of an object which is, briefly, unperceived. However, this special case of recovery is only accomplished immediately after the manifestation ceases, and only by a particular action which is the inverse of the action that canceled the manifestation. By catalyzing the construction of a synthetic item, the pair of inverse actions functions not only as a special case of recognizing persistence, but also as a precursor of a less limited version of persistence recognition.

6.4.3 Persistent details

Tactile and visual details also serve as manifestations of conditions representable by synthetic items. Figure 6.30 shows some synthetic items that designate the persistence of the particular details associated with objects at particular locations. Such items let the mechanism represent more than the continued existence of an unperceived object—its persistent identity is now representable as well, at least to the extent that its apparent details specify its identity.

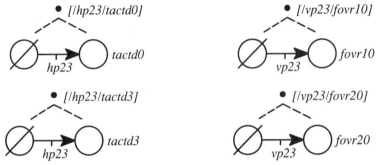

Figure 6.30 Persistent identity. Some synthetic items correspond to a persistent object's specific identity.

6.4.4 Inversely indexed persistence

In addition to persistent-object synthetic items such as *[/hp23/tactl]* and *[/vp21/vf14]*, the schema mechanism builds what might be called *inversely indexed* representations of persistent objects—for example, *[/tactf/hp33]* and *[/vf43/vp23]*. The standardly indexed representations may be thought of as posing the question *What is at this position?*, and answering: an object. In contrast, the inversely indexed representation asks *Where is the object?*, and answers: at this position. The question posed by an inversely indexed representation may lack a unique answer—objects may exist at several locations—but, if details are specified (as, for example, by the inversely indexed item *[/tactd3/hp23/]*, which the mechanism builds), the answer becomes more constrained, and possibly unambiguous. An eventual, more complete object concept must include a coordination of both indexing schemes—knowing that a given position now harbors a particular object, and knowing that a given object is now to be found at a particular position.

6.4.5 Coordinating visible- and palpable-object representations

The synthetic items *PalpableObj@1,3* and *VisibleObj@1,3* in the previous section actually designate the same state of the world as one another—the state in which there is an object at body-relative position (1,3). In principle, though, invisible or intangible objects could exist. Were there such objects, a palpable object at some location would not assure the presence of a visible one, or vice versa. But since such objects do not exist in the microworld, *PalpableObj@1,3* and *VisibleObj@1,3* are in fact *coextensive*—whenever one of those states obtains, so does the other.

However, the schema mechanism is unaware of these items' coextension. What turns On *PalpableObj@1,3* need not affect *VisibleObj@1,3*, or vice versa; initially, in fact, each is turned On only by the successful activation of its own host schema. Thus, the two items can be in opposite states at the same time; like a third-stage Piagetian infant, the mechanism may know that it can touch a currently unperceived object, but not know that it can look at it—or vice versa, depending on the modality by which the object recently manifested itself to the mechanism. Of course, once the object has been recovered by, say, touching it, intermodal schemas can anticipate seeing it by turning to look at what is touched (section 6.4.5); thereupon, the visual item will turn On as well. Thus, intermodal schemas effectively bridge between different modalites of persistent-object representation, as well as between different modalities of sensory representation. Still, in the absence of taking the bridging action—looking at the object that is touched, or vice versa—the mechanism has to clue as to the persistent-object synthetic items' correspondence to one another.

Although the mechanism does not manage to discover the correspondence between that particular pair of items, it does learn of the effective synonymity between among some similar items. For example, the schema */vp23/fovl33* spawns the reliable context spinoff *[/hp23/tactl]/vp23/fovl33*; similarly, */hp23/tactl* spawns the reliable context spinoff *[/vp23/fovl03]/hp23/tactl* (figure 6.31). As described in section 4.2.2, a synthetic item's state is maintained in part by reliable context spinoffs spawned by the host schema. Such schemas' contexts specify conditions under which the host schema is reliable; hence, its reifier turns On. Hence, *[/hp23/tactl]* now turns On *[/vp23/fovl33]*.

As for the converse, the schema *[/vp23/fovl33]/hp23/tactl* does not form, so the item *[/vp23/fovl33]* does not directly turn On *[/hp23/tactl]*1. However, the mechanism does build *[/vp23/fovl03]/hp23/tactl*; and, as it happens, the visual details *03* and *33* tend to co-occur, so seeing an object that turns On *[/vp23/fovl33]* will also tend to turn On *[/vp23/fovl03]*—and turning On *[/vp23/fovl03]* does turn On *[/hp23/tactl]*, due to *[/vp23/fovl03]/hp23/tactl*. Thus, the mutual correspondence of *[/hp23/tactl]* and *[vp23/fovl33]* is effectively recognized.

When this coordination is achieved, each host schema's extended context also determines that when the other synonymous item is Off, that host schema is unre-

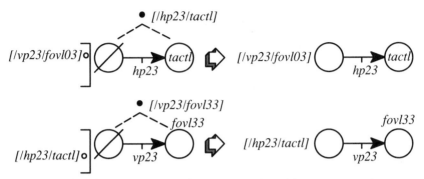

Figure 6.31 Cross-modal persistence. Palpable-object representations admit visual evidence, and vice versa.

liable; hence, its reifier turns Off. When two items thus help maintain one another's state, there is a danger of oscillation when their states differ (and if their states never differed, neither would ever be in a position to turn the other On or Off—the other would already be in that state). Two factors prevent such oscillation: 1) that each item is in an Unknown state when it has received no recent evidence; and 2) as discussed in section 4.2.2, host-trial evidence takes precedence over other verification conditions, and memory of previous evidence yields to current evidence; hence, seeing or touching an object—or failing to when looking or reaching for it—definitively sets the state of one of the two synonymous items, which then sets the state of the other.

The mechanism begins to learn about intra-modal synonymity as well as the inter-modal coordination just described. For example, the items *[hp23/tactr]* and *[/hp32/tactf]* both designate palpable objects at (3,3); the mechanism begins to recognize this correspondence by building the schema *[/hp23/tactr]/hp32/tactf.*

6.4.6 Relational items

The synthetic items of the last few sections all designate persistent objects in a body-relative frame of reference (except for the inversely indexed objects, which might be said to designate the body's position relative to some object). Alternatively, it is possible to describe one object's position relative to another, thereby describing the spatial relationship between the objects. For example, the mechanism builds the item *[/vf02/vf10]*; when On, this item asserts that there are two objects separated by (1,-2) units, since mapping one to *vf02* results in seeing another at *vf10*.

6.4.7 Saturation

The schema mechanism's reference run runs out of space after 10,912 time units (about one day of real time on the CM2). At that point, it has built 7,371 schemas (in addition to 10 primitively supplied bare schemas), 184 synthetic items (in addition to 175 primitive items), and 343 composite actions (in addition to 10 primitive actions).

6.5 Hypothetical scenario of further developments

This section describes some hypothetical further achievements of the schema mechanism—developments that build directly on the substrate of knowledge that the implementation has in fact constructed, and that would perhaps be exhibited if the same software were to run on a larger machine. I present these hypothetical developments both to call attention to what the implementation has not yet achieved, and to specify part of a target scenario for future work.

6.5.1 Grasping and moving objects

Touching what is seen is a useful precursor for grasping and manipulating what is seen. Figure 6.32a shows a schema for moving a grasped object incrementally, as expressed in terms of the visual manifestation of that motion. (The image to the right of the circular object is what the hand looks like when it is grasping something.) Figure 6.32b shows a schema that expresses similar knowledge in terms of persistent objects.

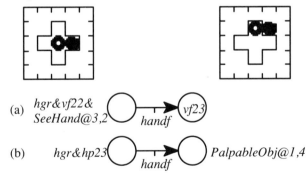

(a) $hgr\&vf22\&$
$SeeHand@3,2$ — $handf$ → $vf23$

(b) $hgr\&hp23$ — $handf$ → $PalpableObj@1,4$

Figure 6.32 Moving an object. These schemas depict moving a grasped object. The depiction is visual (a) or in terms of persistent-object representations (b).

Moving an object not only puts it in a new place, but also removes it from its previous place. Schemas such as those in figure 6.33 express such knowledge.

These are similar to, but more sophisticated than, the schemas of figure 6.15 that show the negation of previous hand and glance orientations, and of visual images, after taking a hand or glance action. The earlier schemas expressed direct, nearly unconditional results of primitive actions on primitive items; the present schemas, in contrast, express effects on grasped objects, and are therefore subject to context conditions that describe the appropriate graspedness.

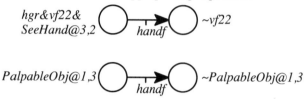

$hgr\&vf22\&$
$SeeHand@3,2$ ⟶ *handf* ~ ~$vf22$

$PalpableObj@1,3$ ⟶ *handf* ~ ~$PalpableObj@1,3$

Figure 6.33 Moving an object away. Moving an object removes it from its previous position.

6.5.2 Hidden objects

Suppose the microworld were modified so that an object is obscured from the robot's view if some other object (other than the robot's own body) lies directly behind it (figure 6.34). This ad hoc modification introduces the problem of representing hidden objects.

Figure 6.34 Hiding from view. The hollow object hides the solid object from view. The robot looks directly at the solid object, but does not see it.

If the robot centers its gaze on the location of the hidden object (as in the figure), the schema /$vp23$/$vf22$, host to the synthetic item $VisibleObj@2,3$, implicitly activates, but its result fails to obtain. The synthetic item thus turns Off. Due to cross-modal coordination similar to that described above in section 6.4.5, the synonymous item $PalpableObj@2,3$ also turns Off—incorrectly, since the hidden object is still palpable. Thus, the mechanism, like a third-stage Piagetian infant, is ignorant of the possibility of touching the hidden object.

There are several ways that the schema mechanism might represent the continued existence of a hidden object. A preliminary step (as in the case of representing persistent objects in the first place) is to designate persistence with respect to a pair of inverse actions. In this case, the actions are those of replacing and displacing the visual obstacle (figure 6.35). Given the discovery of this special-case recoverability, the mechanism can recover a hidden object by displacing the obstacle that hides it—but only immediately following having placed the obstacle there.

Figure 6.35 Uncovering what is hidden. Moving the grasped obstacle to and fro (by moving the hand) alternately reveals and hides the object in front of the obstacle.

One expression of an object's persistence while hidden appears in figure 6.36. A schema for moving the hand while grasping the obstacle, thus displacing the obstacle, has the unreliable but locally consistent result of causing the manifestation to reappear. This schema could serve as host to a synthetic item that designates an object hidden behind the obstacle.

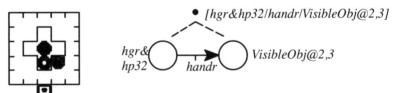

Figure 6.36 An uncovering schema. Displacing the obstacle reveals a hidden object, locally consistently.

This representation would be vulnerable to making a curious mistake. Suppose the host schema activates successfully, turning On its reifier, the hidden-object item. Next, the previously hidden object moves to a new location, in full view of the robot. However, the hidden-object item remains On; there has been no unsuccessful activation of the host schema to turn it Off. If the object were now hidden behind another obstacle at its new position, and the first obstacle returned to its original position, the mechanism could exhibit a Piagetian fourth-stage place error (section 2.5) by still expecting to be able to find the object behind the first obstacle.

This place error can be corrected by representing the displacement of the obstacle on a less subjective level of abstraction. The schema in figure 6.37a has a composite action designating the very displacement of the obstacle, rather than using the primitive hand action of the previous host schema. Now, if the object moves to another location after its original hidden position is uncovered, the continuing uncoveredness of that position entails the continuing implicit activation of the schema whose action is that there be no obstacle covering that position. As soon as the object moves away from the uncovered position, that implicit activation is an *unsuccessful* activation, which turns Off the associated synthetic item. To eradicate the place error, the more subjective host schema must come to designate the new item as a synonym, as shown in figure 6.37b.). (The current implementation of the schema mechanism does not make a composite action with a negative goal state; that ability would have to be added for the non-obstacle action to form.)

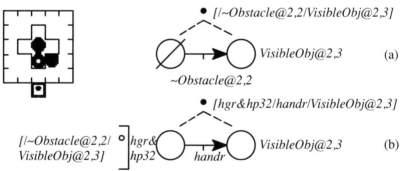

Figure 6.37 Uncovering objectively. A more objective representation of the action fixes fourth-stage place error.

6.5.3 Large-scale space

The spatial framework developed in the scenario is centered on the mechanism's own body; proprioceptive inputs serve as spatial coordinates. This framework suffices for a stationary infant. But after a while, the infant begins to crawl and then walk. By displacing herself, the infant moves *all* the objects in her body-relative space (by moving that space itself). But in externally-based, large-scale space, it is the infant that moves, while the other objects remain still. Coordinates in large-scale space are not given proprioceptively, but can be expressed in terms of fixed landmarks. The infant herself is just one of many objects that can move about in large-scale space.

It is plausible to imagine the schema mechanism going on to build a representation of large-scale space much the way it constructs its "personal" spatial framework (though I have worked out no details for this). The probing action (recall section 4.2.1) for the concept of an object at some landmarked position in large-scale space is to move oneself to the landmark there; the manifestation is for the object then to be present in body-relative space. As in the synopsis above, extended views could be coordinated together, allowing an object's position also to be recognized by seeing the object from a remote landmark, or from a position between landmarks.

One might regard the entire schema mechanism as essentially a large-scale-space facility, in which the terms of representing positions have been generalized—any primitive or constructed item can be used, not just views of landmarks—and the actions that connect places in the space have been generalized to arbitrary state-achievements, not just moving among landmarks. (Something like the schema mechanism may even have arisen, in the course of evolution, as a variation of a large-scale-space facility.) The scenario shows how this generalized large-scale-space facility can be "retrofitted" to the reconstruction of personal space; the extrapolations below speculate about the extension of this facility to the representation of more-abstract "spaces."

6.5.4 Reality and beyond

One might be willing to imagine the schema mechanism constructing arbitrarily elaborate models of the current state of the world. But can such a mechanism possibly move beyond sensorimotor-level representations, to construct *episodic* memories that designate the state of propositions that concern things other than immediate physical reality? Consider, for example, the assertion that a certain object was in a given location *yesterday*, rather than *now*. Its position *now* can be expressed as the coordinated reification of the validity of various schemas, as discussed in the scenario. But *past* state cannot be similarly represented, unless there is some accessor condition by which some manifestation of the state can be revealed.

Sometimes this is the case, as when a sea gull walking along the beach leaves tracks in the sand that indicate its past presence. But it is unusual for past events to be so obliging as to leave conspicuous remnants—or is it? One very general way for a past event to "leave tracks" is to be *remembered by a person*. In principle, one's memory of a past event can serve, for purposes of maintaining a synthetic-item state, as one "view" (among many intercoordinated ones) of that past state. Other possible views include:

- Physical remnants of the event, such as tracks in the sand.

- One's cognitive remnants of the event, other than explicit memories; for example, new abilities or attitudes acquired as a result of the event.

- *Other people's* cognitive remnants of the event, in the form of memories or new abilities, as manifested verbally and by other behavior.

Such views serve as fragments of a representation of past state; the real representation is their coordinated ensemble.

This account may seem circular. After all, the representation of a past state cannot arise from a representation of a memory of the past state, since that memory requires that the past state is already representable. But then, in the same way, it is circular to say that the representation of an object's presence at some location when hidden arises from a representation of the object's presence there when not hidden, since that assumes there is already a representation of the object's presence at that location. On closer examination, though, the circle becomes a spiral: the new representation is not stated in terms of *itself*, but rather in terms of a cruder approximation to itself. This chapter proposes the details of a few turns of that spiral for the development of the physical-object concept; with regard to the speculation about representing past states, I have no such details to offer. So, rather than giving a plausibility argument here, I am just presenting a bare-possibility argument. Still, the thought seems intriguing.[20]

This idea generalizes to the representation of abstractions. At a given moment, the state of any item in the schema mechanism is always some function of the past and present state of primitive, sensory items; hence, it would seem that an item can only represent some physical reality, as reflected in the sensory data on which the item's state (solely) depends. But whenever one's cognitive apparatus includes machinery to perform a certain computational task, it may be possible, by representing that machinery, to make (indirect) statements about the abstraction that the computation embodies. For example:

---

20.   Another possibility is to have a distinct episodic-memory module accessible to the central system, as a kind of internal VCR. Traces of memories stored there could serve as one kind of manifestation of past events, to be coordinated with the others mentioned above. Something resembling Minsky's *k-lines* [46] might provide an interface for storing and retrieving central-system states as memories.

- A thing's *name* is accessed by (something like) holding it up to an adult and manifested by the adult's saying "That's an *x*."

- *Classification* is like naming, except that a class names only one of a thing's many attributes, so the same thing can belong to many classes. Piaget shows that the child gradually coordinates an extensive view of a class—defined by the actual set of members—with an intensive view—defined by a distinguishing attribute of all members of the class

- The *cardinality* of a group of things is the number one arrives at by counting them—that is, by reciting a number sequence in synchronization with touching the objects, touching each exactly once. That process is the accessor, and the final number the manifestation, of the cardinality of the collection. The individual must discover that this is a persistent property of a collection—that if the process is repeated, one gets the same number (conservation of number). Note that this proposes an inductive basis for the discovery—the individual notices that cardinality is persistent, without understanding why. On the other hand, given a facility for performing thought experiments (such as the *subactivation* facility proposed in section 7.1.3), the induction can be carried out on trials on which the individual merely *imagines* placing some objects and performing the counting ritual on them; the induction need not depend on actual events in the environment, as an extreme of the empiricist tradition has held.

- In formal reasoning, the *validity* of an argument (as opposed to the truth of its conclusion) has the accessor of inducing belief in the argument's premises; the manifestation is believing the conclusion. In each of these examples, a new abstraction is conceived in terms of how a person's computational machinery—one's own, or another's—behaves in some situation. The new conception reifies the set of circumstances under which a piece of one's computational machinery behaves a certain way.[21] Even more than with the physical-object concept, each such conception eventually requires an ensemble of many fragments of representation. As with the physical-object concept, Piaget presents snapshots of various incomplete versions of the

---

21. This is not to say that one explicitly or introspectively thinks of one's conception of abstractions as being the representation of properties of certain machines; it need not "feel like" that is what is going on. One's explicit ideas about one's representations are implemented by other structures that express a theory about those representations; and that theory, like any other that one holds, can be arbitrarily far off base.

eventual coordinations. In these, one sees bizarre bugs in a child's behavior that would be inexplicable if a more "appropriate" representation were in use—appropriate, that is, to the given representation considered in isolation, rather than as part of the developmental system—just as the spatial nonlocality of hidden objects is a bizarre property of the infant's fourth-stage conception. The conservation protocol in section 2.8 is one striking illustration of this phenomenon.

In general, then, self-modelling might provide a route to the representation of abstractions, allowing an intelligent system to move beyond representing only the state of the physical world. We can compare this possibility with Papert's speculation [49] that exposure to the abstractions embodied in computers will profoundly change the way people think, once intellectually accessible computer systems become widely available, especially to children; by working with the concrete embodiment of a computational abstraction, a person may appropriate a model of that abstraction for her own internal use. In effect, what I suggest here is that (much of) the necessary access to sophisticated computer systems has long been provided to people—in the form of people themselves. And the resulting cognitive revolution was quite as spectacular as what Papert predicted.

Additionally, modelling one's own mind, and others', is important in its own right. Understanding other people makes them more predictable and easier to interact with in beneficial ways. Understanding oneself provides the opportunity to better exploit one's own abilities, by forming a model of strengths and weaknesses and means of improvement. And what we call consciousness requires a memory of the occurrence of a thought or experience, understood as such. Nothing in the schema mechanism's sensorimotor-level development, for example, qualifies as conscious. One might say metaphorically that the mechanism is aware of the things that it represents; but to take that awareness literally, in the sense of humanlike consciousness, would be to indulge in a kind of animism. Consciousness requires knowledge (and hence representation) of one's own mental experiences as such; the schema mechanism does not come close to demonstrating such knowledge.

7 Extrapolations: virtual structures, mechanisms

The schema mechanism implementation has made rudimentary but encouraging progress in the direction of the Piagetian infant's development of the concept of physical object. Replicating this development is of special interest because of the possibility that it is just the earliest achievement of a learning mechanism with far-reaching capabilities. The present results certainly do not establish that the schema mechanism is capable of going far beyond its achievements so far; but the mechanism's arguable similarity to what is arguably a powerful human learning mechanism warrants at least the speculation that extended achievements are possible.

This chapter elaborates the speculation by exploring some hypothetical further activity of the schema mechanism—activity that is tantamount to the development by the schema mechanism of virtual structures and mechanisms. Some of the hypothetical developments presented here depend on two proposed (i.e., unimplemented) extensions to the schema mechanism, subactivation and inverse-action identification, which are introduced below.

7.1 Virtual generalizations

Many conventional formal systems make it easy to express generalizations. In the predicate calculus, for example, one writes *For all x, P(X) implies Q(x).*, where *P* and *Q* are predicates that apply to some arbitrary object. From the foregoing proposition, and the proposition *P(a)*, *Q(a)* follows; it can be deduced that a particular object *a* that satisfies *P* must also satisfy *Q*. Other systems, such as semantic networks and knowledge-representation languages, provide analogous ways to perform a deduction that instantiates a generalization, that is, that applies the generalization to a particular instance.

The schema mechanism has no comparable facility for expressing generalizations. Disconcertingly, the mechanism must re-learn essentially the same fact in numerous different guises, rather than learning it in a general form and deducing the instantiations. For example, learning about persistent palpable objects at a given body-relative position is independent of learning about them at other positions. Similarly, the effect of grasping a persistent object and then moving the hand incrementally must be learned separately for each body-relative position; there is no automatic generalization from one position to another, and no way to parameterize position in order to express a more general, position-independent principle (such as *Moving an object at* (x,y) *incrementally right brings it to* (x+1,y)) which could then be instantiated for various particular positions (e.g., *Moving an object at (3,2) incrementally to the right brings it to (4,2)*).

One approach would be to augment the schema mechanism with parameterized representations. But it is unclear how the mechanism itself might devise appropriate parameterizations. A parameterization scheme limited to a few built-in special cases would be of little use or interest.

Instead, I suggest a way that the schema mechanism might behave *as though* it expressed and instantiated generalizations; the mechanism might then be said to embody *virtual generalizations*. This capability is speculative; the scenario to follow has not been demonstrated by the schema mechanism implementation, and even the speculation relies in part on currently unimplemented extensions to the mechanism, as described below.

The realization of virtual generalizations relies on representations of the same event in different frames of reference—for example, representing an event visually, relative to the visual field, and also in terms of visible-object synthetic items, in body-relative terms. A representation with respect to a particular position in one field of reference—say, the visual field—applies to a number of different positions in the other frame of reference—in this example, the body-relative frame. Call these the *source* and *target* reference frames, respectively. A specific, fixed-position representation in the source frame thus implies a general, position-independent statement about the target frame. Shifting the glance orientation changes the mapping from source to target, instantiating the generalization at a different target position, as shown in figure 7.1.

Figure 7.1a shows a schema for moving a grasped object incrementally forward; the schema expresses the visual manifestation of this event (*vf23* turning on). In each of the two examples in figure 7.1b, the glance orientation is such that a grasped object appears in the same part of the visual field as in the context of the schema in figure 7.1a. The schemas in figure 7.1b describe the same event as the schema in figure 7.1a, but in terms of persistent objects at particular body-relative positions, rather than in terms of visual appearance.

The visual-field view shown in figure 7.1a serves as a *canonical perspective* of the event that is represented. Suppose the mechanism learns that it is interesting to orient the glance so as to bring about a canonical perspective; in effect, the mechanism learns the heuristic, the rule of thumb, that achieving that perspective is a good idea. Given the opportunity, the mechanism will then tend to bring about that perspective. Doing so serves to instantiate the generalization with respect to whatever target position is mapped onto. If a canonical perspective is achieved by foveation, as in this example, the primitive value associated with the visual-detail items promotes the canonical perspective: trying to turn on the foveal items

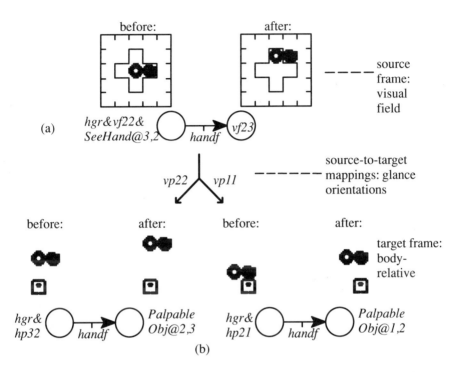

Figure 7.1 A virtual generalization. A virtual generalization is instantiated by mapping one reference frame to another.

achieves the canonical perspective. In other examples, the items designating the canonical perspective may achieve delegated value (section 3.4.1) by virtue of the things of value that are made accessible by achieving the canonical perspective.

7.1.1 Implicit and explicit instantiation

A virtual generalization can be instantiated either implicitly or explicitly. *Implicit* instantiation merely consists of achieving the canonical perspective, making the source-frame schema applicable. *Explicit* instantiation consists of building a target-frame schema that pertains to the current target-frame position. Instantiation requires no special machinery; after a number of trials in the given target-frame position, the marginal attribution facility builds a schema describing the event in terms of the target frame—presuming, of course, the availability of target-frame representational elements (in this case, visible-object synthetic items). (Furthermore, such elements can themselves be formed by the instantiation of virtual generalizations, as discussed below.) Activation of the source-frame schema brings about the event that serves as the basis for building the target-frame representation, thus explicitly instantiating the virtual generalization for a particular target-frame position.[22]

To repeat, virtual generalizations and their implicit and explicit instantiations do not correspond to particular built-in features of the schema mechanism. Rather, they are epiphenomena, higher-level emergent tendencies of the mechanism. (They are also hypothetical—that is, not yet demonstrated by the implementation.) It may seem that so important a capability should be built in. Actually, though, the importance of this capability argues only for assuring its presence; whether it is best to do so by building it in or by building a powerful learning mechanism remains open to question. Piagetian development suggests that many cognitive abilities that are both important and universal (among adults) are learned rather than directly built in—suggesting that evolution found it easier to take the learning route to those abilities, and that efforts to reverse-engineer the fruits of evolution should do likewise. Moreover, the relative ease of learning in terms of non-parameterized units of representation may offer an engineering rationale for relegating parameterizing generalization to the category of having to be learned.

Once a generalization has been explicitly instantiated in a target-frame schema, that schema can participate in a chain of schemas leading to some goal. Thus, the target-frame schema, like any other schema, can be identified by a rapid, parallel process as being of use for a given purpose at a given moment. In the case of implicit instantiation, there is no target schema to be so identified. Thus, the mechanism must heuristically perform an action to achieve a canonical perspective *before* the mechanism can recognize the generalization's pertinence. This requirement makes generalization by implicit instantiation is an inherently serial process, since it is not possible to adopt arbitrarily many perspectives simultaneously. But, since implicit generalization promotes explicit generalization, the initial slow serial process gives rise with repetition to the fast parallel process.

The computational space requirements of stamping out explicit instantiations of virtual generalizations may prove burdensome. But the burden could be offset by encouraging the garbage collection of unimportant target-frame schemas. The

---

1.   The idea of virtual generalization via canonical perspectives appears in Drescher [20], and in Agre and Chapman's notion of *deictic* representations [3]; see section 9.7. (More specifically, deictic representations correspond to implicit, but not explicit, instantiation of virtual generalizations.)

mechanism might identify unimportant target-frame schemas by a conjunction of two criteria:

- *Rederivability.* The marginal attribution facility records each spinoff schema in the extended context or result of the spinoff's parent schema. This record suppresses subsequent, redundant attempts to spin off the same schema. The process could be modified to keep track of the frequency with which such redundant attempts are thwarted. A schema that is a target-frame instantiation of a virtual generalization would tend to be the subject of frequent such attempts, promoted by implicit instantiation of the generalization. There could be a presumption in favor of garbage collecting readily rederivable schemas, on the grounds that they will tend to reappear as needed.

- *Importance.* A schema that serves as an explicit target-frame instantiation is important in proportion to its frequency of activation, and the value of the result in aid of which it is activated. If such a schema is used more frequently than rederivation attempts arise, then its garbage collection based on rederivability should be suppressed.

7.1.2 Generalizing to other positions in the same reference frame

Virtual generalizations depend on a mapping between source and target frames of reference. This mapping may be bidirectional; that is, the reference frame that sometimes serves as the source frame used to express a virtual generalization may at other times serve as the target frame, used to express an instantiation of a generalization from the other frame. For example, in figure 7.2, a body-relative schema now expresses a generalization with respect to the visual field; the body-relative source frame here maps to the visual-field-relative target frame, rather than vice versa.

A bidirectional mapping between two frames of reference also makes it possible to have a virtual generalization that is instantiated at other positions in the same frame of reference that serves to express the generalization. The instantiation occurs in two steps: first, an explicit instantiation is made at some position in the other frame; then, that instantiation serves as a generalization, which is instantiated at various positions in the first reference frame, thus applying the original generalization to other positions in the same reference frame.

Of course, the extrapolation of a schema from one position to another in the same frame of reference does not follow deductively; the reference frame might

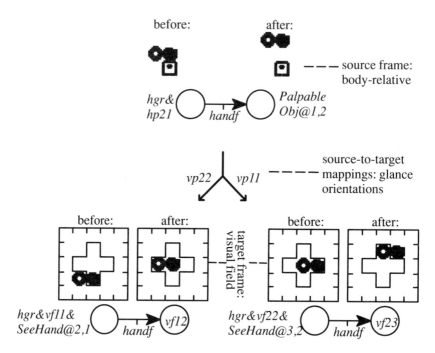

Figure 7.2 Another virtual generalization. Here, the body-relative perspective is the source frame; the visual field is the target frame.

be inhomogeneous, so that objects behaved differently at different positions. (Indeed, even the extrapolation to multiple positions in a distinct target frame of reference does not follow deductively.) Consequently, the processes described here may be regarded as inductive. But it is equally reasonable to say that a given schema represents a virtual generalization over all positions; and although that generalization was itself arrived at inductively, its instantiation at various positions is then a matter of deduction.

7.1.3 Subactivation

Empirical evidence from real-world events is not the only source of knowledge; much can be learned from detached reflection and deliberation as well. A plausible cognitive mechanism must be able to imagine events, as well as participate in actual events. This section sketches a proposed extension to the schema mechanism that would enable it to do this.

To activate an applicable schema is to initiate its action. To *subactivate* an applicable schema is essentially to *simulate* taking its action, by forcing its result items into a simulated-On state (or, if negated, a simulated-Off state). In addition, any other applicable schemas which share the subactivated schema's action are considered to be implicitly subactivated; their results of their activation are also simulated by giving the appropriate items a simulated-On or simulated-Off state. If a subactivated schema's action is composite, the mechanism may elect either to subactivate the action's components, or simply to treat the action as atomic.

An item's simulated state is distinct from its actual state. If a schema's context conditions are all satisfied with respect to those items' simulated state, then that schema is deemed applicable for the next subactivation (but not necessarily for actual activation, which requires that the actual states satisfy the context). In other words, the simulated state from a prior subactivation serves as a point of departure for the next simulated action. The mechanism thus engages in a multi-step "thought experiment."

Such an experiment would be useless if the mechanism could not learn from it. But if the marginal attribution machinery took notice of simulated states as well as of actual states, then learning could proceed from imaginary as well as actual events. This claim might seem perplexing—it might seem that there would be nothing new to learn from a subactivation, which only involves the re-enactment of results already represented by extant schemas. In fact, however, the side-effect of implicitly subactivating some schemas when others are explicitly subactivated can bring about novel sequences of (simulated) events, leading to new knowledge—or at least to newly-expressed knowledge which, like the end point of any deduction, was implicitly present all along. This re-expression is especially promising when explicit subactivation at one level of abstraction has side-effects on another level; the following section outlines some examples of this form.

7.1.4 Subactivation and virtual generalization

As noted above, implicit generalization is a serial process; an action must first bring about a canonical perspective in order for the generalization's applicability to the present situation to become apparent. In addition to being serial, this instantiation process also relies on a physical action (to bring about the perspective), rather than just involving some internal calculation. Although being serial is inherent in implicit generalization, relying on physical action is not. This section discusses the hypothetical use of subactivation in lieu of physical action to achieve the implicit or explicit instantiation of virtual generalizations.

Not surprisingly, the idea is for the schema mechanism to *imagine* achieving a canonical perspective—that is, to subactivate rather than activate a schema which achieves the perspective. Given an adequate substrate of schemas that describe the source and target frames of reference, subactivation can accurately simulate what it would be like to bring about the canonical perspective. Figure 7.3 illustrates the subactivation of the schema /*vf22*/ to shift an image from *vf11* to a canonical perspective at *vf22*. The chain of schemas in figure 7.3a carries out the action /*vf22*/ in this situation. The schemas in figure 7.3b are (implicitly) subactivated in succession as side effects of the schemas which implement the composite action. In this illustration, the initial visual orientation is *vp22*. The orientation after foveation would be *vp11*; the subactivation simulation shows this new orientation, due to the schemas in figure 7.3b, which are implicitly subactivated as a side-effect of the explicit subactivation of the schemas in figure 7.3a. (Other implicitly subactivated schemas, not shown, turn Off the original visual-field item *vf11* and proprioceptive item *vp22* in the subactivation simulation.)

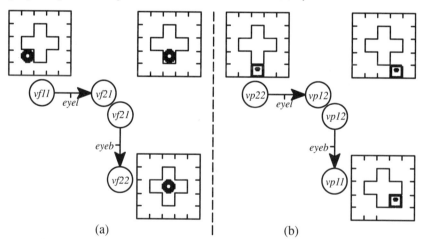

(a)   (b)

Figure 7.3 Subactivation side-effects. Explicitly subactivating the sequence in (a) implicitly subactivates the sequence in (b), changing the subactivation-simulated glance orientation.

Correctly simulating the new visual orientation is crucial, since maintaining the subactivation-state of the relevant visible-object synthetic items depends on that orientation. In this example, suppose the subactivation next simulates moving the hand beside the object and grasping it; suppose the schema in figure 7.1 a is then subactivated, showing the visual effects of moving the grasped object forward. In consequence, and because the subactivation now shows *vp11* On, *VisibleObj@1,1* and *PalpableObj@1,1* turn Off and *VisibleObj@1,2* and *PalpableObj@1,2* turn On in the subactivation simulation; on the basis of such subactivated trials, the mechanism can spin off a target-frame schema similar to those in figure 7.1b. Thus, a virtual generalization is explicitly instantiated, just as though the entire experiment had been carried out in reality, rather than by subactivation.

Thus, when schemas exist that supply enough information about the source and target frames of reference, implicit instantiation (leading to explicit instantiation) can take place by subactivation; it suffices for the mechanism to imagine assuming the canonical perspective, rather than having to do so physically. The implicit instantiation is still a serial process, however, since the mechanism cannot simultaneously carry out arbitrarily many distinct subactivation simulations at once. But, as usual, when a target-frame schema is built, making the instantiation explicit, that schema can subsequently participate in fast, parallel chaining searches—effectively caching the knowledge obtained from the slow, serial search.

7.1.5 Conservation by instantiation of inverse-action generalizations

Section 6.4.2 described the role of inverse actions in promoting conservation discoveries by synthetic item formation. For example, the mechanism might move the hand backward and forward again to withdraw from and move back in contact with an object; this sequence promotes the formation of a synthetic item designating a palpable object at that location.

The successive activation of inverse actions promotes the formation of synthetic items by demonstrating the local consistency of their host schemas. Consider, for example, the inverse hand actions of figure 7.4a. Their successive activation when the hand is at, say, *hp22* implicitly activates the schema /*hp22*/*tactl*. The implicit activation is successful—the schema's result does obtain; several repetitions of the pair of successive activations thus amount to successive successful activations of /*hp22*/*tactl*, exhibiting that schema's local consistency, and spurring the construction of a synthetic item for that schema (if none exists already). Similarly, of course, for other hand positions (and for visible-object items; for those, inverse eye actions, rather than hand actions, give aid).

We may regard this synthetic item formation as the explicit, position-specific instantiation of a position-independent generalization expressed in terms of the successive inverse actions. Furthermore, this explicit instantiation can even be accomplished by subactivation of the relevant schema and its inverse action—assuming one further extension to the schema mechanism. Currently, the mechanism does not recognize that moving the hand forward again, immediately after moving it backward, is likely to recreate the tactile sensation; but let us suppose that the mechanism is extended to be able to make discoveries of that sort, and that it makes this discovery regarding the successive activation of the schemas in figure 7.4a. Then, subactivating those schemas will simulate the recovery of the tactile sensation. But subactivating those schemas will also have the side-effect of subactivating the schemas in figure 7.4b, keeping track of the hand's position as it moves back and forth, and thus simulating the repeated achievement of *hp22* simultaneously with the repetition of *tactl*. The simulation thus demonstrates the local consistency of */hp22/tactl*, and thereby promotes the reification of that schema's validity by the synthetic item *PalpableObj@1,2*.

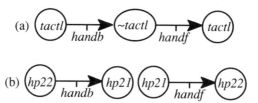

Figure 7.4 inverse subactivation. Subactivating the inverse actions in (a) implicitly subactivates the schemas in (b), showing the actions' side-effects on hand position.

Thus, the need to replicate the discovery of persistent objects at different positions may be mitigated by systematically promoting that replication, as the instantiation of a virtual generalization.

7.1.6 Deductive overriding of default generalizations

Commonsense reasoning is *nonmonotonic*; we may believe the generalization that *For all X, P(X) implies Q(X)*, and then learn that for some *A*, *P(A)* is true but *Q(A)* is false, contradicting the generalization. Typically, we retain the generalization as a default assertion, which we can override in special situations in which the default is known not to hold. (Such reasoning is called nonmonotonic, in reference to the fact that the set of statements believed to be true does not just increase with additional knowledge; sometimes, additional knowledge forces the retraction of a prior view held by default.) Use of extended-context information

to override an (imperfectly) reliable schema (section 4.1.5) implements a rudimentary kind of nonmonotonic reasoning: the reliable schema makes a default assertion, which is trusted except when some specific overriding condition obtains.

Overriding conditions pose a special problem for virtual generalizations. If an
ordinarily reliable schema that expresses a virtual generalization is overridden by
some particular condition, then all instantiations of the generalization ought to be
overridden by that condition too. In figure 7.5a, for example, the schema *SeeDisplace* expresses the visual effect of moving the hand while grasping an object.
The schema exhibits an overriding condition for a particular object that (by stipu-
lation) is too heavy to move; thus, the object remains in place when the hand
moves. Another schema, *SeeHeavy* (figure 7.5b), asserts that the heavy grasped
object stays in place when the hand moves.

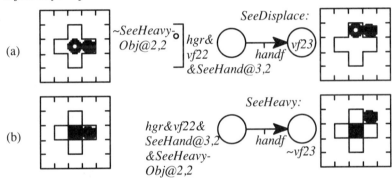

Figure 7.5 An exception to a generalization. Displacing an object
fails if it is too heavy.

Suppose a heavy object is present, and the schema mechanism uses subactivation to simulate achieving the canonical perspective that makes *SeeDisplace*
applicable. That schema's override condition then also turns On , suppressing the
schema; and furthermore, *SeeHeavy* becomes applicable. Thus, this implicit instantiation appropriately gives *SeeHeavy* precedence over *See-Displace*.

However, suppose *SeeDisplace* has been explicitly instantiated at some
body-relative position—say (2,3); call the schema that expresses this instantiation *ObjDisplace2,3* (figure 7.6). Suppose further that the overriding heavy-object schema has not been explicitly instantiated at that position. Now, when the
canonical perspective has been achieved, there is a conflict between the prediction made by the now-applicable *SeeHeavy* schema—which asserts that the
grasped object will remain in place if the hand moves—and the target-frame schema *ObjDisplace2,3*, which predicts that the grasped object will move when the

hand does, contradicting *SeeHeavy*. The contradiction arises at the item *VisibleObj@2,3*; *ObjDisplace2,3* predicts that that item should turn On, while *SeeHeavy* predicts a visual scene that doesn't show the object there.

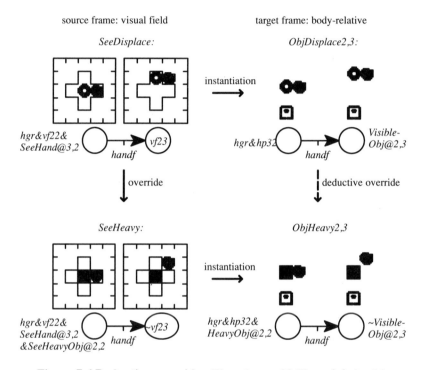

Figure 7.6 Deductive override. The schema *ObjHeavy2,3* should override *ObjDisplace2,3*.

Of course, if the hand action actually occurs in this situation on several occasions, the overriding generalization expressed by *SeeHeavy* will be explicitly instantiated for that position; that is, the schema *ObjHeavy2,3* will be created (figure 7.6), and the schema *ObjDisplace2,3* will come to recognize an override condition (the condition of there being specifically a heavy object at that position). But until then, there are conflicting predictions; worse still, if the canonical perspective has *not* been achieved, then the schema *SeeDisplace* will assert, wrongly but without opposition, that the object will move—even though the mechanism should know better than that, because the visual virtual generalization already properly takes note of the exceptional condition.

It is desirable that the mechanism be able to apply an overriding condition to each target-frame position, rather than having to physically try the relevant action several times at each such position in order to learn the exception there. In the absence of this ability, the utility of virtual generalizations would be severely curtailed, given the prevalence of imperfect generalizations that admit specific exceptions.

The ability to project a general schema's overriding conditions onto target-frame instantiations can be achieved if it is possible to appropriately resolve the conflict just noted between an overriding source-frame prediction (here, *SeeHeavy*), and a non-overridden target-frame prediction (*SeeDisplace*). Given a proper resolution of that conflict in the course of a subactivation, the exceptional event would be correctly simulated—the heavy object would be shown to remain stationary. On that basis, the *ObjHeavy2,3* schema would be built, explicitly instantiating the overriding condition at that position.

I speculate that the required conflict resolution might be achieved by augmenting the schema mechanism to be able to tell that the general target-frame schema (here, *ObjDisplace2,3*) was derivable by subactivation from another schema or schemas (*SeeDisplace*), and to suppress the prediction made by a derivable schema when the schemas from which it is derivable are applicable (even if overridden, as *SeeDisplace* is here). Intuitively, SeeDisplace *accounts for* ObjDisplace2,3 (and for other instantiations, in other positions); so something that supersedes *SeeDisplace* (e.g., *SeeHeavy*) should also supersede what is accounted for by *SeeDisplace*, e.g., *ObjDisplace2,3*. The target-frame override is thus *deduced* from the source-frame override, even though the overriding condition may never have been encountered at the target-frame position in question.

The crux of this approach to deduced overrides is the detection of the derivability of one schema from others by subactivation. The schema mechanism could recognize derivability by detecting what is in fact derived (or rederived) from what during subactivation.

Here is a sketch of how this detection might be accomplished. Suppose that the mechanism kept track of the schemas used to maintain each item's state in the course of a subactivation, and that it also kept track of which items' states were relied on for the creation of a new schema in the course of that subactivation. Then, for each schema derived (or rederived, as defined above in section 7.1.1) by subactivation, the mechanism could note which schemas' result items caused the simulation of state-transitions of the items that appear in the result of the derived schema. Those are schemas from which that schema is derivable. (Counting rederivation, as well as derivation, ensures the recognizability of a schema's derivability even if it arose independently, empirically, before being derived from other schemas.)

As mentioned above, there are two ways to view the instantiation of virtual generalizations. From one standpoint, a virtual generalization quantifies over positions in some space (either physical positions, as in the above examples, or positions in some abstract space); the generalization itself is arrived at inductively, and its instantiation by subactivation may be regarded as a deduction. Alternatively, each application of the original schema to a new position may be regarded as an inductive generalization. From this standpoint, the projection of overriding conditions onto new instantiations may be seen as resolving a conflict between two inductive generalizations at different levels of description. (In the above example, one level of description is in terms of visual images, the other in terms of objects that persist at body-relative positions.)

7.2 Virtual mechanisms

An individual's intelligence develops; an adult's thought is more advanced than an infant's. Piagetian development involves not only more elaborate representations of the world—the focus of this thesis—but also more advanced forms of reasoning, understanding, and problem solving.

7.2.1 Virtual mechanisms and Piagetian development

Some of the stages of sensorimotor development chronicled by Piaget follow directly from representational advances. For example, Piaget's fourth stage brings the ability to coordinate schemas so as to use one object to act upon another (section 2.5). This has the prerequisites of representing the behavior of the acting-on and the acted-upon objects individually (as the results of schemas; first, there must be items capable of expressing those results), and being able attribute the latter to the former (by having composite actions whose goal states correspond to the behavior of the acting-on object—for example, in the hypothetical schema of figure 6.37[23]).

Other advances in intelligence, however, require more than representational advances. For example, fifth-stage tertiary circular reactions (section 2.6) involve the on-the-fly development of new techniques for acting upon an object. Or, to take an example from much later development, the stage of formal operations

---

23.   If the acting-on object is the hand, then less representational sophistication is required, since hand motions are primitively represented as actions.

brings, among myriad new intellectual powers, the ability to systematically consider hypothetical explanations for an event by exhaustively generating all possible permutations of candidate factors. (For example, an individual may be asked to devise a series of experiments to discover which subset of a group of combined chemicals was responsible for a particular reaction.) Such a capability undoubtedly depends in part on new representations—of an abstract space that organizes permutations, for example—but it requires more than that too. It requires the ability to deploy the representation as needed to generate explanations that depend on such permutations.

The schema mechanism's built-in problem-solving behavior is crude, consisting of finding an explicit chain of extant schemas leading from a current state to a goal state. Moreover, the schema mechanism itself does not develop; the mechanism remains constant as its constructs—schemas, actions, and items—evolve. Superficially, this constancy is at odds with the need for intelligence to grow. But just as virtual structures (e.g., the virtual generalizations of the previous section) can overcome some of the limitations of the actual data format, so *virtual mechanisms* can develop and improve despite the schema mechanism's own invariance.

At a given moment, what action the schema mechanism initiates, and what internal structures it creates or alters, are a function of the extant data structures (and, of course, of the mechanism's inputs). This function is invariant; it is in that sense that the mechanism itself does not change. But the schema mechanism, taken together with its acquired structures, operates according to some function of its inputs—and that function can change, as the structures themselves change. What I call a virtual mechanism is simply the operation of the invariant schema mechanism in concert with some or all of its evolving structures. Thus, the invariant schema mechanism can support virtual mechanisms that change, as figure 7.7 illustrates schematically. Depending on the structure that implement them, virtual mechanisms might be domain-independent (e.g., a mechanism for formal reasoning), domain-specific (e.g., a chess-playing mechanism), or some mixture of the two.

In fact, the schema mechanism's hypothetical manipulation of virtual generalizations, discussed in the previous section, is an example of a virtual mechanism as well as of virtual structures; the tendency to activate a source-to-target mapping schema implements a virtual mechanism for instantiating virtual generalizations. But even this rudimentary example, although sketched here in some detail, remains undemonstrated by the implementation; the further-reaching virtual mech-

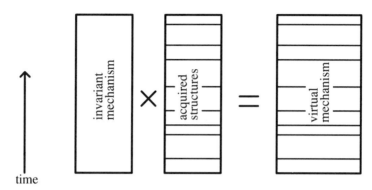

Figure 7.7 Virtual mechanisms. An invariant mechanism, operating with acquired structures, forms a virtual mechanism. As the structures evolve, so does the virtual mechanism.

anisms required for even sensorimotor-level Piagetian development are, at this point, no more than a bare possibility for a system like the schema mechanism.

7.2.2 Virtual mechanisms and the mind's expressibility

Perhaps human cognitive development culminates in some virtual mechanism that is fixed from then on. In this case, adult intelligence can be explained at that level, without reference to its development. But there is an alternative possibility which I think more likely. It may well turn out that the work of the developmental process is never complete—that the elusive human attributes of "creativity" and "common sense" (a kind of routine, practical creativity) depend in part on continual revision and extension of the constructed virtual mechanism. Then, I see no reason to expect that the precise rules of revision are expressible on any level of abstraction higher than that which describes the developmental system.[24] If this is so, an artificial intelligence designed on a higher level of abstraction is sure to exhibit some degree of stereotypical mechanical rigidity in the face of certain unanticipated contingencies; if this is so, humanlike flexibility must be explained in terms of a long-term developmental system, rather than as a later, static, higher-level virtual system.

The prospect of there being no precise, static, higher-level mechanism of intelligence is related to arguments by some authors (e.g., Dreyfus [23], Winograd and Flores [76]) that intelligence is inexpressible as a rule-like system. But if the hu-

---

24.   This is related to Hofstadter's argument [34] for describing the mind at what he calls the *subcognitive* level, the details of which are inaccessible to conscious cognition. However descriptions of the mind at the developmental-mechanism level need not be subcognitive.

man mind is a mechanism, and if the Church-Turing thesis [45] is correct, then a formal (hence rule-like) description of the mind is surely possible. Nonetheless, if we think of rules in the sense of *consciously followed* prescriptive steps—such as those of a recipe or other explicit plan of action—then indeed there may be no precise description of intelligence at that level.[25]

25. Of course, one might imagine a person explicitly following rules that prescribe a hand-simulation of a mechanism of intelligence; the person would thereby be acting intelligently by consciously following explicit rules, as in (one version of) Searle's Chinese room [61]. But this approach is worse than impossibly cumbersome (although it is that, too); it is useless, even in principle, at least as a prescription for rational thought. For whatever the simulation thinks or does might just as well have been thought or done by the person in the first place, in lieu of carrying out the simulation.

8 Nonnaive Induction

As the field of artificial intelligence matures, it begins to address the philosophical conundrums that have confronted older disciplines' contemplation of the mind. The symbol grounding problem, discussed in section 4.2.5, is one such problem. Another is a foundational riddle about induction; any learning system, such as the schema mechanism, which is charged with performing inductive reasoning must eventually face the problem of this riddle.

8.1 The problem with naive induction

Inductive reasoning draws general conclusions from particular examples. For instance, one might conclude that objects falling on this planet accelerate at 32 ft./sec.^{2}, or that the sun will rise again tomorrow, because things have been observed to always work that way before. Inductive reasoning is nondemonstrative, meaning that the conclusions are not guaranteed to follow (in the sense that, for example, 1+1=2 is guaranteed)—yet-unobserved events *could* proceed entirely differently than ones encountered so far. Still, in a universe in which all events conform to a compact set of uniform, exceptionless physical principles—principles which in turn implement higher-level, approximately uniform principles, such as those of cosmology, chemistry, biology, psychology, or economics—inductive reasoning will yield true conclusions to the extent that it discerns such underlying principles from some set of examples.

There is a version of inductive reasoning, called *naive induction*, which, although plausible on the face of it, turns out to be seriously awry. Naive induction proposes that if there is a generalization of the form *All X's are Y*—for example, *All emeralds are green*—that has been tested many times (that is, many X's have been examined for their Y-ness), and found true each time, then there is reason to believe that the generalization applies to examples not yet tested (e.g., to believe that other emeralds are probably green, too); further, the more true examples have been encountered (still in the absence of any false ones), the greater the evidence that the generalization applies as well to untested examples.

Goodman's famous *grue* paradox [29] demonstrates the problem with naive induction. Define *grue* to mean *green if before the year 2000, blue if after 2000*. All observations of emeralds so far are consistent with the generalization *All emeralds are grue* (all have been seen to be green, and it has always been before the year 2000). But it would be absurd to expect the generalization to continue to hold true after the year 2000—in order for emeralds to remain grue then, they would have to suddenly turn blue.

More generally, any set of observed examples is consistent with an infinite number of mutually inconsistent generalizations. If *All X's are Y* is an (intuitively) reasonable generalization, arbitrarily absurd alternatives, also consistent with the data, may be constructed by:

- Conjoining the predicate *Y* with any condition *P* not tested in the examples, to form *All X's are Y and P*, a gratuitous extension to the reasonable generalization; or

- Conjoining the predicate *X* with any condition *Q* common to all the examples tested so far, to form *All X's that are Q are Y*, a gratuitous restriction of the reasonable generalization.

The hidden crux of inductive reasoning is to decide which generalizations consistent with all the encountered data are reasonable, and which—despite their full accord with the data—are absurd. This is the problem that naive induction ignores. In examples such as *grue* vs. *green* generalizations, the distinction is intuitively clear, but the principles on which that intuition operates have proven difficult to formulate. But for purposes of building a humanlike artificial learning system—or for purposes of explaining how the mechanism of human learning works—the underlying principles must be understood.

8.2 The problem with proposing only nonabsurd generalizations

Almost all machine learning research ignores the naive induction problem; extant systems verify proposed generalizations simply by seeing if in fact they accord with the available examples. Such systems succeed only to the extend that absurd generalizations are not entertained in the first place. Holland—an exception to the tendency to ignore the problem—explicitly proposes [35], as a theory of the inductive reasoning performed by his system, that its method for proposing generalizations simply does not entertain absurd ones [26] (though, of course, it may entertain false ones); we may regard this stance as taken implicitly by the authors of learning systems who are silent on the question.

The basis for Holland's claim is that his system—like the schema mechanism's marginal attribution facility—tends to add new conditions only as needed to con-

---

26. Developmental theories in cognitive science also tend to be oblivious to the naive induction problem, although Carey [12] is an exception. Carey proposes a solution along the lines of Goodman's *entrenchment*, described below.

form to the data, and thus avoids incorporating gratuitous extensions or restrictions into the proposed generalizations. However, in the schema mechanism and Holland's system alike, the success of this approach depends on the vocabulary in which the conditions are expressed in the first place. If a bizarre condition, such as grueness, is already expressed as a state element, then nothing blocks the proposal of generalizations in terms of that condition. Goodman uses the term *projectable* to describe predicates which lend themselves to reasonable generalizations; grue is unprojectable (except in certain bizarre generalizations that Goodman discusses). Holland's solution therefore passes the buck from the generalization-proposal machinery to the vocabulary in which the proposals are couched— and hence, in a constructivist system, to the machinery for synthesizing that vocabulary.

For that reason, I believe that relying on the proposal machinery not to generate absurd generalizations in the first place is inadequate to solve the naive induction problem for constructivist systems that are powerful enough to invent arbitrarily complicated and obscure concepts, and to formulate generalizations in terms of their invented concepts. The reasonable-proposal solution works well enough initially, when primitive concepts, and others closely tied to the primitives, predominate; hence the schema mechanism's avoidance, so far, of proposing absurd generalizations. But, as I now argue, that solution eventually must fail.

8.3 The problem with using only projectable concepts

One might propose that even as powerful a concept-inventing facility as human beings' might never have occasion to propose generalizations in terms of bizarre predicates such as *grue*. The mere fact that we can entertain that concept (by reading and writing about it, for example), does not necessarily mean that the concept is available as a vocabulary item to our induction machinery (e.g., does not mean there must be a corresponding synthetic item in the schema mechanism). If our induction machinery does avoid *grue*-like concepts—even when we discuss the grue paradox—then not proposing absurd generalizations might be a viable solution after all.

Unfortunately for that proposal, there is good reason to conclude that the concept *grue*—or, at least, a concept coextensive with it, which presents the same problems—is indeed available to the induction machinery. Suppose I build a grue-detector box; such a device can be built by wiring together a color-detector and a calendar-clock. Whenever I point it at some object, a light turns on if and only if that object is grue. Surely a mechanism of humanlike cognitive power would be able to formulate, and confirm, the generalization that *When this box points at an emerald, the light turns on*; this is just a matter of representing some objects in the environment, and making a straightforward empirical discovery about their behavior. But this generalization is coextensive with (i.e., true under the same circumstances as) *Emeralds are grue.*

Suppose one experimented with the grue-detector box and with various objects, including emeralds. Suppose further that one had no awareness of what was in the box, how it was wired, or what it was computing. One would then come quite reasonably to believe that *When this box points at an emerald, the light turns on*, and one would certainly have no grounds to suspect that this would stop being true at the year 2000; on the contrary, one would quite reasonably (albeit mistakenly) believe that the generalization would continue to be true then.

However—and here is the point of this example—if one were now informed of the circuitry of the box, and understood how it worked, one would then realize that the box's light will start to react differently after the year 2000, and that the above generalization will cease to be true then; this realization is isomorphic to believing that emeralds will continue to be green, and hence not continue to be grue, at the year 2000. Yet the false generalization—*When this box points at an emerald, the light turns on*—has, in fact, been proposed, and extensively and exceptionlessly confirmed, by the induction apparatus. So we cannot rely on a constraint on the vocabulary available to the proposal-generator to explain how the incorrect generalization is rejected.

Rather than not proposing the false generalization in the first place, the induction apparatus must somehow let this well-confirmed generalization be overridden by other generalizations (e.g., those about the behavior of color-detectors, clocks, etc.); after all, one could imagine concluding that the box will continue to give the same answer after 2000, and that it is instead the physics of colors that will change at that time. The question, then, is what criteria the induction apparatus can use to reasonably decide which generalization prevails. (And if the apparatus can decide correctly in this example, it can presumably, by the same principles, override the original *emeralds are grue* generalization. There, knowing the definition of *grue* in terms of green and time is analogous to knowing the circuitry of the box. And there is the analogous problem of figuring out which generalizations override which.)

8.4 The problem with preferring entrenched concepts

The problem has now been recast. It is no longer a matter of not proposing absurd generalizations in the first place, whether by avoiding bizarre (i.e., non-projectable) vocabulary, or by any other means. Rather, the above argument establishes that a humanlike learning system must be powerful enough to entertain such generalizations, and even to believe them, until confronted with conflicting generalizations. The recast problem then is how to resolve that conflict properly.

One approach would be to give priority, when generalizations conflict, to those expressed in terms of more familiar predicates (i.e., older ones, or ones more often encountered or used, or some such basis); Goodman's proposed *entrenchment* criterion is along these lines. In this approach, it is still a matter of assessing the reasonableness of the conceptual vocabulary for expressing generalizations; but now, instead of making a binary distinction between acceptable and unacceptable concepts, it is a matter of the *relative* reasonableness of the competing concepts.

There is some justification for resolving conflicts in favor of more entrenched concepts. Earlier-formed concepts are likely to be both more entrenched than recent ones, and also closer to the primitives, in the sense of being more directly expressed in terms of the primitives; they may thus be closer to sharing the primitives' projectability. The primitive concepts are designed to be plausible terms for expressing generalizations, i.e., to be projectable; indeed, any physical detector that behaves uniformly from place to place and time to time is a promising basis for generalization, given the spatiotemporal uniformity of the physics of our universe (and given the consequence that even higher-level laws tend to be approximately uniform over a wide range of places and times). But even if there is thus some correlation between entrenchment and projectability, it is often the case (for example, in the history of science) that newer concepts better support generalizations than older concepts; indeed, they often supplant the older concepts, overriding the older generalizations, even before any data mitigate in favor of the new concepts and generalizations. Thus, to always resolve conflicts in favor of more entrenched concepts seems arbitrary, unlikely to be correct, and contrary to how people actually work.

In particular, no matter how many times one had used one's grue-detector box—no matter how deeply entrenched the concepts designating that box had become—the discovery of the box's circuitry should be no less decisive in predicting that emeralds will cease to turn on the light after the year 2000. Intuitively, this is because the circuitry already accounts for the box's oft-observed behavior, as well as predicting a different behavior after 2000; both behaviors are derivable from the circuitry. Trusting the circuitry-based prediction is parsimonious, because it requires no separate, additional principle to say how the box works.

8.5 Induction conflicts and deductive overrides

The observation that the grue box's post-millenial behavior is deducible from the box's circuitry is reminiscent of the schema mechanism's facility for deductive overrides (section 7.1.6). There, the schema *SeeDisplace*, and the overriding condition it admits for a heavy object, already accounts both for why *ObjDisplace2,3* moves the object, and for why *ObjHeavy2,3* (which hasn't been tried yet) would not; that is, *ObjDisplace2,3* and *ObjHeavy2,3* are both deducible from *SeeDisplace*, together with its overriding schema *SeeHeavy*. The schema *SeeHeavy* thus deductively-overrides *ObjDisplace2,3*—regardless of which of the schemas or items involved has been used more (is more entrenched).

The suggestion, then, is that deductive-override machinery may permit the schema mechanism to escape the fallacy of naive induction. The key is to regard the conflict between a reasonable generalization and an absurd but always-confirmed generalization as just another conflict between generalizations expressed at different levels of description—and to use the same technique, deductive override, to resolve the conflict. Seen in this light, the grue problem is just like the heavy-object problem.

Deductive override cannot be the whole answer to the naive induction problem. One could always override the override by inventing another absurd, grue-like confirmed generalization from which the previous overriding schema can in turn be deduced. This new generalization will in turn be overridable by some reasonable generalization, but that will in turn be overridable by another absurd one, and so on. Some entrenchment criterion is necessary after all—not to be used by always favoring the more-entrenched schemas and items, but rather by requiring that some threshold of entrenchment be surpassed for an schema or item to be able to participate in a deductive override. That requirement would block an unending cascade of absurd overrides (since only a finite number of bizarre schemas and items can have become entrenched already), while still allowing less entrenched structures to prevail over more entrenched ones when appropriate. (That requirement would also provide a safeguard, in more ordinary situations, against rashly abandoning a robust, proven structure the moment some novel, overriding one comes along.)

8.6 Why nonnaive induction must be built in

There is an alternative to looking to the basic operation of the schema mechanism to keep the mechanism from performing naive induction. Instead, one might propose that the mechanism could form and debug explicit beliefs about reasonable generalizations, much as it might be hoped to form beliefs about, say, chess, or astronomy, or aesthetics. Those beliefs, instead of some built-in facility, could be the mechanism's way of deciding that emeralds are grue rather than green; the problem would thus be solved epiphenomenally, rather than directly by a feature of the mechanism.

But there are two problems with that proposal (not counting its complete lack of detail, since any proposed advanced extrapolation of the schema mechanism's performance is similarly lacking). One problem is that the mechanism's process of forming explicit beliefs about generalizations is itself subject to the naive-induction problem, to the extent that that process has an inductive component. The second problem is that, even if the mechanism succeeded in building a correct explicit theory of induction, and explicitly represented in that theory that the conflict between the green generalization and the grue generalization should be resolved in favor of the former, doing so would still not override a schema that asserts that the grue-box's light will turn on after 2000. The explicit theory may explicitly contradict that schema, but that contradiction just provides yet another conflicting schema, and the mechanism still needs some built-in way to resolve *that* conflict. (Given such built-in machinery, though, an explicit theory of induction built by the mechanism may well assist in resolving induction dilemmas.)

Finally, if there is indeed built-in machinery for resolving induction dilemmas in human cognitive systems, and if that machinery is involved in rejecting grue generalizations and the like, then that machinery must have a plausible use in mundane situations as well; evolution could not have designed a complex apparatus whose only benefit was to help us resolve abstruse modern academic paradoxes. The deductive-override proposal suggests that the relevant machinery is in fact needed to resolve conflicting predictions at differing levels of abstraction, in mundane situations such as the heavy-object example.

Whether or not the particular solution proposed here is on the right track, I think it is clear that there is a problem to be solved—that a constructivist mechanism that performs inductive reasoning cannot be expected to reject grue-like generalizations epiphenomenally, if, at its lowest level, the mechanism is just performing naive induction. Hopefully, the deductive-override proposal is at least an instructive attempt to address the problem.

8.7 Innateness of projectability judgements

It remains true that, whatever experiences an organism or mechanism has had, there are infinitely many mutually contradictory generalizations that are consistent with those experiences. Therefore, any induction apparatus must impose a choice among those consistent generalizations.

However, that choice need not be imposed by innately listing the entire acceptable vocabulary of generalization. Such a measure is both implausibly restrictive—it contradicts the fact that we make generalizations about concepts that could not have been anticipated by evolution—and wholly ineffective, since, as the grue-box example shows, absurd generalizations can be recast in terms of mundane concepts, such as boxes and lights, effectively circumventing any restriction on conceptual vocabulary.

There must instead be a facility for resolving conflicts between reasonable and bizarre confirmed generalizations. The deductive-override machinery, which is necessary anyway for more general and less abstruse purposes, seems a promising candidate. Given such a facility, the mechanism can learn for itself when to trust a confirmed generalization, and when not to.[27]

8.8 Induction and counterfactuals

As noted in section 9.1.1, a schema makes a counterfactual assertion, an assertion about what would be the case if some (perhaps false) premise were true; and a synthetic item reifies the validity conditions of its host schema's counterfactual assertion. The counterfactual statement *Q would be true if P* differs fundamentally from the statement of logical implication *P implies Q;* the latter is equivalent to *P and ~Q are not both true,* and thus is necessarily true if *P* is false—regardless of what *Q* is. In contrast, the consequent of a counterfactual statement must be relevant to the premise, but in a sense that has proven elusive.

In fact, as Goodman points out [29], the problem of characterizing the proper relation between a counterfactual premise and consequent is similar to, and intimately related to, the problem of characterizing projectability. Naively, *Q would*

27. One might maintain, a la Chomsky, that the judgement is not learned, but rather is innately specified, merely by virtue of the fact that an innately specified mechanism mandates the judgement. But this is just a special case of Chomsky's general objection to the notion of learning; see section 1.2.1 for a reply.

be true if P may be taken to be satisfied just in case *All actual instances that have P have Q (but at least some instances with ~P don't have Q).* As with naive induction, however, it is easy to construct counterexamples to this construal—e.g., in all the universe, all instances of George Washington's blowing out the candles on a cake have been accompanied by his receiving gifts (or so we may suppose, for purposes of this example), and otherwise he usually did not receive gifts; yet it would not follow that, on some arbitrary date, he would have received gifts had he only lit and blown out some candles on a cake. Or, to take an example of more practical import to an organism's survival: the assertion *If I step into the road, it is safe to cross,* construed as a logical implication, may well be always true for an individual whose road-crossing behavior is always suitably cautious; moreover, the individual may well know it to be true, either by induction on her past experiences or by knowing about her own characteristic caution. However, the individual would commit a dangerous error to conclude that *If I were to step into the road, it would be safe to cross* is an always-true *counterfactual* assertion; yet that conclusion would follow if the naive criterion of the truth of counterfactuals were used.

To build schemas, which make counterfactual assertions, the schema mechanism must ultimately tackle the problem of nonnaively resolving such assertions (just as it must ultimately tackle the problem of naive induction in order to perform inductive reasoning); taken by itself, the marginal attribution facility's comparison of what happens with vs. without an action corresponds to the naive construal just cited. The problems of counterfactuals and induction converge in the following respect: just as the behavior of the grue-box so far is accounted for by familiar principles which also predict a contrary behavior after 2000, so the truth of *If I step into the road, it is safe to cross* is accounted for by familiar principles (about the physics of oncoming cars, and about how one decides whether to step into the road) which also predict a contrary outcome if, contrary to customary practice, one were to step into the road with many cars rushing by. Goodman's discussion concludes with the yet-unrealized hope that a solution to projectability will lead to a solution to the problem of counterfactuals; I conclude here with the same unrealized hope, in the context of the schema mechanism.

Part IV Appraisal

9 Comparisons

This chapter seeks to situate the schema mechanism in AI-space, relating the mechanism to other research efforts and paradigms. First come some broad observations of where this research fits along several dimensions that characterize AI research programs. There follows a more detailed comparison of the schema mechanism with some proximally related work.

9.1 Modularity for learning: prediction-value vs. situation-action systems

Superficially, a schema resembles a production rule (e.g., [48]). A production rule has two parts: an *antecedent* and *consequent*, also called the *left side* and *right side*, respectively. The antecedent specifies conditions for the rule's applicability; the consequent specifies what happens when the rule is invoked. Some production systems invoke every rule whose antecedent is satisfied; others arbitrate among such rules to invoke just one, or a small number of them.

9.1.1 The basic unit: three parts or two?

A schema differs most obviously from a production rule by having three main parts rather than two. One way to assess the consequence of this difference is to compare the use of schemas and productions for achieving a goal. Productions can serve as *situation-action* rules, in which the left side specifies conditions for taking the action designated by the right side; the conditions may include a specification of a current goal, so that the rule is invoked only when that goal is asserted. Alternatively, productions can represent *situation-result* rules, in which the left side includes an action and some preconditions for taking it, and the right side specifies a result. The production system must identify a sequence of rule invocations that leads to a goal; each rule's result may contribute to the conditions needed for the next one's invocation. Identifying chains of schemas is a similar process.

For purposes of chaining to goals, then, there is little difference between schemas and productions; the information in schemas could be converted to two-part production-rule syntax and used in that form. However, for purposes of learning such rules in the first place, the three-way distinction, I argue, is crucial.[28]

One way to learn how to act is to discover *what would happen* (i.e., a counterfactual assertion) if each of several actions were taken, and to use those pieces of

---

28. Situation-result rules could be annotated to make a three-way distinction by dividing the situation into action and preconditions; but that annotation would amount to having a three-part schema.

knowledge to decide which action to take, based on some designated *values* of the possible outcomes. The schema mechanism takes this approach, forming what we might call a *prediction-value* system. Another possibility is to try to learn directly what action is best in a given situation (rather than deriving that from a representation of what would happen); Holland's *bucket brigade* algorithm [35] exemplifies this approach. First, the system learns the desirability of actions that lead immediately to goals, in certain situations; it then learns the desirability of actions that lead to those precursor situations, in other situations; and so on, extending backward from the goals. The *credit-assignment* problem—attributing an eventual outcome to earlier events or actions—is addressed by passing credit incrementally backward from the goal.

The end result is much the same as with tripartite schemas. In the situation-action paradigm, results are not explicitly represented; still, the actions were learned on the basis of the usefulness of the results obtained. When the rules are invoked, the actions occur in turn, each enabling the next rule in the sequence. Thus, once formed, such rules are as useful as schemas for the purpose of reaching goals—although situation-action rules would not support subactivation, for which results must be explicitly simulated, hence explicitly predicted.

However, situation-action learning is intrinsically, infeasibly slow. One reason has to do with the fact that such learning only takes place along the fringe of the state-space that has already been connected to the goal. Encountering a situation several steps back from the goal is of no use—even if the right action happens to be taken then—if subsequent steps do not lead to the goal, or at least to the recognized fringe. In contrast, with context-action-result structures, various islands of the state-space can be learned as soon as they are encountered, with no forseen applicability to any goal, then quickly chained through to reach a goal when the necessary pieces have been assembled.

Human beings—especially infants and children at play—clearly do seek and obtain knowledge for its own sake, not just to apply to specific goals. Metaphorically speaking, bucket-brigade-style situation-action learning engages only in applied research, whereas schema learning does basic research as well. For infants and technological cultures alike, it is imperative to be able to acquire knowledge without already having on hand a use to which that knowledge can be put.

Empirical learning of situation-action rules is slow for a second reason as well. Different goals arise in different circumstances. For a particular state-space, it may sometimes be desirable to be at a given point in that space, sometimes elsewhere; for example, at different times, one might want to visit a variety of different locations in a room (going to the door, sitting at a table, etc.). In order for the bucket-brigade to deal with this variability of goals, rules' situations must include either the very fact that a certain location is now a goal, or must include a reference to some current circumstance that bears the information that that location is desirable (the doorbell is ringing, the aroma of dinner is present, etc.).

The number of situation-action rules that have to be learned is then proportionate to the product of the size of the state-space and the number of goal indications. In contrast, each piece of a schema-implemented state-space network says what the result of some action would be, and is acquired independently of the system's goals; these pieces are then are used to chain to various goals in order to determine what actions to take. Thus, a prediction-value system, by decomposing the question of what action to take into the distinct questions of where various actions *would* lead (the prediction), and where the next action *should* lead (the value associated with a given state), assumes the right modularity for learning.

If goals were relatively constant—as strategic goals are, compared to tactical goals—then the problem of multiplying positions with goals would not arise. In my view, bucket-brigade-style credit-assignment misapplies a strategic learning algorithm to tactical learning. The schema mechanism instead distinguishes between instrumental value, which facilitates tactical planning, and delegated value, which promotes strategic pursuits (section 3.4.1).

The foregoing considerations—of basic vs. applied learning, and tactical vs. strategic learning—establish the need to represent the result of an action. This, in turn, requires a designation of appropriate context conditions, since, as already discussed at length, a given action may have a variety of distinct results in different situations. Finally, for purposes of learning, the context and action cannot combine to form an undifferentiated antecedent of a two-part rule; the marginal attribution machinery, needed to solve the context-result chicken-and-egg problem, must compare what happens with vs. without the action (given satisfaction of the context conditions), and thus requires an explicit distinction between context and action. Hence, a three-part structure is warranted.

9.1.2 Biological evolution and prediction-value representations

The biological evolution of intelligence must also have faced a design choice between systems using situation-action rules and systems using result predictions and value designations. For organisms whose behavior is primarily innate, situation-action rules are the better choice, for two reasons:

- Situation-action representations are simpler than prediction-value representations; the latter have strictly more information, since the preferred action is deducible from the prediction-value representation, but predicted results are not necessarily deducible from situation-action representations. The extra information in prediction-value representations is both superfluous—the system's purpose is simply to make an organism take the appropriate action in a given situation—and difficult to correct, since evolution (in contrast with, say, marginal attribution) would receive no feedback as to the accuracy of predicted results, except very indirectly, by the viability of the consequent overall behavior.

- Because of this limited feedback, evolution is confined to cumbersome strategic learning (as discussed just above) of innate behaviors, rather than the more efficient tactical learning which can be done by manipulating prediction-value representations.[29] Since evolution therefore cannot avail itself of the advantage of prediction-value systems over the simpler situation-action systems, it has no pressure to develop the more elaborate system for supporting innate behaviors.

Simple organisms' innate behaviors indeed appear to be implemented by situation-action systems rather than prediction-value systems. A classic example is the mating ritual of the stickleback, as described by Tinbergen [69]. Tinbergen's analysis decomposes each participating stickleback's activity into a series of responses to stimuli; each response results in presenting the participant's partner a stimulus which prompts its own response. If an experimenter prevents the next stimulus from reaching the stickleback, the next response does not occur. Conversely, if a fake stimulus is provided, the corresponding response is elicited, even if completely out of sequence. Thus, the sticklebacks do not internally keep track of their progress through the encounter, but rather depend on the environment to keep providing the appropriate next stimulus.

In contrast, more intelligent species, such as our own, engage primarily in learned activity, and so, as just argued, must build prediction-value representations—though not necessarily to the exclusion of having situation-action rules as well. As discussed in section 2.9.3, human beings do embody substantial innate competence, though arguably only in peripheral modules. This innate competence, presumably largely inherited from less intelligent ancestor species, may

---

29.   Here I refer to evolution itself as a learning system (for learning innate-behavior specifications), as opposed to whatever learning system may evolve in the brains of organisms.

well involve situation-action implementations (for example, for visual tracking). Such implementations would not be amenable to augmentation by the central learning system, which, for reasons argued above, needs instead to use a prediction-value representation scheme. Thus, as argued in section 2.9.3, the central system would need to recapitulate in its own terms some of the innate knowledge already embodied in peripheral modules.

For organisms with prediction-value learning systems, evolution can implement innate predispositions by rigging the values associated with innately supplied state elements, turning those states into explicit goals, to be pursued by whatever means each organism can learn. In contrast, systems with only situation-action rules create goals that are only implicit, in that the rules are rigged so that their execution achieves the goals. Without explicit representation of predictions, such systems will not easily learn novel paths to their goals.

9.1.3 Constants and variables

Many production systems allow variables to appear in production rules. A rule's antecedent is checked for satisfaction with respect to any instantiation of those variables; if some instantiation matches, the consequent is asserted using the same variable values that resulted in an antecedent match.

The schema mechanism does not support variables or matching for the elements of schemas. But a sufficiently intelligent system must be able to express and instantiate generalizations; therefore, some other method is needed to support generalizations. Chapter 7 raises the possibility that the mechanism might maintain virtual generalizations, together with virtual machinery for their instantiation. The reason to rely on this hope, rather than building in a variable-matching implementation of generalizations, is just that there is no apparent way to support such an implementation without abandoning the constructivist working hypothesis by including domain-specific build-in structure. For example, if each proprioceptive item were structured as, say *(Prop Hand 3 2)*, with components that designate spatial coordinates, then the mechanism might be augmented to express generalizations of the form *(Prop Hand x y)*, where *x* and *y* can be matched to particular coordinates. Atomic elements, however, do not lend themselves to such generalization.

Perhaps the system itself could be designed to devise explicit structured representations to support variablized generalizations. If virtual generalization turns out to work, the inclusion of such machinery might be gratuitous, even if feasible.

But if virtual generalization fails, devising such machinery may be vital to the schema mechanism.

9.2 The schema mechanism and connectionism

Schemas, although different from production rules, have in common with productions that they are a kind of qualitative, symbolic construct. This contrasts with connectionist systems, which pass numeric values through networks that have adjustable weights.

Yet the schema mechanism's architecture (chapter 5) is connectionist—symbolic structures are composed by setting bits at connection points; data paths transmit only nonsymbolic information, consisting of numbers, truth values, or a small number of atomic, noncomposable tokens (i.e., tokens that do not organize syntactically into larger structures). In fact, as the next section argues, a schema's extended context is essentially a connectionist network solving a classifier problem. The schema mechanism might be viewed as a kind of hybrid system, in which symbolic structures are created and maintained with the help of a connectionist substrate.

9.2.1 Extended context as connectionist network

A connectionist network divides a global computation into numerous simple, local computations. A single-layer, single-output connectionist network has a processing unit which computes a simple function—typically a weighted sum—of the network's numeric input values. A multi-layer network includes *hidden* processing units whose inputs are other units' outputs.

If the inputs are restricted to the values 0 and 1, we can regard a connectionist network as computing a boolean function of its inputs; the function's value is taken to be 0 if the output value is below a specified threshold, else 1. Equivalently, the network classifies all possible input combinations into one of two sets, corresponding to the two boolean outputs.

A classifying network can be *trained* by starting the network with arbitrary weights, presenting a series of example input combinations, and adjusting the weights according to the correctness of the network's classification for each example. There are various algorithms for this adjustment; all share the property that, on each example, each unit's weight is adjusted according to 1) the sign of the unit's contribution to the weighted sum; and 2) whether the network's computation for that example gave the right answer. A positive contribution to a correct answer may be rewarded by increasing the weight's magnitude; a negative contribution to a correct answer may be punished by decreasing the weight's magnitude.

A single-layer network can compute a variety of boolean functions of its inputs. For example:

- If a function is a conjunction of several inputs (e.g., $a(\sim b)c$, a network can realize that function by having a positive threshold k, and dividing that threshold among the weights for the non-negated conjuncts. Negated conjuncts receive negative weights; all other weights are set to zero. Then, only if the non-negated conjuncts are all 1, and the negated ones all 0, can the threshold be reached.

- If a function is a disjunction of non-negated inputs (e.g., $a+b+c$), then each disjunct can be given a weight that exceeds the positive threshold k.

- If a function is a disjunction of possibly negated inputs (e.g., $a+(\sim b)+c$), then the threshold is set to $-k$, where k is the number of negated inputs. Each negated input receives weight $-(1+1/k)$, so that even if all non-negated inputs are 0, the threshold will still be met, unless all negated inputs are 1. Each non-negated input receives weight 1, so that even if all negated inputs are 1, any non-negated input will cause the threshold to be reached if that input is 1.

If there exists a set of weights to compute a given function, a *convergence* theorem [47] shows that a connectionist network can be trained to adjust its weights so as to compute that function. Consequently, a series of incremental adjustments to local computing elements can culminate in computing the appropriate overall computation.

But single-layer networks cannot compute arbitrary boolean formulae. This is made apparent by considering DNF (disjunctive normal form) formulae; a DNF formula is a disjunction of clauses, each a conjunction of (possibly negated) atomic terms. Consider, for example, the formula $ab+cd$. If ab and cd each exceed the threshold, then a's weight or b's must be at least half the threshold, as must either c's or d's. But then the larger weight from one conjunction, plus the larger from the other, also exceeds the threshold; no assignment of weights to a,b,c and d can allow ab and cd to exceed the threshold, while preventing both $ac\sim b\sim d$ and $ad\sim b\sim c$ (or both $bc\sim a\sim d$ and $bd\sim a\sim c$) from doing so.

The problem is that inputs that satisfy the formula are not linearly separable from those that do not. Multi-layer connectionist networks solve this problem by having hidden units that compute functions in terms of which the formula is linear. For example, two internal units might compute the conjunctions *ab* and *cd*; an output unit then computes the disjunction of those internal units' outputs. However, there is no demonstration that such networks converge to the appropriate weights within a practical number of training examples, if the inputs number hundreds or more, and if there may be many (say, dozens) of conjunctive clauses of several terms each.

Marginal attribution in the schema mechanism takes a different approach. A schema's extended context resembles a first-order connectionist network; it faces the classification problem of distinguishing input combinations (i.e., items' states) that correspond to successful activations from those that correspond to failures. (Of course, extant items aren't always adequate to make that distinction.) The classification problems to be tackled come from the mechanism itself, rather than from the supervision of an external teacher—each result spinoff poses a classification problem to be solved by the spinoff schema's extended context. Each extended-context slot's correlation measure is roughly like a connectionist weight; it adjusts after each trial to reflect the corresponding item's contribution to the overall classification. An item's relevance is identified quickly; the identification needs only a handful of successful trials to demonstrate a significant difference in the schema's success rate as a function of the item's state.

Rather than using intermediate processing units to compute conjunctions, the schema mechanism builds spinoff schemas, whose contexts compute conjunctions. Each such schema has its own extended context—in effect, its own entire connectionist network. Having an entire such network support each small, symbolic unit of representation is expensive, though arguably (section 5.1) within neurophysiologically plausible bounds.

9.2.2 Back-propagation and empirical credit assignment

Section 9.1's remarks about the modularity of learning, and about credit assignment, also apply to much connectionist work. (Holland's bucket-brigade algorithm, in fact, has dual citizenship as a production system and a connectionist system; since Holland's rules' antecedents require no variable-matching, and since all applicable rules are invoked in parallel, a network of such rules is isomorphic to a connectionist circuit.) Sutton's *temporal difference* methods [66] generalize the bucket-brigade algorithm, and introduce an important distinction between rewarding that which leads to eventual success vs. rewarding that which leads to a normally reliable precursor of eventual success. Nonetheless, temporal difference methods fall within the scope of the foregoing discussion.

9.3 The schema mechanism and search algorithms

The schema mechanism broadcasts messages in parallel through chains of schemas (section 5.1.2). Backward broadcasts from a goal state find paths to that goal; forward broadcasts from the current state find accessible states. Such broadcasts implement a breadth-first traversal of the state-space described by schemas. Such searches are prominent in conventional AI; they appear, for example, in classic game-playing programs (e.g., [59]), which do a minimax search (e.g., [77]) in a heuristically limited portion of state space; and in SOAR [37], which uses productions that chain to describe series of transformations.

Compared to these other state-space searches, schema mechanism broadcasts are faster but more limited. Both properties derive from the fact that a broadcast merely propagates messages in parallel through existing structures, whereas general state-space searching requires computing at each step a new total world state from which the next step can proceed.

Consider, for example, a goal of placing two toy blocks on a table. It is not enough for there to be a schema for placing each of the blocks (figure 9.1 a). Even though activating them in succession would indeed reach the goal state, those schemas do not chain to the goal state, because neither schema's result shows two blocks on the table; each shows only one. This matters, since, for example, any other schema whose context required two blocks on the table could not be chained to by either of these schemas. Chaining to the goal is possible only if one of the schemas has a result that designates both blocks on the table; and if a schema's action is to place a single block, then a two-block result can only follow reliably if that schema's context asserts that the other block is already there. Such a schema is chained to by a single-block-placement schema (figure 9.1 b), thus chaining to the goal.

In short, each link along the chain must explicitly designate all aspects of the world state that are still needed further down the chain. In contrast, conventional state-space searches can generate that information on the fly by applying successive transformations each of which designates only that part of the world that is locally relevant to that transformation. This difference makes the conventional transformations far more general, because the links in a schema chain must involve not only a widely applicable transformation (e.g., placing a block), but also a specific version of it that is relevant to the goal of the particular situation (e.g.,

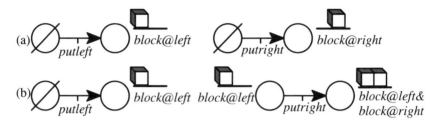

Figure 9.1 Conjunctive planning. Achieving each result separately
(a) does not chain to the conjunctive goal. The schemas in (b) do chain,
by noting the intermediate state.

placing a block when another has already been placed). But such on-the-fly generation cannot be done in parallel by propagating a fixed set of tokens through
pre-established links; hence, the greater expense of the conventional paradigm.

Subactivation, the extension to the schema mechanism proposed in section
7.1.3, offers the possibility of performing the more general and more expensive
kind of search. Subactivating, say, one of the block-placement schemas in figure
9.1a would produce a simulated world state in which the block is on the table; subactivating the other placement schema would then yield a simulated state in which
both blocks are there. From such subactivations (or from actual activations of the
same schemas), the mechanism can derive the dual-block-placement schema of
figure 9.1b (either by marginal attribution, or perhaps by a faster process suggested in section 9.4); that schema is thereafter available for rapid, parallel chaining to the goal.

As with conventional state-space search, subactivation steps are serial. Also,
as with conventional search, there needs to be some systematic or heuristic basis
for selecting the next subactivation step, since the action is not yet known to chain
to the goal; rather, the discovery of that chain will be a consequence of the subactivation. What is needed is the development by the schema mechanism of a virtual
mechanism implemented with the aid of schemas that promote the appropriate
search steps in an appropriate sequence. Such a development is, at this point, entirely speculative and undemonstrated.

9.4 The schema mechanism and explanation-based learning

As noted in section 7.1.3, having multiple levels of representation means that subactivated schemas at a given level might combine to predict results at another level, which can then be described at that level. Were there but one level of representation, subactivation would just re-enact what is already known, without deriving anything new.

One way for the schema mechanism to learn from subactivated events is by using the marginal attribution machinery just as for actual events. But this is needlessly inefficient, for it requires several trials, despite the fact that repeating a sequence of subactivations with the same structures will have the same result; the repeated subactivated trials convey no more information than a single such trial.

Conceivably (though I propose no details here) the mechanism could keep track of the aspects of the world state that the subactivated result depended on, and build a schema on the basis of a single subactivated trial, putting the depended-on state elements in the context of the new schema. Such a technique would resemble chunking in SOAR [57], which, like other explanation-based learning mechanisms, identifies and records the dependencies in a search process, and abbreviates subsequent searches by recording what follows from those dependencies, so that that search need not be recapitulated. (The recording of proximity information in a composite action's controller was also likened to SOAR broadcasting—section 4.3.1—but with respect to the more primitive search process carried out by parallel chaining.) Or, in lieu of explicit dependency tracking, the mechanism might simply grant a subactivated trial exaggerated impact on correlation statistics, having the same effect as several actual trials.

Section 3.4.2 raised the possibility that the hysteresis of schemas' activation value—a tendency to reactivate schemas recently activated—might promote imitation, by inducing the mechanism to explicitly activate a schema that had just activated implicitly. Explanation-based learning by means of subactivation might exploit a tendency toward imitation: a subactivated imitation of an event just observed might include a derivation of an explanation of the event, by deriving schemas that predict the observed outcome.

9.5 The schema mechanism and rational learning

Biological entities are self-constructing and self-maintaining. To be sure, suitably nurturing environments are essential. But the eventual structure of a newly conceived organism is determined primarily from within, by its genetic endowment; likewise, repair of injuries is guided from within.

Artificial machines, in contrast, are built and repaired from without—for example, by technicians at a factory. It is not clear that the biological approach is advantageous if factories (or the like) are readily available to provide synthesis and maintenance. But if they are not available, self-organization is the only possible choice; systems that bootstrap themselves from scratch, as in the case of biological evolution, must therefore organize from within.

In the cognitive domain, the dichotomy of empirical vs. rational learning [36] parallels the distinction between building from within vs. from without. Rational learning analyzes representations in light of their internal structure and their relations to other structures—forming analogies, noticing dependencies, and so on. The building or modifying of a particular structure is determined mostly by the knowledge implemented by myriad other structures; in that sense, the construction and elaboration is directed from without, not from within the structure that is affected.

In contrast, empirical learning proceeds locally; each structure (for example, a schema) maintains its own statistics, and spawns variations of itself. True, the schema's behavior depends in part on its connections to other structures (for example, via the extended context and result). But those structures do not implement an understanding of the subject matter of the schema they connect to; the connections do not allow those structures to analyze the schema, but rather the connections pass data to the schema, which processes the data (e.g., by maintaining correlation statistics), again without having any representation of the meaning of the structures.

Doing empirical learning—having structures that learn from within, rather than from without—is crucial to constructivist bootstrapping, much as self-replication is to evolutionary bootstrapping. Just as evolution had no factories to set it in motion, constructivist systems include no built-in domain-specific knowledge to guide earliest learning. This is most evident with regard to the invention of new concepts by the assembly of autonomously developed precursor fragments of that concept (recall the discussion of this Piagetian theme in section 2.9.1).

For example, in conventional systems of representation, an object's presence at some location is designated by some notation such as (AT-POSITION OBJ-259 25 16); the system's domain knowledge and deductive resources combine with this notation to derive, for example, that to grasp OBJ-259, the hand should move to (25,16) (and that to see it, the glance should be directed there). In contrast, the schema mechanism has to construct the very concept of *at-position* from what other systems would regard as derived fragments of the concept. This is not merely a matter of reasoning in the other direction; the mechanism invents the concept in the first place from the underlying fragments, rather than just discovering the relation between an already-formed concept and its already-formed fragments. This having been done, the system indeed reasons both from the fragments to the concept (by using verification conditions to judge the concept's applicability), and vice versa (by the concept's designation in schemas' contexts and results).

These considerations do not argue for empirical learning to the exclusion of rational learning. Indeed, explanation-based learning is a form of rational learning; and, as the previous section suggests, subactivation may allow the schema mechanism to support such learning—after an adequate substrate of knowledge has been laid down by another process. (Analogously, biologically evolved systems that build from within eventually do implement factories, which build from without; the two systems are thereafter symbiotic.) Empirical rather than rational learning is needed to get off the ground, both at the very origin of individual development, and upon introduction to drastically novel domains; conceivably, even routine situations often require some on-the-fly fine-tuning of skills at levels for which no rational analysis is readily available. Conventional AI proclaims that "in the knowledge lies the power;" the constructivist rejoinder, to paraphrase a well-known adage, is that learning will get you through times of no knowledge better than knowledge will get you through times of no learning.

9.6 Virtual mechanisms and self-modification

There are two ways that a mechanism might change as it learns. As discussed in section 7.2.1, a mechanism might operate in conjunction with its acquired data structures to form a virtual mechanism that evolves as the structures evolve. Alternatively, the mechanism might actually modify itself. For example, Lenat's learning system Eurisko [38] represents its own implementation in a format that the system itself can modify (though not with great usefulness; see Haase [30]}). Similarly, in SOAR, aspects of the mechanism's control structure are represented in a format that the system can change, making the system partially self-modify-ing.[30]

In my view, it is implausible for a constructivist, Piagetian system to modify its own implementation by the same principles it uses to modify its other data struc-tures (the systems just mentioned are not Piagetian systems, so this objection does not apply to them). Representing the system's implementation in structures ame-nable to elaboration by the system itself is vastly more difficult than thus repre-senting, say, the rudiments of physical objects. It would make no apparent sense to design a system that starts with the far more sophisticated built-in knowledge, but has to reinvent the much more basic knowledge.

9.7 The schema mechanism and situated activity

The schema mechanism follows Piaget in emphasizing that an individual's physi-cal activity is the foundation for acquired knowledge—even eventual abstract knowledge far removed from physical domains. A recent trend in AI, highlighted by the work of Suchman [65], Agre and Chapman [3, 2, 14], Brooks [10], and Wil-son [75] also addresses activity that is said to be *situated* in the physical world.

Brooks offers an intriguing methodological rationale for his line of research. Brooks designs robot systems with roughly insect-like abilities; he argues that, on the scale of biological evolution, insects are most of the way to humans, so artifi-cial replication of humanlike intelligence might arise from gradual elaboration of artificial insectlike intelligence. (Wilson puts forth a similar rationale, though Wilson maintains that using simulated organisms in simulated worlds work as well as building real insect-robots; Brooks argues that using the real world is vital, since microworlds may fail to pose problems that their designers did not know about.[31]) In my view, infants are a more fruitful point of departure than insects; but this, like many methodological disagreements, is probably most quickly re-

30. .Even a self-modifying mechanism can be described as an invariant mechanism operating in conjunction with variable data to produce a variable mechanism at a higher level of abstraction. For example, any computer implementation of Eurisko runs on digital hardware that remains con-stant; the hardware maintains data which describe the implementation, and which change. But the level of abstraction at which there is an invariant mechanism is one that describes a general-pur-pose computer, not one that describes anything specific to Eurisko's learning apparatus. In con-trast, the schema mechanism separates into a fixed mechanism and mutable data at an abstraction level that does correspond to the substance of the learning mechanism.

31. I agree with Brooks' criticism of simulated domains, but maintain that real-world robotic do-mains are as vulnerable to the same problem. In both cases, a learning system faces challenges defined by whatever interface has been constructed between it and its problem domain. In both cases, that interface imposes some challenges on the mechanism, and glosses over others; and in both cases, the designer may not anticipate all the challenges posed, or all the challenges not posed.

solved by investing the necessary years of work on both approaches, and seeing which (if either) succeeds.

A central theme of situated-activity work is the use of what Agre and Chapman call *leaning on the world,* as opposed to relying on an explicit internal model of the state of the world. Their sense of leaning on the world has, I belive, two primary components:

- Their systems do not represent the expected results of actions; rather, they have what amount to situation-action rules (and, of course, machinery for adjudicating among them). Section 9.1 argues that such an approach is likely to preclude effective empirical learning; Agre and Chapman's systems do not attempt to learn. Also, not representing results prevents being able to learn from thought experiments as well as from real activity.

- Their systems do not build perspective-invariant representations of objects; rather, the representations of situations are tightly bound to (rather sophisticated) perceptual inputs to the system.

The latter point is similar to the Piagetian view, but with a different emphasis. Sensorimotor schemas, which do not represent an object apart from its perceptual manifestations, indeed provide a basis for the infant's early activity. But, even more importantly, such schemas and activity also form a scaffold for the creation of explicit representations apart from perception, which in turn support more sophisticated activity. The emphasis on perception-based activity's role in bootstrapping up to explicit, perception-independent representations distinguishes constructivist AI from situated-activity AI.

Agre and Chapman, Brooks, and Wilson present three distinct, innovative architectures to support situated activity. Agre and Chapman's system is organized around the use of *visual routines* [70] to direct action; Brooks's system is organized in a *subsumption hierarchy* [11] that allows progressive elaboration of the system's behavior; and Wilson's *animats* (artificial animals) use a Holland-like genetic algorithm [35] to evolve situation-action rules. All three systems avoid explicit models of the predicted state of the world. Agre and Chapman's primary argument against using world models that make explicit predictions is the intractability of conventional planning [13] based on maintaining world models (particularly in the presence of uncertainty); but the schema mechanism's control structure (which implements a special case of planning, by chaining schemas) is efficient; and, like some systems without explicit world models, supports the deferral of low-level aspects of a plan that depend on yet-unknown details of the world, and can respond seamlessly to unanticipated problems and opportunities.

Agre and Chapman's *deictic* (originally *indexical–functional*) representation has much in common with virtual generalization in the schema mechanism. Like virtual generalization, deictic representation expresses a general rule by mapping an instance to a particular perceptual view, and then having a routine that applies to that view (for example, moving the hand to the position of object X can be expressed as: look at object X; then move the hand to where-looking). But the schema mechanism, in keeping with its philosophy of *transcending* leaning on the world, can go on to build explicit instantiations of virtual generalizations, obviating the subsequent need to physically enact the mapping step (section 7.1.1).

Agre and Chapman propose deictic representation as an efficient alternative to variable binding. I am unpersuaded, and do not make a similar claim for the schema mechanism's virtual generalizations. Variable binding is indeed intractable when done exhaustively; but it need not be intractable when good heuristics guide the matching of variables to constants. The mapping step for virtual generalizations, and for deictic representations, effectively embodies such heuristics; the techniques of virtual generalization and deictic representation—along with the conventional technique of variable binding—will stand or fall on the development of heuristics that indeed converge to the correct sliver of an exponentially large search space.[32]

9.8 The schema mechanism and the society of mind

Minsky's Society of Mind theory [46] is an ingenious portrait of the human mind as a huge, intricate agglomeration of perhaps thousands of disparate modules, each fairly simple and unintelligent, some acting as managers for others. In contrast, the schema mechanism is a (comparatively) simple, uniform mechanism.

To some extent, the apparent dichotomy between these two approaches exaggerates the actual difference. The schema mechanism, if indeed present in the hu-

---

32. Also, I believe, Agre and Chapman illustrate the adequacy of the deictic alternative to variable binding only for purposes of the execution of plans, not for purposes of plan generation. Since their microworlds include nondeterministic, unpredictable events, their systems embody a generalized kind of plan. A traditional plan says, unconditionally, what next action to take (and can therefore specify the entire sequence of actions in advance), whereas Agre and Chapman's systems *conditionally* specify the next action to take, as a function of the current state. (Calling their conditional specifications generalized plans is my own description; Agre and Chapman would not necessarily agree.) A traditional planner generates a plan from a description of the rules of the problem domain, and a specification of the goal state. Agre and Chapman's systems have no facility for generating plans, generalized or otherwise; their systems' situation-action rules are hand-coded to converge to the goal.

man mind in some form, undoubtedly coexists with many other modules, some involving sensorimotor interfaces, some strictly internal. Whether one regards these modules as peripheral units hanging off the side of the schema mechanism (which is the perspective suggested by this book), or as co-equal components of the mind, is largely a matter of descriptive convention, rather than being a contentful claim (although some statement of the relative importance of these modules may be implicit in the choice of description). Thus, the schema mechanism could be seen as but one agency in a Minsky-like society.

Moreover, even within the schema mechanism, there is a huge, intricate agglomeration—although it is an agglomeration of acquired structure, rather than a built-in agglomeration. I fully agree with Minsky that human intelligence requires a plethora of techniques and representations, and of competing agencies, some of which may manage others. However, the strong need for such features says nothing, a priori, about whether they characterize the innate architecture, or only its constructs. The schema mechanism shows a rudimentary ability, for example, to construct and choose among differently formulated representations of the same thing (section 6.3.3). And one can readily imagine the development of schemas whose activation systematically puts the mechanism into situations from which it can learn usefully—a kind of self-managerial expertise. The hypothetical virtual mechanisms of chapter 7, for example, involve such management; and section 4.3.3, for example, speculates about the mechanism's development of composite-action pathways that reliably get into trouble, thereby systematically prompting the mechanism to figure out how to repair a path to a goal state. These early steps and speculations are far from a demonstration of societal development, but they at least hint at the possibility that a uniform underlying mechanism can build and use a society of diverse agencies.

9.9 Other Piagetian or sensorimotor learning systems

The previous sections have characterized the schema mechanism with respect to broad paradigms of AI. This section instead compares the schema mechanism with specific research projects that attempt to model Piagetian learning, or sensorimotor learning that resembles early Piagetian learning. I make no attempt to be exhaustive in citing such systems, but rather try to present a representative sample.

9.9.1 Cunningham

Cunningham's work [18] was the proximal inspiration of my own effort; that work first suggested to me the idea of trying recapitulate sensorimotor development, and the mechanism Cunningham proposed served as a point of departure for the schema mechanism. Cunningham presents a hypothetical sensorimotor-level scenario for his unimplemented mechanism. His scenario emphasizes the development of the typical stages of intelligent strategy (the various circular reactions, etc), rather than the development of object concepts. Cunningham does not propose a viable mechanism for empirical learning; his bipartite schemas simply tie together all simultaneously active elements, and there is no other provision for creating new representations.

9.9.2 Becker

Becker [6] proposes a mechanism and microworld for sensorimotor-level learning (though he does not explicitly cast this in a Piagetian context, and he presents no scenario of expected development). Becker's mechanism examines an exhaustive record of serial primitive events. An event designated as a goal is found in the sequence. A sequence starting with this event is taken to be a result, and a sequence of events preceding it is proposed as its cause. Different event sequences leading to a common result are compared, and irrelevant events (and irrelevant ordering-constraints on the events) are discarded. This creates schemas such as

$$[a] \rightarrow [b][c] \rightarrow [d] \rightarrow [e][f][g] \Rightarrow [h][i] \rightarrow [j] .$$

The sequence to the left of the double arrow is a cause, the sequence to the right a result; a single arrow designates an ordering constraint, while events not separated by an single arrow are mutually unordered. The double arrow is placed so that no actions lie in the result sequence. Elements of the cause sequence include actions, and non-actions that serve serve as context conditions, which, as in the schema mechanism, assure that the result will follow the action. Becker argues for this context-action-result structure on the grounds of being able to chain schemas to lead to a goal (although, as argued in section 9.1, two-part rules can be used for that purpose as well).

The state elements that appear in event sequences are structured rather than atomic. His system includes machinery for comparing and generalizing over parts of these structures, but the structuring itself is built in; there is no provision for the system to acquire such structuring of its own. There is no abstraction facility apart from discarding irrelevant components (or orderings) from a compound structure.

Becker's system does not address the chicken-and-egg problem of empirical learning. Rather, the combinatorial problem of associating events is glossed over by considering only serial events. A variant of Becker's unimplemented mechanism was implemented by Bond and Mott [7]. Their system used a simple robot, which learned to turn towards and approach a light source to recharge its battery when it ran low. Despite its being situated in the real world, the robot's trivial sensorimotor interface ensured that recognized events were serial, and were typically related when contiguous.

9.9.3 BAIRN

BAIRN, a program by Wallace, Klahr, and Bluff [71], is a production-system model of cognitive development. BAIRN organizes its declarative and procedural knowledge in structures called *nodes*. A node comprises a set of productions, some of which express procedural knowledge—what action to take given particular circumstances and goals; others express declarative knowledge—what follows from current facts.

Insofar as nodes compete for activation, resulting in the invocation of their constituent productions, a node is somewhat like a schema with a composite action (though a node's productions need not converge to a goal state). In addition, a token corresponding to a node's activation can appear as a condition in a production rule. The node's activation thus effectively defines a state element; in this regard, nodes are like synthetic items.

But nodes and synthetic items represent differently. A schema designates a specific assertion, the counterfactual proposition that a given action, under specified circumstances, would have a particular effect; and a synthetic item represents the validity conditions of a schema, the conditions under which the schema's assertion is true. In contrast, a node need not correspond to a succinct assertion, though it might, depending on the productions in the node.

Wallace et al. report an impressive synopsis of BAIRN's acquisition of conservation of number; the developmental progression closely follows the sequence shown by children [28]. The progression culminates in BAIRN's construction of nodes designating the cardinality of collections, with productions that embody the understanding that a collection of a number of objects keeps its cardinality, despite any rearrangement of the objects, unless something is added or removed.

The construction of these nodes is particularly striking in view of the amorphous nature of what a node represents. The key to BAIRN's ability to build such nodes is the presence of highly structured built-in nodes that serve as predecessors to the eventual number-representing nodes. In particular, Wallace et al. postulate built-in *subitizing* nodes, which perceive the numerosity of a small collection of objects that are in the system's focus of attention. When BAIRN counts actual objects, its differentiation and generalization machinery builds variants of the primitive nodes, appropriately modifying the variants' constituent production rules. A complicated derivation leads eventually to the number nodes.

Wallace et al. cite compelling evidence for the existence of innate subitizing abilities in infants (e.g., Strauss and Curtis [64]); hence, their built-in subitizing nodes are not at all ad hoc. Still, it is an open question how such innate competence might be embodied with respect to the central system. In the spirit of the schema mechanism, for example, there might be a primitive item whose meaning is *There are two objects in view that resemble the object I'm focusing on*, another item that means *There are three of them*, etc. These primitive items could enable a system's behavior to give evidence of subitizing abilities before the system recapitulates any actual understanding of number. In contrast, BAIRN's built-in subitizing nodes have extensive internal structure that is in the same format that BAIRN itself uses, and that is fully accessible to BAIRN; without this accessibility, the construction of number-representing nodes could not proceed. Thus, BAIRN's invention of the number concept does not accord with a constructivist account of human development; whether it accords with the actuality of human development remains to be seen.

9.9.4 Darwin I, II, and III

Gerald Edelman [24, 56] argues for the importance of neurophysiological verisimilitude in models of intelligence (beyond the superficial neural resemblance of connectionist systems and so-called neural nets). In particular, Edelman maintains 1) that the development of the brain—both the maturation of its circuitry, and the adjustment of synaptic weights as the individual learns—follows a Darwinian paradigm of a selection process that takes a set of random variants and replicates or amplifies those which turn out to win some kind of experiential contest; and 2) that in the brain, as in biological evolution, this selection culminates in adaptation to the conditions imposed by the contest. As discussed in section 4.2.5, Edelman maintains that this adaptation leads the organism to autonomously develop categories of experiences, rather than (like many artificial learning systems) presuming that primitive symbols come pre-grounded in the categories of interest.

Edelman's Darwin I, II, and III programs engage in classification and recognition of patterns in the environment. Darwin III, the most advanced of these efforts, includes a simulated organism in a simulated world; the organism categorizes the objects it encounters, and its categorizing is manifested in its behavior toward the objects (grasping or avoiding, examining visually, etc.). The core learning machinery has in common with neural networks the fact that it alters connection strengths among quasi-neural assemblies to punish or reward these assemblies for their role in causing positive stimuli; the initial assemblies, however, are more complex and less uniform than is typical for neural nets.

Edelman's appeal to biology and evolution as models for intelligence are reminiscent of Piaget's approach. Edelman, however, carries the appeal further, not only taking evolution as a metaphor for learning, but taking neurobiology literally as a detailed basis for a learning system. As just noted, Edelman criticizes conventional symbolic AI systems for grounding their symbols in the categories intended by the programmer, rather than autonomously; and, although connectionism has been put forth as a solution to that problem, Edelman criticizes this solution by saying that its appeal to neurophysiology is half-hearted, and ultimately unrealistic. But Edelman does not explain why neurophysiological realism is important to solving the problem. His own mechanism, while different—and more neurophysiologically realistic—in its details than other connectionist systems, nonetheless shares the basic paradigm of training subsystems by strengthening or weakening their responses based on their accord with some indicator of a concept that is to be learned. And, as argued in section 4.2.5, that paradigm per se is missing the crucial step—creating an indicator of a radically novel concept in the first place, before being able to train a subsystem to recognize it.

10 Conclusions

10.1 Methodological underpinnings of constructivist AI

Research in artificial intelligence has two basic goals:

- The scientific goal is to understand human intelligence, which in turn has several motivations; for instance:

    - As a naturalist, one wonders about the workings of the human mind, just as one explores any significant phenomenon in nature.

    - As a philosopher, one seeks to comprehend such things as the structure and limits of our knowledge, and the nature and origins of our feelings and values, our thoughts, beliefs, attitudes, and conscious experiences.

    - As a practicing human being, one wishes to understand one's mind, and others', to help oneself and others achieve fulfillment.

    - As an engineer, one may want to design and build human-like intelligence; this task would be aided by knowing just what human intelligence is.

- The engineering goal is to endow computers with intelligence, for two kinds of reasons:

    - One may promote the practical applications of intelligent machines. Depending on the researcher, these applications may range from enhancing the quality of people's lives to profitable technologies of death and destruction.

    - One may experiment with artificial intelligences as a source of ideas as to how human intelligence might work.

Different emphases on these goals can lead to different AI methods. A practical-minded researcher might be happy with a machine that works efficiently, but in a patently nonhuman way; someone more theoretically inclined might be content with a less efficient mechanism if it mirrored human capabilities in an interesting way.

On the other hand, these two goals can be mutually supportive, as indicated by the last motivation cited above for each of the two. Our theories of how humans accomplish a given feat of intelligence are informed by knowing various ways that it *can* be accomplished. Conversely, insight as to how humans do work—derived from introspection, observation, conversation, experiment, dissection, etc.—may provide a fresh idea as to how a task can be accomplished. Speculations about the machinery of human intelligence can be tested and revised by engineering a mechanism that works the way humans are thought to, and improving it until it performs adequately; which in turn creates new speculations about how humans might work, and so on in a cycle of refinement. Different cycles, for different pieces of the puzzle, influence one another.

10.1.1 Levels of explanation

The scientific and engineering goals for AI support one another to the extent that the artificial mechanisms under consideration do things the way humans do. But this concept suffers from a serious ambiguity. For a mechanism to usefully resemble the human mind, does it suffice for the mechanism to correspond only functionally, performing the same computation from input to output as humans do; or must it *implement* the computation as humans do—and, if so, down to what level of abstraction?

Probably the human mind, like other parts of any biological system, is organized in a hierarchy of levels of abstraction. There may be something analogous to a logic-gate level in electronic computers, with a higher level designating something like registers and data busses, perhaps followed by several layers of virtual machines, some of which (if intelligence is indeed constructivist) are built by the mechanism itself, as discussed in chapter 7. At the highest level of abstraction, only external behavior—actions as a function of cumulative sensations—is described.

Simulating intelligence at the highest level is often without explanatory value for natural intelligence. Consider, for example, a program like Weizenbaum's ELIZA [73], which carries on trivial conversations in English by triggering on key words and performing simple grammatical transformations (e.g., rephrasing a sentence that was spoken to it, changing first-person phrases to the third person). ELIZA roughly approximates the computation—the function from input to output—that is executed in a superficial human conversation; people naively conversing with ELIZA sometimes fail to notice that ELIZA's responses are vacuous. But unlike a human in the same situation, ELIZA lacks the slightest comprehension of what it is talking about. It sheds virtually no light on how (even trivial) human conversation works; it would not even serve as a useful point of departure for an effort to model the machinery of human conversation.[33]

Other such examples abound. For instance, a program might play good chess by doing very fast brute-force search of the game space, pruned by very simple heuristics. But this may have little to do with how a person accomplishes a similar level of play; human chess players apparently perform little explicit search of the game space, relying instead, for example, on noticing analogies between the current board position and other, familiar ones.

On the other hand, simulation at a very low level—say, that of individual neurons, or even individual atoms—is unnecessary and prohibitively impractical. By analogy, to understand how a particular Lisp program performs a certain calculation, one need not know how the structures in the computation map onto the underlying transistor physics of the machine running the program. Admittedly, there are *some* purposes for which understanding to substantial depth is important. As a clinician, one must understand implementation on a variety of levels of abstraction, since problems might arise on any level. (Though even for clinical purposes, understanding the higher levels alone is not without value; that often suffices for addressing issues that arise at those levels.) And as a naturalist, one can be curious about all the various levels of implementation. But as an engineer or philosopher, one needn't always care which of several ways some mundane module happens to be implemented, as long as one understands what the module does, and how it can be done.

For purposes of engineering and philosophy, then, specification at the most superficial level of abstraction provides an inadequate explanation of intelligence, but very deep levels pose too strict a requirement. Some intermediate level is needed. The following section proposes criteria for identifying the appropriate level.

10.1.2 Foundational fragments

If we are addressing human adult intelligence *as a whole*—in contrast to some minute subset, like the ability to add numbers or play chess or exchange verbal salutations—then it would be valuable to know *any* mechanism that matched the

---

33. Weizenbaum does not dispute the superficiality of his simulation. In contrast, Colby regarded his own program, PARRY [16]—an ELIZA-like simulation of paranoid conversation—as an explanatory model of human paranoia. Colby performed a Turning-test-like controlled experiment in which a number of psychiatrists, communicating via teletype with a paranoid patient or with PARRY, were unable to determine which was which. Putting this finding in perspective, Weizenbaum [74] described a program which simulated a form of infantile autism; he speculated confidently that no psychiatrist working via a teletype could distinguish this program—which gives no response to anything you say—from an actual autistic patient.

human mind even at the topmost level of abstraction, without concern for lower-level similarities. This is so for two reasons:

- No one can yet characterize (except in the vaguest terms) what intelligence *is* at the topmost level (i.e., what computation is performed), except indexically—we point to intelligent beings and say that intelligence is *like that*. *Any* artificial implementation of that computation would be, if nothing else, a specification of the computation.

- It is quite possible that there are not many radically different reasonable ways to implement whatever it is that intelligence, as a whole, does. To the extent that this is so, one can zero in on how our intelligence works by setting out to discover any way it reasonably *could* work.

This claim may seem contrary to the remarks above about the inadequacy of the most superficial level of explanation, as illustrated by ELIZA. But the apparent inconsistency can be resolved by considering *fragments* of the task of intelligence—by *fragment*, I mean some partial specification of the computation performed by the system. There are several different dimensions along which fragments of a system can be delineated, including:

- Domain. A fragment can be a module that performs a subset of the task performed by the entire system.

- Precision. A fragment can be a vague sketch of the computation performed by the entire system, as, for example, Piaget's theory sketches a proposed constructivist mechanism, but not with enough precision to say just what structures are created next, or just what action is to happen.

- Accuracy. A model of the system might be very precise—*any* implementation is precise, for example—but, below a certain resolution, its details might be inaccurate, failing to match the original system.

ELIZA's task, for example, is fragmented both by domain—being able to hold a banal conversation is a very small aspect of human intelligence; and by accuracy—ELIZA's conversation seems realistic only by the most casual and naive inspection.

When a fragment is severely limited in its precision, accuracy, or domain, it may have a much more parsimonious implementation by itself than as a component of what the larger system does. In that case, the most reasonable implementation of the task in isolation may bear little resemblance to its most reasonable implementation in the context of the entire system; the former then teaches little or nothing about the latter, severing the symbiosis between studying a natural implementation of the entire system and an artificial implementation of the fragmented task.

But this does not mean that one must attack the whole system at once. A fragment of the system *may* have the same reasonable implementation in isolation as it has as part of the whole system's behavior. Such a fragment can be called *foundational*. Identifying foundational fragments of intelligence is useful because it affords the methodological value of exploring natural intelligence via artificial models, and vice versa—while focusing on a tractable subset of the system.

Insofar as a system's implementation cleaves into cleanly separated modules whose effects show through at top level, each module will tend to perform a foundational fragment of the system's task—the very separation of the modules tends to assure that how each one can best implement its interface to the rest of the system is unaffected by the internal details of the rest of the system. In particular, if there is a module of the human mind devoted to Piagetian learning (e.g., a schema mechanism), then Piagetian learning is a foundational fragment of the mind's behavior; the top-level manifestation of the learning module consists of the changes to the individual's behavior as knowledge is acquired. Constructivist AI is the enterprise of working backward from that manifestation to reverse-engineer the underlying module. (And by thus working backward from a manifestation to the manifested entity, the enterprise exemplifies its own content and converges with itself.)

10.2 Directions for future work

Suggestions for extensions of this work are scattered through preceding chapters. First, as noted in the introduction to chapter 6, the present implementation results are best viewed as a pilot effort; validation of the implementation results presented here requires replication and quantitative characterization of those results. Secondly, some further progress through the Piagetian sequence might be achieved just by moving the existing implementation to a larger machine, and making trivial microworld extensions, such as providing for visually obscured objects. Thirdly, several extensions to the basic mechanism appear worthy of exploration, some of which have been mentioned above:

- *Subactivation.* As discussed in section 7.1.3, subactivation would allow the mechanism to learn from thought experiments, as well as from actual physical events. Furthermore, the learning mechanism might be augmented (section 9.4) to learn from a single subactivated trial, rather than having to do statistical learning based on several identical repetitions.

- *Connectionist contexts.* A schema's extended context data proposes spinoff schemas, and also maintains override conditions for the schema. The latter function could be generalized by allowing the extended context to act as a conventional connectionist network, adjusting its weights to compute some function of its inputs (the state of all items) that corresponds to the validity conditions of the schema. Such a function might usefully complement the validity conditions computed by the contexts of spinoff schemas.

- *Clustering.* Certain primitive items designate states which are special cases of other primitively represented states (e.g., *fovx20* is a special case of *vf22*; *tactd2* is a special case of *tactl*). Representing states at different resolutions facilitates the representation of state-spaces at different levels; having coordinated coarse- and fine-grained spaces mitigates the combinatorics of showing the path from one fine-grained place to another, because the path can be represented as a coarse segment to get in the right vicinity, followed by a fine-tuning segment. It would be helpful if constructed state elements, as well as primitive ones, could avail themselves of such organization. This might be accomplished by noticing states that cluster together, in the sense that they are mutual near neighbors in a network of schemas for transforming among them. A new item might then be defined as the disjunction of several clustered items.

- *Combinatorics and garbage collection.* Marginal attribution does a creditable job of picking out reliable schemas (and their precursors) from the exponential space of expressible schemas. But even among such schemas, there can be combinatorial proliferations of schemas that are useless variations of one another (e.g., schemas expressing the co-occurrence of foveal events); there may also be many schemas that explore useless and sterile corners of state-space. The schema mechanism may benefit from being able to recognize and purge such structures—that is, to *garbage-collect* them. (I borrow the term garbage collection from programming languages that feature automatic reclamation of memory that stores permanently inaccessible—and therefore unusable—structures. The metaphor is used loosely here; in the present sense, the reclaimed structures are estimated to be of lesser value, but need not be flatly unusable.)

The most straightforward garbage collection technique is to purge the least useful schemas, where usefulness increases with the frequency of a schema's activation, and with the goal-value of the result achieved by activating it. Depending on actual activation makes the usefulness measure responsive to all factors that contribute to a schema's selection for activation (including the availability of other, competing schemas in the situations that make a given schema applicable).

The value of actions and items might derive from the value of the schemas in which they appear. Care must be taken when purging a structure to either purge those structures that contain it as a component, or to change such them to remove their reference to that structure.

Garbage collection based on actual use is infeasible until a large enough set of structures has amassed. The threshold is determined by the amount of structure needed to do interesting and useful things; the schema mechanism's basic rather than applied learning (section 9.1) causes it to build fragments of skills that will not become useful until the rest of the necessary fragments also arise. Only then can the usefulness of the useful structures become apparent, supporting an informed choice of which structures to purge.

Other possible garbage collection criteria involve recognizing particular kinds of unnecessary proliferations, and purging the proliferating structures:

- Building up to a context conjunction one item at a time leaves behind a trail of precursor structures with incomplete contexts. If these structures' extended contexts fail over a number of trials to make any progress toward spawning further spinoffs, they might be purged.

- The mechanism might keep track of how often a given schema would be spun off, if it didn't already exist. If re-creating circumstances arise much more frequently than the schema's activation, the schema might be purged, in the expectation that it is likely to be re-created before it is next needed (or at least before the next several times). This reclamation would have the plausible consequence that the mechanism might become rusty at unused skills, due to the need to re-create some components on the fly when the skill is resurrected.

In addition to further extending and experimenting with the schema mechanism itself, the schema mechanism's developmental progression might suggest experiments to perform with actual infants, to find evidence for or against corresponding details of their development.

10.3 Evaluation and summary

It is important that at attempt to engineer a constructivist mechanism be guided by a plausible theory of constructivism in humans; this provides both a point of departure for the mechanism's design, and a road map of target abilities by which the mechanism can be appraised and revised. Moreover, taking such a theory as a working hypothesis for the design of an artificial mechanism provides an elaboration and appraisal of the original theory. The schema mechanism is built upon Piaget's theory of cognitive development; the focus is on sensorimotor-period development, since the underlying mechanism is easiest to discern when acquired structure is still simple.

The schema mechanism is a self-extensible system that constructs schemas, actions, and items. The mechanism uses these constructs to represent the state of the world, to discover regularities in the world, and to organize sequences of actions in the pursuit of goals. The schema mechanism tackles basic problems about empirical learning and concept invention:

- Empirical learning poses the chicken-and-egg problem of identifying an action's results before knowing the corresponding context conditions; the solution is to distinguish relevance from reliability, and to use an exhaustive crossbar to look for relevance.

- Concept invention poses a deeper problem: the need to invent concepts that do not resemble prior ones, and that may indeed be inexpressible (hence undefinable) as any fixed function of prior ones. Here, the solution is to work backward from a previously-conceived manifestation to postulate the previously-unconceived thing that is manifested; the newly conceived entity is defined as the potential to evoke the manifestation.

The mechanism's empirical-learning and concept-invention facilities share the uncommon feature that both take counterfactuals seriously. By making counterfactual assertions, schemas promote a useful modularity for learning by separating the question of what would happen from the question of what should happen. And synthetic items, by reifying the validity conditions of their host schemas' counterfactual assertions, gain the power to make conservation discoveries, acquiring representations of previously unconceived-of aspects of the world that remain invariant when their manifestations change or cease.

Relying on counterfactuals may seem odd, given the relative novelty and obscurity of the concept of counterfactual assertion, in contrast with the far more familiar (and far better understood) concept of logical implication. As noted in section 8.8, counterfactuals pose subtle problems that are related to the problems of nonnaive induction (and which perhaps have related solutions). Clearly, though, counterfactuals are fundamental to what an organism needs to learn. Its most useful predictions are contingent on its actions, which are in turn contingent on its action-contingent predictions—the organism should take that action which, if it is taken, predicts the best result, and that is an inherently counterfactual criterion. The difficulty and obscurity of the concept of counterfactuals is, I suspect, a reason that its fundamental importance for learning systems has been late to be recognized, rather than a reason to consider it an implausible basis for learning.

10.3.1 Evaluating the mechanism's performance

The achievements of the schema mechanism's implementation are on target, but preliminary. The mechanism does use plausibly designed domain-independent learning machinery to recapitulate some early milestones of Piagetian development, including the anticipation of visual effects of hand motions, learning how to bring the hand into view, discovering intermodal coordination (e.g., touching what's seen, and vice versa), conceiving of persistent visible and palpable objects, and discovering their coextension. However, the mechanism just barely reaches the point of constructing some such representations, and does not go so far as to put them to practical use (say, to grasp an object in order to do something with it). And even its rudimentary abilities are acquired in the context of a microworld and sensorimotor interface that are far simpler than what the human environment provides.

The Piagetian milestones accomplished by the schema mechanism do not all occur in the same order as in actual Piagetian development. For example, the mechanism gains facility with recovering hidden objects before it masters intermodal coordination; as noted in section 6.3.3, although the mechanism succeeds in building schemas that anticipate, say, tactile contact resulting from moving the hand next to where an object is seen, the mechanism does not happen to develop chains of schemas that enable it to move the hand there (though it does learn how to move the hand's image elsewhere). Thus, it can predict tactile contact in that situation, but cannot intentionally bring it about.

This out-of-sequence achievement of some milestones are at odds with an interpretation of Piagetian stages that regards them as necessarily uniform, each stage as a whole requiring the structure of the last as a whole. But the more flexible view of stages espoused in section 2.9.2 is compatible with a variable order of achievement; intermodal coordination is not logically prerequisite to persistence, so the order may well depend on contingencies of a learning system's environment. In particular, the schema mechanism's microworld tends to confine the available objects to a small set of "home positions" (four such positions apiece), compared to a larger number of visual-field regions (25); that reason alone might explain why persistence of objects at those positions is more quickly learned than knowledge formulated in part in terms of a visual representation.

The example of learning intermodal coordination raises another point. As just noted, the schema mechanism can predict the tactile results of visible hand motions before being able to purposefully achieve those results. If an experimenter were restricted to observing the actions of the schema mechanism's simulated robot (as Piaget and other early investigators were restricted to observing infants' overt behavior), there would be no apparent indication of the mechanism's anticipation of tactile contact. The invisibility of that anticipation is reminiscent of the results of recent investigators such as Baillargeon (section 2.9.3), who demonstrates, by monitoring subtle indicators of surprise, that infants anticipate more than they can act on. The schema mechanism illustrates how a learning system that operates according to Piagetian themes might indeed know more than its overt behavior indicates, leading to an overly conservative attribution of knowledge if such behavior were the only evidence available.

A concluding caveat is in order concerning several major features of the schema mechanism whose usefulness has been argued for here, but has not been demonstrated by the implementation, even though the features are part of the implementation. First of all, the chicken-and-egg problem tackled by marginal attribution is not seriously posed by the schema mechanism's microworld. The microworld does allow for actions whose reliable effects may be rare without the correct context conditions; still, few events occur at once, and they are almost always the result of the action just performed, so that more naive learning techniques may well suffice to solve the chicken-and-egg problem here. Secondly, although the purpose of the mechanism is to build structures that are both predictive and useful, only the former has been demonstrated; the mechanism puts its structures to so little use that the very existence of those structures probably would not be inferable from the mechanism's behavior. Thirdly, along the same lines, the elaborate control criteria built into the mechanism, including the facility for delegated value, contributes little to its performance. The mechanism's only achievement has to build structures that represent aspects of its world—structures which, at present, are revealed to observers only by monitoring the internal workings of the mechanism.

10.3.2 Extrapolating from the implementation's performance

As with any AI effort, the question arises as to whether we might expect this system ever to go significantly further than it already has. Here is a roundabout argument for such extrapolation.

Prior to its most advanced acquisitions, the schema mechanism weaves networks of spatial knowledge (the visual and proprioceptive networks) that are not predicted by Piaget. Nor do these acquisitions contradict Piaget; there is no conspicuous external manifestation of their presence or absence, so their development is not externally evident. Nonetheless, their development proceeds according to the same themes as explicitly Piagetian acquisitions, and, in the schema mechanism, obtains from the same machinery. Doubtless much of this *micro-Piagetian* knowledge (as we might call it) is also built in to innate cognitive modules; this may be true of much Piagetian knowledge as well, as discussed in section 2.9.3. But, as argued there, a general learning mechanism may need to recapitulate what is built in elsewhere in order to represent that knowledge in the format that the learning mechanism can operate on, to then transcend what was built in.[34]

Indeed, such eventual transcendence is the only apparent reason for any system, natural or artificial, to be designed to rely on recapitulating what is already built in. Thus, if infant cognitive development is in fact a form of learning, there is good reason to expect that later development involves similar learning, so that the principles of the early learning extrapolate to more advanced performance.

I think this argument offers the strongest reason to suspect that something along the lines of the schema mechanism may be capable of more advanced achievements. As just noted, the mechanism's performance so far, while on the

34. The design of the schema mechanism makes no attempt to incorporate in its peripheral modules the sort of innate competence that exists in those modules in human beings. For one thing, not enough is known of this innate competence to support a reasonable job of replicating it. Also, it is unclear what influence, if any, the peripheral competence has on central-system development. If the peripheral competence does help, then not having it in the schema mechanism makes the mechanism's task even more formidable.

right track, is far too rudimentary to convincingly demonstrate extrapolability to adultlike (or even childlike) intellectual capabilities. I think this is true of all artificial intelligence systems to date; extant AI programs either have expert-like abilities in very narrow domains, general methods that work only on toy problems, or are virtual programming languages whose generality and power derive from their specific programming. For that matter, even the behavior of young humans is not convincingly extrapolable—it would never occur to us, when we watched an infant, that the infant might eventually attain adult competence, had we not already known that to happen to others.

The schema mechanism—again, like other AI (and natural) systems—faces combinatorial problems that threaten its ability to scale up to more advanced abilities. Although the schema mechanism incorporates a number of features designed to mitigate aspects of the combinatorial assault, there is no theoretical argument or practical demonstration that these features are necessary or sufficient. But the core features of the schema mechanism—the machinery for empirical learning (marginal attribution), abstraction (composite actions), and conceptual invention (synthetic items)—arguably help explain Piagetian development. To the extent that an artificial system resembles a natural system, the natural system is an existence proof that something resembling the artificial system can indeed work. And if the natural system has a way to keep its combinatorics in check—as it must, since it works—then such an ability can be built into the artificial system as well.

Without Piaget's elaborate observations of actual development, one might react to the schema mechanism by saying that yes, it looks potentially powerful, but the mechanism's early object representations (for example) seem too strange for us to be comfortable with the idea of an intelligence having to pass through that. Similarly, given Piaget alone, one might acknowledge the force of his description of major developmental themes, but be skeptical of how or why a sensibly engineered mechanism would exhibit (for example) the odd bugs evident in early object-understanding. The schema mechanism and Piaget's theory, taken together, explain how the strange, early representations may support the eventual invention of sensible concepts, and explain why a learning mechanism would exhibit some of the odd bugs encountered along the way in Piagetian development.

When a mechanism figures out for itself that there are objects "out there," it dramatically demonstrates an ability to invent new concepts. The schema mechanism implementation has taken preliminary but promising steps in that direction. If this success continues—if it is shown that more of the Piagetian sequence of achievements, and mistakes, would indeed follow from this machinery designed to construct and use novel representations—then I think it likely that such machinery is actually involved in the infant's development.

In sum, to the extent that the schema mechanism might approximate the actual mechanism of early Piagetian development, and to the extent that the mechanism of early Piagetian development might be responsible for later development as well, it is plausible that something like the schema mechanism can account for aspects of later development as well. The most ambitious hope for the present research is that it may be an early step towards an eventual such account—one more verse in the long, strange song of who and how we are.

The End

Bibliography

[1] Harold Abelson and Gerald J. Sussman. (1985) *Structure and Interpretation of Computer Programs*. MIT Press, Cambridge Ma.

[2] Philip E. Agre. (1988) *The Dynamic Structure of Everyday Life*. M.I.T. A.I. Technical Report 1085. M.I.T. A.I. Laboratory, Cambridge, Ma.

[3] Philip E. Agre and David Chapman. (1987) Pengi: An Implementation of a Theory of Activity. *Proceedings of the Sixth National Conference on Artificial Intelligence*. pp. 196-201.

[4] James A. Anderson and Edward Rosenfeld (eds.). (1988) Neurocomputing. MIT Press, Cambridge Ma.

[5] Renée Baillargeon. (1987) Young Infants' Reasoning About the Physical and Spatial Properties of a Hidden Object. *Cognitive Development*. 2, 179-200.

[6] Joseph Becker. (1973) A model for the encoding of experiential information. in Roger Schank and Kenneth Colby (eds.) *Computer Models of Thought and Language*. pp 396-434. Freeman, San Francisco.

[7] A. Bond and D. Mott (1981) Learning of sensory-motor schemas in a mobile robot. In *Seventh International Joint Conference on Artificial Intelligence*. pp. 159-161.

[8] Gordon H. Bower and Ernest R. Hilgard. (1981) *Theories of Learning*. Prentice-Hall, Englewood Cliffs, N.J.

[9] T.G.R. Bower. (1977) *A Primer of Infant Development*. Freeman, San Francisco.

[10] Rodney A. Brooks. (1986) Achieving Artificial Intelligence through Building Robots. M.I.T. A.I. Memo 899. M.I.T. A.I. Laboratory, Cambridge Ma.

[11] Rodney A. Brooks. (1986) A Robust Layered Control System for a Mobile Robot. in *IEEE Journal of Robotics and Automation*. 2 (1), pp. 14-23.

[12] Susan Carey. (1985) *Conceptual Change in Childhood*. MIT Press, Cambridge Ma.

[13] David Chapman. (1987) Planning for Conjunctive Goals. In *Artificial Intelligence*. 32 3, pp 333-377.

[14] David Chapman. (1990) *Vision, Instruction, and Action*. M.I.T. A.I. Technical Report 1204. M.I.T. A.I. Laboratory, Cambridge, Ma.

[15] Noam Chomsky. (1988) *The Managua Lectures*. MIT Press, Cambridge, Ma.

[16] Kenneth C. Colby (1973) Simulation of Belief Systems. In Roger C. Schank and Kenneth C. Colby, eds., *Computer Models of Thought and Language*. Freeman, San Francisco.

[17] F. Crick and C. Asanuma. (1986) Certain aspects of the anatomy and physiology of the cerebral cortex. in James L. McClelland and David E. Rumelhard et al (eds.) *Parallel Distributed Processing: Explorations in the Microstructure of Cognition*. pp. 334-371. MIT Press, Cambridge, Ma.

[18] Michael Cunningham. (1972) *Intelligence: It Origins and Development*. Academic Press, N.Y.

[19] Gary L. Drescher. (1980) Suggestions for Genetic A.I. M.I.T. A.I. Working Paper 198. M.I.T. A.I. Laboratory, Cambridge, Ma.

[20] Gary L. Drescher. (1985) *The Schema Mechanism: A Conception of Constructivist Intelligence*. M.I.T. M.S. thesis.

[21] Gary L. Drescher. (1987) A mechanism for early Piagetian learning. *Proceedings of the Sixth National Conference on Artificial Intelligence.* AAAI-1987.

[22] Gary L. Drescher. (1988) Learning from experience without prior knowledge in a complicated world. *Proceedings of the 1988 Spring Symposium: Parallel Models of Intelligence,* AAAI-1988.

[23] Hubert Dreyfus. (1979) *What Computers Can't Do.* 2nd ed. Harper Row, N.Y.

[24] Gerald M. Edelman. (1987) *Neural Darwinism: The Theory of Neuronal Goroup Selection.* Basic Books, N.Y.

[25] Jerry A. Fodor. (1975) *The Language of Thought.* Harvard University Press, Cambridge, Ma.

[26] Jerry A. Fodor. (1981) Methodological solipsism considered as a research strategy in cognitive science. In Jerry A. Fodor, *Representations: Philosophical Essays on the Foundations of Cognitive Science.* MIT Press, Cambridge, Ma.

[27] Jerry A. Fodor. (1987) *Psychosemantics.* MIT Press, Cambridge, Ma.

[28] Rochel Gelman and C. R. Gallistel. (1978) *The Child's Understanding of Number.* Harvard University Press, Cambridge Ma.

[29] Nelson Goodman. (1979) *Fact, Fiction, and Forecast.* 1983 rev. Harvard University Press, Cambridge, Ma.

[30] Kenneth W. Haase. (1989) Automated discovery. In Richard Forsyth (ed.), *Machine Learning: Principles and Techniques.* pp. 127-155. Chapman and Hall, N.Y.

[31] Kenneth W. Haase. (1990) *Programs Which Invent.* PhD dissertation, M.I.T.

[32] Stevan Harnad. (1989) The symbol grounding problem. Presented at *CNLS Conference on Emergent Computation.* Los Almos.

[33] W. Daniel Hillis. (1985) *The Connection Machine.* MIT Press, Cambridge, Ma.

[34] Douglas Hofstadter. (1982) Artificial Intelligence: Subcognition as computation. Indiana Universtiy Computer Science Dept. Technical Report 132.

[35] John H. Holland, Keith J. Holyoak, Richard E. Nisbett, and Paul R. Thagard. (1986) *Induction.* MIT Press, Cambridge, Ma.

[36] Yves Kodratoff. (1988) *Introduction to Machine Learning.* Morgan Kaufmann, San Mateo, Ca.

[37] John E. Laird, Allen Newell, and Paul S. Rosenbloom. (1987) Soar: An architecture for general intellgence. *Artificial Intelligence.* **33**

[38] Douglas B. Lenat. (1983) The role of heuristics in learning by discovery: three case studies. In Ryszard S. Michalski, Jaime G. Carbonell, and Tom M. Mitchell (eds.) *Machine Learning.* Vol I. pp. 243-306. Tioga, Palo Alto, Ca.

[39] David Lewis. (1973) *Counterfactuals.* Harvard University Press, Cambridge Ma.

[40] Nick Littlestone. (1987) Learning when irrelevant attributes abound. In *Proceedings of the 28th Annual Symposium on Foundations of Computer Science.* pp. 78-87.

[41] David Marr. (1982) *Vision.* Freeman, San Francisco.

[42] Z.S. Masangkay, K.A. McCluskey, C.W. McIntyre, J. Sims-Knight, B.E. Vaughn, and J.H. Flavell. (1974) The early development of inferences about the visual percepts of others. *Child Development* **45** pp. 357-366.

[43] James L. McClelland, David E. Rumelhard, and the PDP Research Group. (1986) Parallel Distributed Processing: Explorations in the Microstructure of Cognition. MIT Press, Cambridge, Ma.

[44] Drew McDermott. (1981) Artificial intelligence meets natural stupidity. In John Haugeland (ed.), *Mind Design*. pp. 143-160. MIT Press, Cambridge, Ma..

[45] Marvin Minsky. (1967) *Computation: Finite and Infinite Machines*. Prentice-Hall, Englewood Cliffs, N.J.

[46] Marvin Minsky. (1986) *The Society of Mind*. Simon and Schuster, N.Y.

[47] Marvin Minsky and Seymour Papert. (1969) *Perceptrons*. MIT Press, Cambridge, Ma.

[48] Alan Newell and Herbert A. Simon. (1972) *Human Problem Solving*. Perntice-Hall, Englewood Cliffs, N.J.

[49] Seymour Papert. (1980) *Mindstorms*. Basic Books, N.Y.

[50] Jean Piaget. (1952) *The Origins of Intelligence in Children*. Norton, N.Y.

[51] Jean Piaget. (1952) *The Child's Conception of Number*. Norton, N.Y.

[52] Jean Piaget. (1954) *The Construction of Reality in the Child*. Ballentine, N.Y.

[53] Jean Piaget and Bärbel Inhelder. (1969) *The Psychology of the Child*. Basic Books, N.Y.

[54] M. Piattelli-Palmarini. (1980) *Language and Learning: The Debate between Jean Piaget and Noam Chomsky*. Harvard University Press, Cambridge, Ma.

[55] Hilary Putnam. (1975) The meaning of "meaning." In Keith Gunderson, ed., *Language, Mind, and Knowledge*. pp. 131-193. University of Minnesota Press, Minneapolis.

[56] George N. Reeke, Jr. and Gerald M. Edelman. (1988) Real brains and artificial intelligence. In *Daedalus: Journal of the American Academy of Arts and Sciences, Winter 1988.*

[57] Paul S. Rosenbloom and Allen Newell. (1983) The chunking of goal hierarchies: a generalized model of practice. In Ryszard S. Michalski, Jaime G. Carbonell, and Tom M. Mitchell (eds.) *Machine Learning*. Vol II. pp. 247-288. Tioga, Palo Alto, Ca.

[58] Bertrand Russell. (1945) *A History of Western Philosophy*. Simon and Schuster, N.Y.

[59] A.L. Samuel. (1963) Some studies in machine learning using the game of checkers. In E.A. Feigenbaum and J. Feldman (eds.) *Computers and Thought*. pp. 71-105. McGraw-Hill, N.Y.

[60] Marcel J. Schoppers. (1987) Universal Plans for Reactive Robots in Unpredictable Environments. *Proceedings of the Tenth International Joint Conference on Artificial Intelligence*. pp 89-104.

[61] John Searle. (1980) Minds, brains and programs. *Behavior and Brain Science*. **3**, pp. 63-109.

[62] Claude E. Shannon and W. Weaver. (1949) *The Mathematical Theory of Communication*. University of Illinois Press.

[63] Guy L. Steele. (1984) *Common LISP: The Language*. Digital Press, Burlington, Ma.

[64] M. S. Strauss and L. E. Curtis. (1981) Development of numerical concepts in infancy. In C. Sophian (ed.), *The Origins of Cognitive Skills*. Lawrence Erlbaum, Hillsdale N.J.

[65] Lucy Suchman. (1987) *Plans and Situated Action*. Cambridge University Press, Cambridge.

[66] Richard S. Sutton. (1988) Learning to predict by the methods of temporal differences. *Machine Learning*. **3** pp. 9-44.

[67] Thinking Machines Corporation. (1988) **Lisp Reference Manual*. Cambridge Ma.

[68] Thinking Machines Corporation. (1988) *Paris Reference Manual*. Cambridge Ma.

[69] N. Tinbergen. (1951) *The Study of Instinct*. Clarendon Press, Oxford.

[70] Shimon Ullman. (1984) Visual Routines. *Cognition*. **18**, pp. 97-159.

[71] Ivan Wallace, David Klahr and Kevin Bluff. (1987) A self-modifying production system model of cognitive development. In David Klahr, Pat Langley and Robert Neches (eds.) *Production System Models of Learning and Development*. MIT Press, Cambridge, Ma.

[72] B. White and R. Held. (1966) Plasticity of sensory-motor development in the human infant. in W. Allinsmith and J. F. Rosenblith (eds.) *The Causes of Behavior.* Allyn and Bacon, Boston.

[73] Joseph Weizenbaum. (1966) ELIZA—a computer program for the study of natural language communication between man and machine. In *Communications of the Association of Computing Machinery*. **9**(1) pp. 36-45.

[74] Joseph Weizenbaum. (1974) Letter to *Communications of the Association of Computing Machinery*. **17**(9) p. 543.

[75] Stuart W. Wilson. (1985) Knowledge growth in an artificial animals. In *Proceedings of the International Conference on Genetic Algorithms and their Applications, July24-26, 1985.* Carnegie-Mellon University, Pittsburgh.

[76] Terry Winograd and Fernando Flores. (1986) *Understanding Computers and Cognition*. Ablex, Norwood, N.J.

[77] Patrick H. Winston. (1984) *Artificial Intelligence*. (2nd edition) Addison-Wesley, Reading, Ma.

Index

Artificial Intelligence

Patrick Henry Winston, founding editor
J. Michael Brady, Daniel G. Bobrow, and Randall Davis, current editors

Model-Based Control of a Robot Manipulator, Chae H. An, Christopher G. Atkeson, and John M. Hollerbach, 1988

A Robot Ping-Pong Player: Experiment in Real-Time Intelligent Control, Russell L. Andersson, 1988

Robotics Research: The Fourth International Symposium, edited by Robert C. Bolles and Bernard Roth, 1988

The Paralation Model: Architecture-Independent Parallel Programming, Gary Sabot, 1988

Concurrent System for Knowledge Processing: An Actor Perspective, edited by Carl Hewitt and Gul Agha, 1989

Automated Deduction in Nonclassical Logics: Efficient Matrix Proof Methods for Modal and Intuitionistic Logics, Lincoln Wallen, 1989

Shape from Shading, edited by Berthold K.P. Horn and Michael J. Brooks, 1989

Ontic: A Knowledge Representation System for Mathematics, David A. McAllester, 1989

Solid Shape, Jan J. Koenderink, 1990

Expert Systems: Human Issues, edited by Dianne Berry and Anna Hart, 1990

Artificial Intelligence: Concepts and Applications, edited by A. R. Mirzai, 1990

Robotics Research: The Fifth International Symposium, edited by Hirofumi Miura and Suguru Arimoto, 1990

Theories of Comparative Analysis, Daniel S. Weld, 1990

Artificial Intelligence at MIT: Expanding Frontiers, edited by Patrick Henry Winston and Sarah Alexandra Shellard, 1990

Vector Models for Data-Parallel Computing, Guy E. Blelloch, 1990

Experiments in the Machine Interpretation of Visual Motion, David W. Murray and Bernard F. Buxton, 1990

Object Recognition by Computer: The Role of Geometric Constraints, W. Eric L. Grimson, 1990

Representing and Reasoning With Probabilistic Knowledge: A Logical Approach to Probabilities, Fahiem Bacchus, 1990

3D Model Recognition from Stereoscopic Cues, edited by John E.W. Mayhew and John P. Frisby, 1991

Artificial Vision for Mobile Robots: Stereo Vision and Multisensory Perception, Nicholas Ayache, 1991

Truth and Modality for Knowledge Representation, Raymond Turner, 1991

Made-Up Minds: A Constructivist Approach to Artificial Intelligence, Gary L. Drescher, 1991.

The MIT Press, with Peter Denning as general consulting editor, publishes computer science books in the following series:

ACM Doctoral Dissertation Award and Distinguished Dissertation Series

Artificial Intelligence
Patrick Henry Winston, founding editor
Michael Brady, Daniel Bobrow, and Randall Davis, editors

Charles Babbage Institute Reprint Series for the History of Computing
Martin Campbell-Kelly, editor

Computer Systems
Herb Schwetman, editor

Explorations with Logo
E. Paul Goldenberg, editor

Foundations of Computing
Michael Garey and Albert Meyer, editors

History of Computing
I. Bernard Cohen and William Aspray, editors

Information Systems
Michael Lesk, editor

Logic Programming
Ehud Shapiro, editor; Fernando Pereira, Koichi Furukawa, Jean-Louis Lassez, and David H. D. Warren, associate editors

The MIT Press Electrical Engineering and Computer Science Series

Research Monographs in Parallel and Distributed Processing
Christopher Jesshope and David Klappholz, editors

Scientific and Engineering Computation
Janusz Kowalik, editor

Technical Communication
Ed Barrett, editor